Rhetoric and Philosophy
in Renaissance Humanism

RHETORIC AND PHILOSOPHY IN RENAISSANCE HUMANISM

The Union of Eloquence and Wisdom,

Petrarch to Valla

JERROLD E. SEIGEL

PRINCETON, NEW JERSEY

PRINCETON UNIVERSITY PRESS

1968

Publication of this book has been aided by
the Whitney Darrow Publication Reserve Fund
of Princeton University Press.

This book has been composed in Caledonia type.

Printed in the United States of America
by Princeton University Press,
Princeton, New Jersey

For Jayn

PREFACE

THIS BOOK has a double aspect. It seeks first to contribute to the understanding of an important chapter in European intellectual history: the humanism of the early Renaissance. It also tries to tell part of the history of an ideal which inspired (and troubled) men of thought both in the Italian Renaissance and in other times and places: the combination of rhetoric and philosophy, the union of eloquence with wisdom. The book is primarily concerned with the culture of the Renaissance humanists, but the study of their attempt to unite wisdom and eloquence leads to a consideration both of the problems raised by this ideal and of its broader meaning. The humanists the reader will meet in these pages were primarily men of eloquence rather than men of wisdom. Their understanding of the combination of rhetoric and philosophy was shaped by their basic commitment to the art of the orator. Each of them understood this commitment differently: this makes an inquiry into their individual versions of the combination interesting and rewarding. Moreover, all of them shared certain assumptions about the requirements of eloquence on the one hand and of wisdom on the other, and these assumptions were present not only among Renaissance men, but among earlier and later thinkers as well: this lifts the issues faced by Petrarch and his successors out of the specific Renaissance context, and makes them the concern of a much broader group of men.

In part, the study of early humanist thought is inseparable from the study of "the combination of rhetoric and philosophy," since this formula was a central element in the early humanist ideal of culture. To say this is not to propose a novel view of early-fifteenth-century humanism; the enthusiasm of the humanists for eloquence, and their desire to join it to philosophy, are well-known features of humanist thought. What distinguishes this book from other studies of humanism is rather the point of view from which the humanist passion for rhetoric is approached and, per-

vii

haps, the seriousness with which it is taken. Modern men are not at ease with rhetoric; to declare our independence from it often seems a necessity of all our discourse. For this reason, many students of the humanist movement have been unable to involve themselves closely enough in the humanists' passion for rhetoric to arrive at a sympathetic understanding of it. Instead, they have interpreted the humanist praise of rhetoric to mean something else: beauty of form, for instance, or civic activity, both things to which rhetoric can contribute, but neither identical with it. Those who have taken the humanist commitment to rhetoric at face value have usually limited their analyses to such matters as literary form or technique of composition. These subjects are not considered here. Rather, what the reader will find is a discussion of some of the consequences which the humanists' commitment to rhetoric brought to their lives as thinkers and intellectuals. The author hopes to show that the humanists found in their passion for rhetoric a basic intellectual identity, a style of thinking which shaped and colored their view of man's mental and moral life.

This is not to say that early humanist culture can be reduced to an elaboration of the humanists' cultivation of oratory. Though it is difficult to think of any humanist concern that had no connection at all with the ideal of eloquence, such activities as their classical scholarship, and their writing of poetry and history did not remain mere appendages to the culture of the orator. Moreover, the demands to which humanism responded were not all in the realm of ideas. Many arose from problems of political and social life. The reader will find some reference to these aspects of humanism in Part Two of this study, and in the Conclusion; however, they are treated in a rather summary fashion. The book's basic concern is with the single question of the relationship between rhetoric and philosophy. The brief examination of other questions about the humanists—their place in Renaissance society, their relationship to certain features of medieval intellectual history—is conducted, so to speak, through the prism provided by the discussion of rhetoric and philosophy in humanist thought.

READERS of this book will find in the notes and text many evidences of the author's debts to others who have studied the subject before him, but some scholars and friends have contributed to the final work in ways which can be acknowledged properly only at the beginning, and in the first person. Of these, I think first of E. Harris Harbison, under whose guidance this study was presented in its first form as a doctoral thesis in 1963. Professor Harbison provided both kind encouragement to follow my interests where they seemed to lead, and perceptive criticism of the conclusions that emerged. His death in 1964 deprived me—as it did other students of the Renaissance—of wise and gentle counsel. Had he lived longer, this would have been a better book. While preparing this study as a doctoral thesis, I received valuable advice and criticism also from W. S. Howell, and from Joseph R. Strayer. Paul Oskar Kristeller's help has been indispensable from beginning to end. It was from his writings on Renaissance thought that I received the first impulse to study humanism in the terms employed here. Almost from that first moment he has both encouraged my work and rescued me from many errors and inadequacies. He read the whole manuscript in nearly final form; the factual accuracy of many statements would not have met the rigorous standards of scholarship without his help. William J. Bouwsma's reading of the manuscript improved it in a different way, making me aware of several general problems of interpretation, organization, and tone. I have not solved all these problems to my own satisfaction, but I think the book is better for their having been raised. To Felix Gilbert I owe many things that cannot be stated here, as well as some that can. His friendship and encouragement have lightened my work, and added much pleasure to it. He read this study both in its earlier version as a thesis and in its penultimate one as a book, and improved every aspect of it—conception, content, and style. At the Princeton University Press, R. Miriam Brokaw helped me by her kind and continuing interest in this book, and Linda Peterson lent her fine sense of clarity and style to the improvement of every page. Many other friends and colleagues have also helped me—some of them in less immediate, but no less appreciated ways. To name them all would be to write another, different kind of book.

Most of the research for this study was carried out in the Princeton University Library, and in the Biblioteca Nazionale Centrale of Florence. My work was aided by Princeton University, which provided me with a Procter Fellowship in 1960-61, and by the State Department, which granted me a Fulbright Fellowship for research in Italy in 1961-62. The final revisions were done while I was a Fellow of the Harvard University Center for Italian Renaissance Studies, Villa "I Tatti," Florence, in 1966-67.

An earlier version of Chapter II appeared in the *Journal of the History of Ideas*, XXVI (1965); portions of Chapters VII and VIII were published in *Past and Present*, No. 34 (1966). I am grateful to the editors of these journals for permission to reprint this material here. I also wish to thank the Harvard University Press for permission to quote from the Loeb Classical Library editions.

To my wife, Jayn, I owe a debt which may be mentioned here, but which can be specified and acknowledged only on pages written for her alone.

J. E. S.

Princeton
November 1967

INTRODUCTION

IN HIS *De inventione rhetorica*, Cicero observed that man was distinguished from other animals by his power of speech. Petrarch, coming upon this passage in his copy of Victorinus' commentary on Cicero, was moved to make a note. "Here Cicero spoke as an orator," Petrarch remarked. "He spoke as a philosopher however in the second book of the *De finibus*, where he said: 'Although men differ from the beasts in many respects, they do so chiefly in this, that they have reason. . . .'"[1] Petrarch's comment may seem odd to many people today. It seldom occurs to us to juxtapose the orator and the philosopher, much less to attribute to each a particular view of what distinguishes man from the beasts. To the humanists of the Renaissance, however, Petrarch's remark was not at all strange. The relationship between the orator and the philosopher, between rhetoric and philosophy, was one of their continual interests. Nor were the humanists alone in their concern with this question. Many classical and medieval writers had shared it, and some later thinkers would too.

The contrast between oratory and philosophy had many meanings. In a sense, the one that Petrarch voiced in his comment on Cicero was the most fundamental: the philosopher and the orator held different views of what made man unique. Both accepted the Greek word *logos* as a description of man's distinctive quality, but for the philosopher *logos* had the Latin sense of *ratio*, reason, whereas for the orator it meant *oratio*, speech. To regard man primarily as a thinker was to posit different potentialities and expectations for him than to view him first of all as a speaker. The history of the relationship between philosophy and rhetoric shows that they have been regarded not only as separate studies in themselves, but as alternative centers around which to organize broad programs of education. The choice of one or the other as the central intellectual discipline de-

---

[1] Pierre de Nolhac, *Pétrarque et l'humanisme* (Paris, 1907), I, 249-50.

termined the way in which other arts—grammar, logic, poetry, history, ethics—would be defined and pursued. The contrast between a cultural program organized around rhetoric and one structured around philosophy has been the focal point of some dramatic and significant encounters in the history of Western thought. In these moments of sharp conflict, rhetoric and philosophy emerge as the bases for contrasting perspectives on the whole of man's intellectual and moral life.[2]

One of the earliest clear descriptions of rhetoric and philosophy as competing cultural ideals appeared in the Socratic dialogues of Plato.[3] There Socrates advanced a program of culture and education, a *paideia*, based on philosophy. In doing so he set himself against the rhetorical sophists such as Gorgias, for whom the foundation of *paideia* was the art of oratory. As developed by Plato,

[2] On the role of these different perspectives in the history of medieval and Renaissance thought, see Richard McKeon, "Renaissance and Method in Philosophy," *Studies in the History of Ideas*, ed. Dept. of Philosophy, Columbia University, III (1935), 37-114, also *idem*, "Rhetoric in the Middle Ages," *Speculum*, XVII (1942), 1-32, and "Poetry and Philosophy in the Twelfth Century," *Modern Philology*, XLIII (1946). McKeon's essays are extremely suggestive, and the present study owes much to them, although the terminology and substance of what follows differs widely from his. On rhetoric as a category in intellectual history, see also I. A. Richards, *The Philosophy of Rhetoric* (New York, 1936); Chaim Perelman, *Rhétorique et philosophie, pour une théorie de l'argumentation en philosophie* (Paris, 1952), and *idem*, *Traité de l'argumentation, la nouvelle rhétorique* (2 vols., Paris, 1958); P. Albert Duhamel, "The Function of Rhetoric as Effective Expression," *Journal of the History of Ideas*, X (1949), 344-56.

[3] For classical rhetoric and its relations with philosophy, see Werner Jaeger, *Paideia: The Ideals of Greek Culture*, trans. Gilbert Highet (3 vols., New York, 1943); Hans Friedrich von Arnim, *Leben und Werke des Dio von Prusa, mit einer Einleitung: Sophistik, Rhetorik, Philosophie in ihrem Kampf um die Jugendbildung* (Berlin, 1898); August Burk, *Die Pädagogik des Isokrates als Grundlegung des humanistischen Bildungs-Ideals* (Würzburg, 1923); H. Gomperz, *Sophistik und Rhetorik* (Leipzig, 1912). Also, H. I. Marrou, *A History of Education in Antiquity*, trans. George Lamb (New York, 1956); Charles Sears Baldwin, *Ancient Rhetoric and Poetic* (New York, 1924), and Donald Lemen Clark, *Rhetoric in Greco-Roman Education* (New York, 1957).

Socratic philosophy challenged the claims of the rhetorical sophists that the training they offered was appropriate to man's rational faculty, his *logos*. Plato's Socrates sought to replace a form of education based on training in speech with one founded on the rational search for truth. Whereas the rhetorical sophists had trained men to succeed in an existing world of politics, the new philosophical *paideia* was based on "the effort to form one's life along lines which are philosophically understood, and to direct it so as to fulfill the intellectual and moral definition of man."[4] The confrontation of rhetoric and philosophy in the Socratic dialogues thus went well beyond a competition between two intellectual methods. Rhetoric and philosophy imposed different expectations on their students; each asked its followers to accept a different image of the properly educated man.

The qualities which rhetoric and philosophy sought to produce in the men who pursued them were, respectively, eloquence and wisdom. What was meant by eloquence? To many people today the word suggests an aesthetic quality: an eloquent speech is beautiful, harmonious, dignified. This was not the primary meaning of eloquence to classical and Renaissance writers. To them eloquence meant, above all, persuasive power. The orator sought to teach and to entertain his hearers, but most of all to move them, to persuade them. This was his proper task. As a man of eloquence he was a leader in public assemblies; his speech gave him power over other men.[5] The public nature of rhetorical eloquence distinguished it from the wisdom of the philosopher. Wisdom was defined in a number of different ways by classical writers, but the various definitions had much in common. Wisdom was knowledge of human and divine things, knowledge of first causes and principles, or knowledge of the highest things.[6] Though such knowledge might lead to power over the external world, wisdom was first of

[4] Jaeger, *Paideia*, II, 69-70.
[5] See, e.g., Cicero, *De oratore* I, viii, 33.
[6] See Eugene F. Rice, Jr., *The Renaissance Idea of Wisdom* (Cambridge, Mass., 1958), pp. 1-3.

all an inward excellence, a private achievement of the wise man.

The question of the relationship between rhetoric and philosophy included the problem of the relative value of eloquence and wisdom, and of the proper place of each in men's lives. Most writers, in antiquity and later, agreed that wisdom was morally superior to eloquence. Even a rhetorician like Cicero admitted that the power of eloquence could be made to serve evil ends. True wisdom could not be misused in the same way (assuming, of course, that it was distinguished from such lesser qualities as prudence or mere cleverness). Genuine knowledge of goodness and virtue could not aid evil or vice.[7] While wisdom was placed above eloquence, however, it was subject to a characteristic weakness. By itself it had no necessary power over men, no inherent ability to make its message active in the world. Thus the danger that the power of eloquence might not serve wisdom was matched by the fear that wisdom itself would lack power over men. To avoid these pitfalls, many writers embraced an ideal which promised to cure both evil and weakness. This ideal was the union of eloquence and wisdom, the combination of rhetoric and philosophy. If the two could be joined together, then wisdom would be made active and eloquence committed to the service of truth. This was Plato's purpose in the *Phaedrus*, and Cicero's in several of his treatises.[8]

The ideal of the combination of rhetoric and philosophy appears over and over again in the history of the relationship between these two arts. Yet many problems about its meaning have always remained. To propose a union of wisdom and eloquence was simple enough; to show how it could be accomplished was much more difficult. The same considerations which made the combination seem so desirable could, if looked at in reverse, impede it. Philosophers, absorbed in the pursuit of truth, sometimes scorned mere custom and popular opinion. To orators, practical

[7] See the introductory paragraphs of Cicero's *De inventione.*
[8] See below, Chap. I.

men who sought to work in a world ruled by custom and opinion, this scorn gave evidence of the small utility of philosophical truths to practical life.[9] Similarly, the possibility that rhetorical power might be used to serve questionable ends, and the necessity—admitted by most orators—of appealing to their audiences on grounds other than pure reason and undiluted truth, sometimes caused men whose passion was for reason and truth alone to look with disgust on "mere rhetoric." To combine the two arts required either that philosophy modify its commitment to abstract truth, or that rhetoric compromise its drive for persuasive success. The combination of the two arts always threatened to deprive each of something essential to itself; in fact no form of the union could be devised which fully satisfied all the demands of both. The version which met a philosopher's needs appeared impractical or ineffectual to an orator; the one envisioned by the rhetorician seemed to the philosopher insufficiently tied to truth. Thus the ideal of the combination of rhetoric and philosophy did not completely solve the problem of the proper relationship between the two arts. Often it became simply the framework within which this relationship was discussed.[10]

The discussion below treats the problems of combining wisdom and eloquence as they appeared to men whose main roots were in the tradition of rhetoric rather than of philosophy. The reason for this is simply that the author is a historian seeking to understand particular moments in the development of European culture, not a philosopher

[9] For example, Callicles in Plato's *Gorgias*, 485A-486D. On the early Roman suspicion of Greek philosophy, see Marrou, *A History of Education in Antiquity*, pp. 329-30.

[10] The full justification of these statements rests on the discussion below. But note that Plato in the *Phaedrus* answered doubts about the practicality of his rhetoric by declaring that "even to fail in an honorable object is honorable," and added: "If we had the truth ourselves, do you think we should care much about the opinions of men?" (*Phaedrus*, 274A-C). The rhetorician Isocrates, however, insisted that in public discourse "we should not seek novelties, for in these discourses it is not possible to say what is paradoxical or incredible or outside the circle of accepted belief" (*To Niccocles*, 41; Loeb edn., I, 63).

attempting to clarify a general question. However, the main elements of the general question, as they would have to be considered by a philosopher, should emerge from our historical inquiry.

Something should be said about the organization and scope of the present study. We begin with Cicero. To understand humanist discussions of the relationship between rhetoric and philosophy, one must be aware of their Ciceronian background. The unique completeness of Cicero's treatment, and his particular perspective, made the Roman orator a model for the humanists in their search for eloquence and wisdom. In the main body of the study we shall discuss the reemergence and working out of the questions that Cicero raised, as they appear in the writings of four major Renaissance humanists: Petrarch, Coluccio Salutati, Leonardo Bruni, and Lorenzo Valla. Petrarch heads the list because he was the father of humanism in the Renaissance. In the present context, this means that he rediscovered certain basic elements of Ciceronian rhetorical culture which medieval men had not seen. His articulation of these elements made it possible for those who followed to work out their own perspectives on the orator's place in the intellectual world. Salutati and Bruni, outstanding followers of Petrarch in the next two generations, each pursued the union of wisdom and eloquence in a different direction. Valla was more radical in his devotion to rhetoric than any of his predecessors; he is our stopping point, because in his writings the humanist celebration of eloquence reached its culmination. After his death, the problem of the relationship between rhetoric and philosophy remained alive, but it no longer contributed as much to the development of humanist thought.

Following this account of the development of humanist views on rhetoric and philosophy we shall consider, in Part Two, humanist culture in relation to three relevant contexts. The first is the background provided by characteristic medieval discussions of the same set of questions; the second is the comparison of humanism with professional

rhetoric in Italy before Petrarch; the third is the relationship between humanism and the other main intellectual
tendency of the period, scholasticism, and the place of each
in the life of the time. This part of the study differs in approach and in texture from the chapters of Part One: here
the argument is more speculative and the documentation
less complete. Despite the tentative nature of these chapters,
they are included because of the importance of the questions on which they bear. They seek to expand the understanding of the humanist movement along lines suggested
by the analysis in Part One. No doubt their reach exceeds
their grasp, but if they contribute to the overcoming of
some old clichés and suggest further lines of inquiry, they
will have served their purpose.

CONTENTS

Part One

Philosophy and the Humanist
Defense of Rhetoric

CHAPTER I

RHETORIC AND PHILOSOPHY: THE CICERONIAN MODEL

O great father of Roman eloquence! I am not alone in offering you my gratitude; with me are all those who deck themselves with the flowers of Latin speech. We sprinkle our meadows with water from your fountains; you are our guide; it is you who sustain and enlighten us." The writer was Petrarch.[1] The recipient of his praise could only have been Marcus Tullius Cicero. To the humanists of the fourteenth and early fifteenth centuries, Cicero was the central figure of classical culture, the inspiration and guide for those who sought to return to the classical world. "According to the opinion, judgment and acknowledgment of the most authoritative men," one of Petrarch's followers wrote, Cicero was "the most excellent teacher and ornament of all those among the Latins who were distinguished by their writings in any past age, or who will be so in the future."[2]

Above all else, it was Cicero's eloquence which fitted him for this part. "Cicero is the source of eloquence," Coluccio Salutati wrote; "any later writers who treat the art of rhetoric derive from that source." "Nor was anyone eloquent after Cicero's time who did not take him for a leader and authority," Poggio Bracciolini agreed. "To the power of the

[1] *Le Familiari* (*Familiarium rerum libri*), ed. V. Rossi (Florence, 1933-42), XXIV, 4, 4. This edition of Petrarch's letters will hereafter be cited as *Fam.* The translation is taken from Pierre de Nolhac, *Petrarch and the Ancient World* (Boston, 1907), p. 109. For a translation of the whole letter, see Mario Emilio Cosenza, *Petrarch's Letters to Classical Authors* (Chicago, 1910), pp. 21-28.

[2] Sicconis Polentoni, *Scriptorum illustrium Latinae linguae libri XVIII*, ed. B. L. Ullman (Rome, 1928), p. 266: "Me quoque id commovit quam maxime, quod existimarem ignavie potius quam modestiae tribui, si eum pretermitterem qui omnium qui praeclare aut scripserunt ulla aetate superiori aut in posterum scribent unquam apud Latinos, gravissimorum hominum sententia, iudicio, confessione sit magister summus et lumen."

3

Roman Empire he added eloquence, the ruler of human
affairs," Leonardo Bruni proclaimed.[3] Cicero's role as the
prince of Latin eloquence might by itself have recommended his writings to the humanists, but the power of
speech was not all they found in him. When Bruni said that
Cicero "disclosed the light of learning and wisdom" to men
of Latin speech, he suggested that the orator was not important only for his style. "He was the first to explain philosophy in Latin," Bruni went on. "Previously philosophy
was unknown in our language, and almost shrank from
Roman speech; many learned men thought it could neither
be written about nor spoken of in Latin."[4] Cicero helped
men learn to think as well as to speak.

A careful consideration of humanist comments on Cicero
would reveal many reasons for their devotion to him. As a
Roman, he aroused sympathy in Italians who felt a nostal-
gic attachment to their own classical past. His works were
accessible to readers who knew no Greek and his discussions of philosophy were conducted in nontechnical terms.
Since he lived at a time when all the basic work of classical
philosophy had already been accomplished, he was able
to summarize much of what could be learned about ancient
thought. No doubt other general reasons could be added to
this list. In the present context, however, they are less rele-

[3] *Epistolario di Coluccio Salutati*, ed. Francesco Novati (4 vols.,
Rome, 1891-1911), I, 307: "Cicero quidem fons est eloquentie; qui-
cunque post eum artem rhetorice tradiderunt, ab illo fonte derivant."
(This work will be cited as *Epistolario*.) Poggius, *Epistolae*, ed.
Thomas De Tonellis (Florence, 1832), III, 176: "Neque enim eloquens
quisquam post Ciceronem fuit quin illum eloquentiae habuerit ducem
et auctorem." (These letters have been reprinted as Vol. III of Poggius
Bracciolini, *Opera Omnia*, con una premessa di Riccardo Fubini
[Turin, 1964].) Leonardo Bruni Aretino, *Cicero novus seu Ciceronis
vita*, in *Humanistisch-Philosophische Schriften*, ed. Hans Baron (Leipzig and Berlin, 1928), pp. 114-15: "Hic ad potestatem Romani imperii
dominam rerum humanarum, eloquentiam, adiunxit." Cf. *Vita di
Cicerone scritta da messer Lionardo Bruni Aretino* (Parma, 1804),
pp. 75-76.
[4] *Cicero novus*, ed. Baron, pp. 114-15: "Hic enim primus philosophiam antea nostris litteris incognitam et paene a Romano sermone
abhorrentem, de qua nec Latine scribi nec disputari posse plerique
docti viri arbitrabantur, Latinis litteris explicuit."

4

vant than a more specific appeal that Cicero held for the humanists, partly suggested in the statements just quoted. Cicero was both a man of eloquence and a man of philosophy. He had an enormous respect for the great figures of Greek philosophy, and he found in their endeavors the answers to certain human needs which social life could not fully meet; thus he recommended the study of philosophy to his fellow citizens. But his own basic commitment was to the life of man in society, and his primary intellectual allegiance was to the culture of rhetoric. Balancing these two sets of loyalties, Cicero gave more attention than perhaps any other classical writer to the question of the relationship between rhetoric and philosophy. It is this aspect of his work which we shall see reflected in the concerns of the Renaissance humanists, and it is on this aspect of his thought that we must now focus our attention.[5]

Cicero dealt specifically with oratory in several treatises, of which the *De oratore* is the most elaborate, and for our purposes by far the most interesting. The picture of the orator given there was derived from earlier writers, from Cicero's own experience, and from his memories of some of the great orators of Rome. Two of these, Crassus and Antonius, took the largest parts in the dialogue. Much of the usual subject matter of rhetorical treatises was included. The speakers described the orator's tasks as *docere, delectare, movere*: to teach, to please, and to move; recounted the five-part division of oratory into invention or discovery, arrangement, style, memory, and delivery; listed the three kinds of speeches: forensic, deliberative, and pane-

[5] The fullest and most recent treatment of Cicero's thought from this perspective is Alain Michel's *Rhétorique et Philosophie Chez Ciceron* (Paris, 1960). Michel's approach and emphasis differ somewhat from those adopted here, but his work is solid and complete (664 pages of text), and should be consulted for further information about Cicero. See also, for general discussions of Cicero, M. L. Clarke, *The Roman Mind* (Cambridge, 1960); C. N. Cochrane, *Christianity and Classical Culture* (New York, 1940; reprinted 1957), pp. 38ff.; also the works of Marrou, Baldwin, and D. L. Clark, cited in the notes to the Introduction. The bibliography on Cicero is too vast to list here.

gyric; and discussed the division of the speech into sections, namely the exordium (aimed at securing the attention and good will of the audience), the statement of the case, the proof, the refutation of the opponent's case, and the peroration or summary. Many other topics concerning the orator's training, his talents, and his place in public life were treated, sometimes traditionally, sometimes in conscious opposition to earlier writers.[6] Underlying the whole discussion, however, was a more general question: Should the orator seek to acquire a wide general culture—especially learning in philosophy—or should he instead concentrate his training on more restricted and intense practice in oratory itself?

Despite the disagreement between Crassus and Antonius on the first day of the discussion, Cicero's answer to this question was never really in doubt. Here, as elsewhere, Cicero affirmed his allegiance to the ideal of the combination of rhetoric and philosophy. In the prologue to Book II of *De oratore*, Cicero wrote to his brother Quintus: "No man has ever succeeded in achieving splendor and excellence in oratory, I will not say merely without training in speaking, but without taking all knowledge [*sapientia*] for his province as well."[7] Similar statements can be found in Cicero's other works. The opening affirmation of *De inventione* was often quoted by later writers: Wisdom without eloquence was of little use to civic life, eloquence separate from wisdom was often of great harm; only the man who joined the two could bring true benefit to himself and to his fellow men. Cicero invoked the same ideal

[6] On Cicero's exposition, his sources, and his relation to other writers on rhetoric, see D. L. Clark, *Rhetoric in Greco-Roman Education*, esp. pp. 68-80; Baldwin, *Ancient Rhetoric and Poetic*, esp. pp. 37-61; Eduard Norden, *Die Antike Kunstprosa* (Leipzig and Berlin, 1915), I, 212-33; Martin Schanz and Carl Hosius, *Geschichte der Römischen Literatur*, in *Handbuch der Altertumswissenschaft . . .* neu herausgegeben von Walter Otto, Sec. VIII, Part I (Munich, 1927), pp. 459-63, with extensive bibliography to 1927.

[7] *De oratore* II, i, 5; Loeb edn., I, 201. (All translations from Cicero's works given in the text and notes are those of the Loeb Classical Library editions, except where otherwise indicated.)

when he wrote on philosophical subjects. In the *Tusculan Disputations* he declared that he intended to make use of rhetoric in his discussions of philosophy, "for it has ever been my conviction that philosophy in its finished form enjoys the power of treating the greatest problems with adequate fullness and in an attractive style."[8] Such statements reflect the actual attempt Cicero made to adapt philosophical learning to the tasks of the forum, as well as his effort to present philosophy itself in an elegant and persuasive way. No ideal better characterizes Cicero's vision of culture than the combination of rhetoric and philosophy.

Despite the central place this ideal occupied in Cicero's work, however, certain of his statements show that he regarded it as difficult and perhaps impossible to achieve. What made it so problematical, Cicero recognized, was that the orator, in contrast to those who pursued certain other arts (clearly including philosophers), was limited in his intellectual range by the capacities of the ordinary men who made up his audience: "Whereas in all other arts that is most excellent which is farthest removed from the understanding and mental capacity of the untrained, in oratory the very cardinal sin is to depart from the language of everyday life, and the usage approved by the sense of the community."[9] The orator shared the common life of his community, and in the exercise of his office he had to accept its basic standards. This meant not only that he had to conform to its linguistic habits, but that he must respect its moral standards as well. We shall see that Cicero in *De oratore* regarded the ethical doctrines of the Stoics as incompatible with oratory because they clashed with the common beliefs of ordinary men. Philosophy, however, was among the arts that were free of such restrictions. In the *Tusculan Disputations* Cicero said that philosophy "of set purpose avoids the multitude and is in her turn an object

[8] *De inventione* I, i, 1; *Tusc. Disp.* I, iv, 7. Cf. Plato, *Phaedrus*, 269-70; Isocrates, *Antidosis*, 47-49.
[9] *De oratore* I, iii, 12; Loeb edn., I, 11. Compare the passage from Isocrates, quoted above in note 10 of the Introduction.

7

of suspicion and dislike to them." He quoted with approval Plato's description of philosophy as a preparation for death, adding that its task was "to sequester the soul from pleasure . . . ; from private property . . . ; from public interests; from any kind of business."[10]

This contrast between rhetoric and philosophy caused the two disciplines to have opposing attitudes toward the problem of knowledge. Philosophy sought a kind of knowledge which was superior to mere opinion or customary belief. But the speakers in *De oratore* agreed that oratory did not take part in the search for this sort of knowledge. It was not an "art" in the sense of "the knowledge and clear perception of facts, all tending to a single conclusion and incapable of misleading." Its subject matter did not consist "in things thoroughly examined and clearly apprehended, and which are also outside the control of mere opinion, and within the grasp of exact knowledge." The reason for this was that the orator used popular rather than philosophical language. "For all the kinds of language we ourselves use in public speaking are changeable matter, and adapted to the general understanding of the crowd."[11] The orator's commitment to the intellectual and linguistic standards of his audience prevented him from fully participating in the search for knowledge carried out by the philosopher.

These considerations suggest a large and perhaps unbridgeable gap between rhetoric and philosophy as Cicero conceived them. Despite this distance, however, Cicero never gave up the attempt to bring the two arts together. Not only did he discuss philosophy in his rhetorical works; he also continued to insist on the relevance of oratory to philosophical discourse, even when it concerned the most rigorous and uncompromising of philosophers, the Stoics.[12]

---

[10] *Tusc. Disp.* II, i, 4; Loeb edn., pp. 149-51; and I, xxx, 74-75; Loeb edn., pp. 87-89.

[11] *De oratore* I, xxiii, 108; Loeb edn., I, 77. Cf. Isocrates, *Antidosis*, 271; Loeb edn., II, 335: "It is not in the nature of man to attain to a science by the possession of which we can know positively what we should do or what we should say. . . ."

[12] See Cicero's *Paradoxa Stoicorum*, and the discussion below.

How did Cicero justify his continued faith in the ideal of the combination of rhetoric and philosophy? From his point of view, what precisely did this ideal entail?

One of the most significant features of Cicero's version of this union was that it differed markedly from those of both Plato and Aristotle. In order to clarify Cicero's position—and therefore the position of his admirers, the humanists—in the history of the matters we are considering in this study, we must indicate something of the way in which these two greatest figures of Greek philosophy understood the union of philosophy and oratory, and how the most eminent Roman orator differed from them in his understanding of it.

Plato's historical position and his cultural program both demanded that he be concerned with the relation of rhetoric to philosophy. Sophistic education in his day was largely education in rhetoric. Effective speech was one of the chief needs of politically active men in a Greek city-state. In fact, the classical Greek word for a politician was simply *rhetor*. "Eloquence then was the point from which any attempt to educate a man for political leadership was bound to start."[13] Necessarily, sophistic education also touched on many philosophic issues, but the sophists did not regard philosophy as an independent discipline, capable of measuring existing cultural or political life by its own standards. The elements of later Greek philosophy and science contained in the sophists' program were restricted by their dependence on the underlying rhetorical ideal. As soon as these elements became independent of rhetoric, they would provide powerful opposition and competition for the sophistic *paideia*.[14]

The leader in the struggle for this independence was the Socrates of Plato's dialogues. By putting forth a new conception of knowledge and insisting that education was not possible apart from such knowledge, Socrates demanded that rhetoric be joined to philosophy in a sense quite differ-

---

[13] Jaeger, *Paideia*, I, 287-88. [14] *Ibid.*, pp. 293-95.

ent from the sophistic one. Both to fulfill his moral obligation as a leader of men, and to succeed in his own task of
creating persuasive speech, the orator needed to devote
himself to the knowledge of man provided by philosophy.
No one, Socrates asserted, "will ever be able to speak about
anything as he ought to speak unless he have a knowledge
of philosophy."[15]

To Plato this meant not only that the orator must study
philosophy, but much more: he must take its intellectual
and moral standards for his own. In the *Phaedrus*, Socrates
asserted that the true art of rhetoric would not be built on
the principles of the rhetoricians, but along the lines of dialectic: definition of the subject, its division into its smallest
component parts, and arrangement of the speech according
to the logical structure of the subject itself.[16] Socrates' new
rhetoric rejected the common reliance of orators on prob-
ability or verisimilitude. The sophists argued that men were
persuaded by what seemed to them to be true, and that
this was not always the same thing as truth itself; it followed, they said, that the rhetorician need concern himself only with what was probable, not with what was true.
In Socrates' view, the orator who acted thus did not teach
his hearers, but deceived them. If a man mistakenly persuaded a soldier to ride to battle on an ass, thinking it a
horse, he would not have benefited the soldier. "And when
the orator, instead of putting an ass in the place of a horse,
puts good for evil, being himself as ignorant of their true
nature as the city on which he imposes is ignorant; and
having studied the notions of the multitude, persuades
them to do evil instead of good—what will be the har-
vest which rhetoric will be likely to gather after the sowing
of such fruit?"[17] Thus, for Socrates, the orator had to combine rhetoric with philosophy in a way which made no
compromise with the weaker understanding of those who

---

[15] *Phaedrus*, 261A. See Jaeger, *Paideia*, Vol. II, Bk. 3.
[16] *Phaedrus*, 265Dff., and 277 B-C.
[17] *Ibid.*, 260C; cf. 272Dff.

10

were not themselves philosophers. He boasted that orators
trained as he suggested would be "worthy of a higher
name . . . —lovers of wisdom or philosophers is their modest
and befitting title."[18] Plato's reform of rhetoric was a part
of his hoped-for reform of Athenian politics and morality.
The Greek politician was the *rhetor*. In the *Phaedrus*, as in
the *Republic*, Plato's aim was to transform him into the
philosopher.

As we have already seen, this is precisely what Cicero
denied could be done. The orator's subject matter, he insisted, could not be placed "outside the control of mere
opinion, and within the grasp of exact knowledge." His language was inconstant, because it had to be adapted to the
understanding of the crowd. It is not necessary to rely on
the implications of this observation to demonstrate Cicero's
rejection of the Socratic or Platonic view of the proper relationship between rhetoric and philosophy. In *De oratore*
Cicero included Socrates among those Greeks "who, being
themselves copiously furnished with learning and with
talent, but yet shrinking on deliberate principle from politics and affairs, scouted and scorned this practice of oratory." Socrates won whatever argument he entered, but in
Cicero's view Greek culture was the loser by his work.

> Whereas the persons engaged in handling and pursuing
> and teaching the subjects that we are now investigating
> were designated by a single title, the whole study and
> practice of the liberal sciences being entitled philosophy,
> Socrates robbed them of this general designation, and in
> his discussions separated the science of wise thinking
> from that of elegant speaking, though in reality they are
> closely linked together; and the genius and varied dis-
> courses of Socrates have been immortally enshrined in
> the compositions of Plato, Socrates himself not having left
> a single scrap of writing. This is the source from which
> has sprung the undoubtedly absurd and unprofitable and

[18] *Ibid.*, 278D.

11

reprehensible severance between the tongue and the brain, leading to our having one set of professors to teach us to think and another to teach us to speak.[19]

In Cicero's view, therefore, rhetoric and philosophy had been correctly joined together before Socrates appeared on the scene, i.e., by the rhetorical sophists. The Socratic version of the union of the two arts, based as it was on the dominance of philosophy, appeared to Cicero as the opposite of a proper combination of them. "The followers of Socrates cut connection with the practicing lawyers and detached these from the common title of philosophy, although the old masters had intended there to be a marvellously close alliance between oratory and philosophy."[20] Cicero's version of this alliance depended on the recognition of the right of practicing orators to be called philosophers, whereas Plato's demanded that the methods of philosophy be adopted by rhetoric.

Cicero's position becomes still clearer when we contrast his attitude with that of Aristotle's *Rhetoric*. Here the differences are less fundamental, but no less real. As is well known, Aristotle differed from his master Plato in that he had a more practical bent, was less utopian in his political program, and granted greater philosophical value to realms of contingency. He admitted that practical life contained many problems to which only probable answers could be given. Thus his view of rhetoric admitted that oratory could not be turned into a science of certainty, and he agreed that rhetorical discourse should remain content with probable demonstrations.[21] On this point his position was much closer to Cicero's than Plato's was. Cicero often remarked

[19] *De oratore* III, xvi, 59-61; Loeb edn., II, 47-49. Cf. Isocrates' criticism of Athenian usage of the term "philosophy" in Plato's time, *Antidosis*, 285.

[20] *De oratore* III, xix, 73; Loeb edn., II, 59. Cicero gave a somewhat different explanation of this in *De inventione* I, iii, 4. On Cicero's ties to the sophists, see Michel, *Rhétorique et Philosophie Chez Ciceron*, pp. 87, 101-04, 658.

[21] See Aristotle, *Rhetoric* I, 4, 1359b, where rhetoric is distinguished from the sciences.

on Aristotle's interest in rhetoric, and he sometimes claimed to follow his precepts. He praised Aristotle's style, and once spoke of his "golden stream of eloquence."[22]

Where Aristotle's attitude toward rhetoric in relation to philosophy clashed with Cicero's was on the question of what fields of knowledge the orator was competent to treat. For the Stagirite, the competence of rhetoric was strictly limited. He wrote in his *Rhetoric*: "To enumerate and classify accurately the usual subjects of public business, and further to frame, as far as possible, true definitions of them, is a task which we must not attempt on the present occasion. For it does not belong to the art of rhetoric, but to a more instructive art and a more real branch of knowledge; and as it is, rhetoric has been given a far wider subject-matter than strictly belongs to it."[23] This view of the province of the orator was poles apart from that of *De oratore*. We have already noted Cicero's belief that the man who sought perfection in oratory would take all knowledge, all *sapientia*, for his domain. Cicero was well aware who some of the opponents of his conception had been:

> To us belong—assuming that we are really orators, that is, persons competent to be retained as leaders and principals in civil actions and criminal trials and public de-

[22] Regarding Aristotle's "aureum flumen orationis," see Cicero's *Academica* II, 119; cf. *De oratore* I, x, 43; I, xi, 49, and elsewhere. On Cicero's use of Aristotelian rhetorical precepts, see *Topics* I, i-ii and *De inventione* I, v, 7; I, vii, 9; I, xxxv, 61; II, ii, 6, and elsewhere. On the harmony of "Peripateticism" with oratory, see below. It should be pointed out here that the Aristotelian treatises available to Cicero were not the ones known to modern readers, but an earlier and more popular group of Aristotle's writings, only fragments of which now survive. These were certainly written in a more polished style than the works we know today, but Professor Jaeger doubts that their style reflected a concern for rhetorical splendor. While the youthful Aristotle sometimes included rhetorical ornaments in his treatises, his chief concern was with scientific clarity. Later Peripatetics, beginning with Theophrastus, gave much more attention to rhetorical precepts; it may be that Cicero's praise of Aristotle's eloquence was influenced by their writings, as his ideas of Aristotelian doctrine definitely were. See Werner Jaeger, *Aristotile* (Ital. edn., Florence, 1935), pp. 37-38 and note.

[23] *Rhetoric* I, 4, 1359[b].

13

bates—to us, I say, belong the broad estates of wisdom and of learning, which having been allowed to lapse and become derelict during our absorption in affairs, have been invaded by persons too generously supplied with leisure, persons who actually either banter and ridicule the orator after the manner of Socrates in Plato's *Gorgias*, or else write a few little manuals of instruction in the art of oratory and label them with the title of *Rhetoric*—just as if the province of the rhetoricians did not include their pronouncements on the subjects of justice and duty and the constitution and government of states, in short the entire field of practical philosophy.[24]

Since Cicero praised Aristotle's treatment of rhetoric elsewhere, it may not seem likely that it was he who was being castigated here. Yet it is clear from the words of Aristotle quoted above that he held exactly that view of the orator's proper sphere which Cicero attacked. That Cicero was aware of this is suggested by another long passage from *De oratore*. Contrasting Aristotle with others who had written about rhetoric, Cicero said:

And between this Aristotle (I read also that book of his, setting forth the rhetorical theories of all his forerunners, and those other works containing sundry observations of his own on the same art), and these true professors of this art, there seemed to me to be this difference,—that he surveyed these concerns of the art of rhetoric, *which he disdained*, with that same keen insight, by which he had discerned the essential nature of all things; whereas those others, considering this the only thing worth cultivating, have dwelt upon the treatment of this single subject, without his sagacity, but, in this one instance, with larger practice and closer application.[25]

[24] *De oratore* III, xxxi, 122; Loeb edn., II, 95-97. See also III, xxvii, 107-08.
[25] *De oratore* II, xxxviii, 160; Loeb edn., I, 313-15. Italics mine. Cicero sometimes spoke of Aristotle as one who had joined rhetoric to philosophy, and he even compared his own task with the Greek's (e.g., *Tusc. Disp.* I, iii, 6f.). But whereas Cicero sought to combine

14

But often put in compendium w/ Eth. Pol.

Thus in Cicero's view Aristotle was not a "true professor" of rhetoric, because he lacked a proper respect for the subject. Like Plato, he limited the competence of professional orators in a way which clashed sharply with Cicero's exaltation of them. Despite the genius of these two men, Cicero preferred the teachings of the Greek rhetoricians to theirs.

Notwithstanding all his insistence on a rhetorical culture informed by philosophy, then, Cicero preferred the treatment accorded rhetoric by those who considered it "the only thing worth cultivating" to the approach of one of the greatest Greek philosophers to the subject. Though Cicero often praised philosophers and their concerns, his works reveal a recurring suspicion of philosophy, and particularly of the attitude of philosophers toward rhetoric. Cicero wanted to combine rhetoric with philosophy, but not in the way that philosophers had. Their attempts to unite the two arts had been misdirected. They had tried to restrict the province of the orator, whereas in Cicero's view his domain actually included a large part of philosophy. What Cicero called "practical philosophy," or the study of *vitam et mores*—"the topics of virtue, duty, equity, and good, moral worth and utility, honor and disgrace, reward and punishment" and the like—this was properly at the orator's command.[26] He, not the philosopher, was the proper person to effect the desired union of the two arts.

It will not do, however, to say simply that Cicero wished to join rhetoric and philosophy by subordinating the second to the first. On the contrary, he often specifically stated that philosophy was the higher pursuit. In the *Tusculan Disputations* he said it was "grander and more fruitful" than oratory.[27] In *De inventione rhetorica* he said, "I have been led by reason itself to hold this opinion first and foremost, that wisdom without eloquence does too little for the good of states, but that eloquence without wisdom is generally

---

the two arts willingly, Aristotle had been driven to it by the competition of the rhetorician Isocrates. See *De oratore* III, xxxv, 141.

[26] *De oratore* I, xv, 68-69; III, xxvii, 107-08.

[27] *Tusc. Disp.* I, iv, 7.

highly disadvantageous and is never helpful." The study of
philosophy and moral conduct was "the highest and most
honorable of pursuits," and only through it could oratory
be turned to the true good of the community.[28] How could
Cicero reconcile the superior place given to philosophy in
these statements with his suspicion of its effects on oratory
elsewhere?

Cicero made his peace with philosophy by admitting its
superiority to rhetoric, while at the same time approaching
the various philosophical schools along a path which was
especially suited to the orator. He did not attempt to restrict philosophy within predetermined limits, but he constructed a point of view which hid the threat to rhetoric
that philosophy contained, and which made philosophy appear to fit the orator's requirements. Philosophy was not
absorbed by rhetoric, but neither was it allowed to restrict
the orator's competence, or to demand that rhetoric be
transformed along philosophical lines.

All this could not be accomplished simply by taking over
the doctrine of one of the existing philosophic schools. The
one which most nearly satisfied Cicero's requirements, however, was Academic skepticism. To the Ciceronian orator,
skepticism was a natural philosophic attitude, for reasons
we have already encountered in *De oratore*: rhetoric was
not an "art" in the sense of "the knowledge and clear perception of facts, all tending to a single conclusion and incapable of misleading." If, as Cicero insisted, practical philosophy was properly the domain of the orator, then one
should not expect complete certainty in this field. To be
sure, the skepticism which Cicero embraced was not based
solely on the orator's limitations. It also derived from the
Academics. Their criticism of knowledge was based on the
criterion for truth set forth by the Stoic Zeno, namely that
true perceptions "were of such a sort that there could not
be a false one of the same sort." Arcesilas, the founder of
the "New Academy," accepted this criterion, but he denied
that men could ever attain such perceptions. None of our

[28] *De inventione* I, i, 1.

notions convince us of their truth by their character of being utterly different from false or misleading ones. Therefore nothing can be perceived—no knowledge is possible.[29]
While Cicero thus built his skepticism on a philosophical
base, however, he also made quite explicit his awareness of
its harmony with rhetoric. The clearest statement of this
occurs in his *De natura deorum*. In this treatise, the speakers attribute the force of Cotta's discourse to his combination of training in oratory with learning in the techniques
of the Academics. Velleius says that he "would not carelessly try to dispute with someone who is at once an orator
and an Academic. I would not greatly fear someone who
was only an Academic, or an orator, however eloquent,
who was not versed in this philosophy, for I am not dis-
turbed either by a stream of empty words or by subtle arguments couched in a dry style." The two together made a
formidable mixture, however. A bit later in the discussion,
Cotta is praised for "those powers of eloquence which your
rhetorical exercises have bestowed upon you and which the
Academy has fostered."[30]

The reasons for this harmony go beyond the orator's own
practical skepticism. The orator and the skeptic were united
not only negatively, in their refusal to accept the teachings
of any dogmatic philosophical school as true, but also positively, in their claim to be able to speak persuasively on
any side of any philosophical question. The orator, as
orator, used the method of rhetoric to accomplish this, the
skeptical philosopher employed dialectic. The perfect orator would use dialectic as well as rhetoric in constructing
his speeches; to do so he had to learn the use of dialectic
from philosophers who also taught men to argue on both
sides of a case.[31] He would combine rhetoric with philosophy, but in a way which preserved his independence from

[29] *Academics* II, xxv, 113; Loeb edn., p. 613.
[30] *De natura deorum* II, i, 1; II, lxvii, 168 (my translation). See
also *Tusc. Disp.* II, ii, 5, and II, iii, 9.
[31] *De oratore* III, xix, 71; cf. *De finibus* V, iv, 10. The Peripatetics
are mentioned here together with the Academics, since they too taught
students to argue on either side of a question.

those philosophers who thought that the true love of wisdom dictated the acceptance of certain philosophic propositions.

Thus the orator could combine eloquence with philosophy while still preserving his freedom to uphold whatever position his situation demanded. But this dialectical ability was still not enough for the "truly cultured eloquence" Cicero envisioned in the *De oratore*. To fulfill this ideal required a different kind of knowledge of philosophy. It demanded not only that the orator know how to argue in a philosophical manner, but also that he have available a supply of philosophic opinions and maxims. These would enable him to "turn aside from the particular matter in dispute to engage in an explanation of the meaning of the general issue, so as to enable the audience to base their verdict in regard to the particular parties and charges and actions in question on a knowledge of the nature and character of the matter as a whole."[32] Cicero's orator would seek this knowledge, as Cicero himself did, in the teachings of the dogmatic philosophers. Since he would have to argue many diverse cases and points of view, he required a full supply of philosophical opinions. Different maxims would be needed to exhort an audience than to restrain one; the view of human nature which provided the best basis for praising a soldier might not serve for condemning a murderer; a different definition of patriotism would be employed in urging war than in praising peace.

Where would Cicero's orator find this learning in philosophy? To answer this question we must briefly state Cicero's position with regard to the philosophical schools which were popular in late republican Rome. Those with the most adherents seem to have been the Epicurean and the Stoic.[33] Of the two, Epicureanism did not attract Cicero at all. He admitted that some followers of Epicurus led admirable lives, but he denied that their virtues reflected their

[32] *De oratore* III, xxx, 120; Loeb edn., II, 95.
[33] On the philosophical interests of Romans in this period, see M. L. Clarke, *The Roman Mind.*

18

doctrines. The Epicurean praise of pleasure—however chastely one sought to define it—repelled Cicero morally and appeared to him indefensible intellectually. Moreover, the school's praise of a life of withdrawal from public duties made its teaching unfit for an active statesman of Rome. Though Cicero mentioned the Epicureans in *De oratore* and explained their moral doctrines in *De finibus*, in both cases he seemed anxious to be done with them quickly; they were the philosophers who interested him least.[34]

The Stoics, on the other hand, fascinated Cicero. This does not mean that he always approved of their doctrines; on the contrary, he often combated them. Even when he did, however, a note of admiration sometimes crept in. The outstanding characteristic of Stoic moral philosophy was its picture of the *sapiens*, a man convinced that happiness depended entirely on virtue and that moral worth (*honestas*) was the only genuine good, and fundamentally indifferent to lesser considerations such as health, riches, and fortune. Cicero often scoffed at this Stoic wise man; in his oration *Pro Murena* he subjected the image to outright ridicule: "Only the wise are beautiful—however deformed they may be; they alone are rich—even if utter beggars; kings—even if in a state of slavery. And we who are not wise men are runaways, exiles, enemies, madmen. All wrong actions are equal; every misdeed is a foul crime, and it is as bad to strangle a cock unnecessarily as to strangle your father."[35] Yet the very features of Stoic doctrine which drew Cicero's scorn here—its harshness to the common ear and its uncompromising rigor—evoked his praise elsewhere. As we shall see, Cicero sometimes thought of the Stoics as "the only true philosophers."

In Cicero's day, Stoic doctrine was changing. Next to the original Stoicism of Zeno and Chrysippus there grew up a reformed Stoic school, "Middle Stoicism," associated with the names of Panaetius and Posidonius. These philosophers

---

[34] For Cicero's arguments against the Epicureans, see *De finibus* II.
[35] *Pro Murena*, §61; trans. by Clarke, *The Roman Mind*, p. 33.

softened the earlier insistence on *honestas*. They said that the wise man should also devote himself to *decorum*, which they interpreted in a way that justified actions appropriate to existing situations. In earlier Stoicism, *decorum* meant only what was fitting to man as a rational being. Now, however, it was understood in a way which justified behavior in accord with existing social norms, and which took account of an individual's age and social position. Defined in this way, the Stoic *sapiens* could serve as a model for the Roman citizen: a man devoted to virtue, but in a way which reinforced rather than weakened his patriotic devotion to the state. Cicero took this Middle Stoicism as the basis for his description of the duties of a Roman aristocrat in his treatise *De officiis*.[36]

Yet the existence of this softer version of the Stoic ideal did not lessen Cicero's fascination with the earlier, more rigorous doctrine. If Middle Stoicism harmonized easily with the conventional wisdom of the Roman governing class, the original Stoic doctrines struck Cicero precisely because they did not: they were either foolishness, or a higher wisdom. Cicero ridiculed them in *Pro Murena*, but he praised them as the truest form of moral philosophy in the *Paradoxes of the Stoics*, and it was these teachings, rather than those of Panaetius, which he chose to represent Stoicism when he alternatively criticized and praised it in the *De finibus* and the *Tusculan Disputations*.[37] As we shall see in a moment, it was this stricter Stoicism which Cicero had in mind when he considered the suitability of Stoic philosophy to the orator. Before we come to that,

[36] For Cicero's sources in *De officiis*, see Clarke, pp. 37-38; also Friedrich Ueberweg and Karl Praechter, *Die Philosophie Des Altertums* (Berlin, 1926), pp. 474-75.

[37] On the sources of these treatises, see Ueberweg and Praechter, pp. 472-74. H. Rackham suggests that the source for the Stoic exposition in Bk. III of *De finibus* was Diogenes of Babylon; see his introduction to the Loeb edn., p. xiii. On Diogenes of Babylon—a disciple of Chrysippus, the "second founder" of Old Stoicism—see Ueberweg and Praechter, p. 410. See also the general statement of Cicero's philosophical position, *ibid.*, pp. 465, 474.

however, we must glance at a school of moral philosophy with which Cicero often contrasted the Stoics.

The leader of this school was Cicero's own teacher, Antiochus of Ascalon. Originally a skeptical follower of the "New Academy" (and a successor to Philo of Larissa, who introduced Cicero to skepticism), Antiochus deserted skepticism in favor of a set of moral doctrines which he attributed to the "Old Academy." By this he did not mean Plato's Academy, but a much wider group of thinkers, whom Cicero variously called "the ancients," "Aristotle and the other disciples of Plato," or "the early Peripatetics and Academics, who agreed in substance though they differed in terminology." By means of this eclectic grouping Antiochus sought to demonstrate that there had been a generally accepted point of departure for moral philosophy before Zeno the Stoic appeared on the scene, namely the belief that moral worth (*honestas*) was not the only "good." Health and external circumstances were also classed as goods. Thus the teaching of Antiochus contrasted with that of the Stoics on the basic question of ethics, the definition of "the good." It followed that Antiochus' conceptions of virtue and happiness would differ from the Stoic ones. According to his teachings, health and fortune could make genuine contributions to a happy life.[38]

This was the doctrine which Cicero set against Stoicism in such treatises as the *De finibus* and the *Tusculan Disputations*. In what follows, we shall refer to this doctrine as "Peripateticism." Though historically it would be more accurate to call it "the Academic-Peripatetic doctrine of Antiochus," we will avoid this designation both for its clumsiness and for the following reasons of substance. First, Cicero often described this doctrine simply as "the teaching of the Peripatetics" (never as that of the Academics alone); in giving the sources of his account of it, he named only Aristotle's *Nicomachean Ethics* and the works of Aristotle's

[38] *De finibus* V; Rackham's introduction, Loeb edn., pp. xxiii-xxv; Ueberweg and Praechter, p. 474.

immediate disciple Theophrastus. While he often insisted on the agreement of Academics and Peripatetics, when he spoke of "the Academics" by themselves he usually meant the skeptical "New Academy"; this is true even in *De finibus*, where the system of Antiochus received its fullest exposition. In many places, both in *De finibus* and elsewhere, Cicero referred to the opposition he had in mind simply as one between Stoics and Peripatetics.[39] This was the terminology which the humanists would take over from his writings; it would play an important role in the development of their thought. It was the nomenclature Cicero himself usually employed when he considered the relevance of the various dogmatic schools to the culture of the orator.

The difference between Stoicism and "Peripateticism," as it appears from Cicero's writings, may be summarized as that between a rigorous, consistent, often harsh and narrow devotion to philosophical rationalism (the Stoics), and a less exalted, softer, more realistic teaching, which admitted the necessities of human nature and everyday life (the "Peripatetics"). Both schools agreed that man's happiness lay in a life in accord with his nature, and both called those things good which helped to perfect such a life. The Peripatetics listed three classes of "goods." Virtue itself was the highest, since it pertained to man's highest part, his soul. But there were also goods of the body, for man was a composite creature, and goods of circumstance, since man was affected by the conditions of his environment. Health and riches were examples of these last two classes of goods. For the Stoics, however, there was only one good: *honestas*, moral worth. Such things as health and riches were not genuine goods, since they could be turned

[39] For the description of Antiochus's doctrine as "the teaching of the Peripatetics," see *De finibus* V, iv, 9ff.; V, xxv, 75; for Aristotle ("and his son Nicomachus") and Theophrastus as the specific sources, see V, v, 12; for the more general description of the doctrine as characteristic of all Greek philosophy between Plato and Zeno's teacher Polemo, see IV, iii, 3; IV, ii-iii, 5; IV, xxii, 61, and elsewhere. For the contrast specifically between Stoics and Peripatetics, see III, xii, 41ff.; IV, i, 2; IV, iv, 10; IV, xxvi, 77-78. For the use of the term "Academics" as equivalent to skepticism, see V, xxviii, 85.

to evil ends; moreover, to make happiness depend on them was to give man's life into the hands of fortune, which could bring or take them away. The wise man would remain indifferent to health and riches; while he might regard them as "preferable" to their opposites, he knew that neither was truly good or a part of true happiness. The only source of genuine virtue was perfect knowledge of the good. The wise man therefore possessed at once all virtues; lesser men could never achieve any.

Cicero admired the Stoics for their consistency and their unyielding devotion to virtue, but he found their system of doubtful relevance to life as it is lived. The doctrines of the Peripatetics were less consistent and in a sense less admirable, but they spoke to man's condition more than Stoicism did. To the Peripatetics, Stoic teachings did not seem to take account of the exigencies of man's composite nature. From a Stoic viewpoint, however, the Peripatetics appeared as crowd-pleasers who suffered from inconsistency and an incomplete devotion to virtue and moral worth.[40]

These two philosophical schools would occupy very different places in the culture of the orator. Cicero discussed their value in the *De oratore*. There he asked "not which system of philosophy is the truest, but which is the most fully akin to the orator."[41] This was a prize the Stoics could not win. As philosophers, Crassus affirmed, "I by no means disapprove [of them]." But:

> Clearly there is something in them that is quite out of keeping with the orator whom we are depicting: in the first place their assertion that all those who are not wise are slaves, brigands, enemies, madmen, and that all the same nobody is wise—yet it would be the height of folly to place a public meeting or the Senate or any assembly of people under the direction of a person who holds the view that not one of those present is sane, or a citizen, or

---

[40] This paragraph is based mainly on the *De finibus* III-V.

[41] *De oratore* III, xvii, 64; Loeb edn., II, 53. Cicero quickly dismissed Epicureanism because of its rejection of the concerns of the everyday world.

a free man. There is the further point that even the style of their discourse, though possibly subtle and undoubtedly penetrating, yet for an orator is bald, unfamiliar, jarring on the ear of the public, devoid of clarity, fullness and spirit, while at the same time of a character that makes it quite impossible to employ it in public speaking; for the Stoics hold a different view of good and bad from all their fellow citizens or rather from all other nations, and give a different meaning to "honor," "disgrace," "reward," "punishment"—whether correctly or otherwise does not concern us now, but if we were to adopt their terminology, we should never be able to express our meaning intelligibly about anything.[42]

The basis for this attitude toward the Stoics had appeared earlier in *De oratore*: "other arts" might reject the common-sense notions of ordinary men, but oratory had to accept them, along with "the language of everyday life." The refusal of Stoic philosophy to respect these requirements made Stoicism unsuitable for the public orator. The same Stoic indifference to common opinion and everyday language made their writings on rhetoric itself of little use. The treatises of Cleanthes and Chrysippus were composed "in such fashion that anyone who has conceived a desire to become dumb has only to read" them. They were flawed by the Stoic insistence on a terminology which was not easily understood by ordinary men. Some Stoics had written well, borrowing methods from practical oratory. But Stoic pronouncements on virtue were not of the sort to in-

[42] *De oratore* III, xviii, 65-66; Loeb edn., pp. 53-55. Note also *De finibus* IV, ix, 21-22, where the speaker complains that Stoic philosophy "could not possibly be produced in civic life, in the law courts, in the Senate. For who could tolerate such a way of speaking in one who claimed to be an authority on wise and moral conduct? . . . Could an advocate wind up his defence of a client by declaring that exile and confiscation of property are not evils? that they are 'to be rejected,' but not 'to be shunned'? that it is not a judge's duty to show mercy? Or supposing him to be addressing a meeting of the people: Hannibal is at the gates and has flung a javelin over the city walls; could he say that captivity, enslavement, death, loss of country are no evils?" (Cicero, *De finibus*, trans. James S. Reid [Cambridge, Eng., 1883].)

flame men to pursue it. They were like little pinpricks, of no effect.[43]

The Peripatetics were a different breed. It was their teaching which the aspiring orator should study if he wanted to progress toward perfection. They were the philosophers "most fully akin to the orator." In the *De oratore* itself the explicit reason given for this was that Aristotle had developed a dialectic which taught one to argue on either side of any question.[44] Implicitly, however, the Peripatetics emerged as superior to the Stoics also in not departing as far from everyday life as their rivals had. Cicero stated this view of the difference between the two schools more openly in *De finibus*. There he criticized the Stoics several times for their departures from common usage. "How is it," he demanded of them, "that when the Peripatetics deal with the same subject matter, I do not find a word I cannot grasp?"[45] The language of the Peripatetics, unlike that of the Stoics, could be understood in the marketplace. Their philosophy did not carry the orator beyond the bounds his tasks set for him. The rhetorician who spoke in their terms would be intelligible even to men "who have never set eyes on a philosopher."[46]

At this point, therefore, Cicero's version of the combination of rhetoric and philosophy seems to consist of two elements. The first is the free critical spirit of the Academic skeptics. The second is the moral doctrines of the Peripatetics. If this were the whole range of Cicero's philosophic culture, then his philosophical interests would be strictly limited ones. They would conform approximately to the limits set on the usefulness of philosophy by one of the speakers in *De oratore*: "for us who are involved with the people and in the forum, it is enough to know and say those things about the way men live which are not inconsistent with their way of living."[47] This statement recalls

[43] *De finibus* IV, iii, 607 (trans. Reid).
[44] *De oratore* III, xix, 71.
[45] *De finibus* IV, i, 2; also IV, ix, 21ff.; IV, xxii, 61; IV, xxvi, 72.
[46] *De finibus* V, xxvii, 80.
[47] *De oratore* I, li, 219: "nobis tamen, qui in hoc populo foroque

the attitude of Socrates' opponent Callicles in the *Gorgias*; he approved of a little learning in philosophy for the man of action, but warned that too much was a dangerous thing.[48] Despite this resemblance, however, Cicero's philosophical attitude was not that of the sophist Callicles. If he occasionally sounded like him, he also sometimes directly contradicted him. At the beginning of Book II of the *Tusculan Disputations* he insisted that the pursuit of philosophy cannot go only "a little way": "It is difficult to have a little knowledge in philosophy without having either a great deal or all that there is; for neither can a little be selected except from much, nor, when a man has learnt a little, will he not also go on with the same eagerness to master what remains."[49] In this passage Cicero sounded less like Callicles than like Socrates himself. The Roman orator was not consistent in his attitude toward philosophy. As Petrarch observed in the remark quoted at the beginning of our study, Cicero spoke sometimes as an orator, sometimes as a philosopher. At times he limited the province of philosophy in order to make it serve the needs of the orator in the forum; at other times he denied that such limits could be set.

Even when he spoke in this philosophical way, however, Cicero did not entirely desert the standards of rhetoric. In two ways he remained loyal to them. First, he insisted that training in rhetoric could be useful in discussions of philosophy. In treating of philosophy in the *Tusculan Disputations* he said, "it is my design not to lay aside my early devotion to the art of expression, but to employ it in this grander and more fruitful art: for it has ever been my conviction that philosophy in its finished form enjoys the power of treating the greatest problems with adequate fullness and in an attractive style."[50] Moreover, not only would Cicero thus retain the orator's concern for style, he would

versamur, satis est, ea de moribus hominum et scire, et dicere, quae non abhorrent ab hominum moribus" (my translation).

[48] Plato, *Gorgias*, 485A-486D.

[49] *Tusc. Disp.* II, i, 1; Loeb edn., p. 147.

[50] *Ibid.*, I, iii, 6–I, iv, 7; Loeb edn., pp. 9-11.

also continue to be aware of the need to address his audience in terms that would be intelligible and acceptable to it. The philosopher's audience, however, was not the same as the orator's: "For philosophy is content with few judges, and of set purpose on her side avoids the multitude and is in her turn an object of suspicion and dislike to them, with the result that if anyone should be disposed to revile all philosophy he could count on popular support."[51] Philosophy spoke not to the marketplace but only to the "educated," to those fit to listen to her. She would speak with grace and eloquence, but her message was her own.

The content of this message would be the teachings of the Stoics. Even in the *De finibus*, where he concluded largely in favor of the Peripatetics, Cicero noted the superiority of the Stoics in certain respects. By departing from common sense and everyday language they attained a degree of consistency which placed them above other philosophers. By insisting that only virtue was good, and thus that happiness depended wholly on moral rectitude, the Stoics had produced a system which "is a marvellously consistent whole": "The conclusions agree with the first principles, the middle steps with both, in fact every part with every other. They understand what inference follows from and what contradicts a given premise. It is like geometry: grant the premises and you must grant everything. Admit that there is no good but Moral Worth, and you are bound to admit that happiness consists in virtue. Or again conversely: given the latter, you must grant the former."[52] The Peripatetics lacked this consistency. Once they had admitted that goods of the body and external circumstance existed and could affect man's happiness, they should have drawn the inference that fortune—which often brings good health or riches—rules the life of men.[53] Thus the Peripa-

---

[51] *Ibid.*, II, i, 4; Loeb edn., pp. 149-51.

[52] *De finibus* V, xxviii, 83; Loeb edn., p. 487. Cf. *De natura deorum* III, i, 4.

[53] Aristotle's disciple Theophrastus had actually drawn this conclusion, which Cicero called consistent with Peripatetic premises. *Tusc. Disp.* V, viii, 24-25.

27

tetic teachings which Cicero preferred when he looked at
them from the point of view of an orator could also seem,
from a more philosophic point of view, to be weak, inconsistent, and "like the crowd."[54] From this perspective, the
Peripatetics' harmony with rhetoric became a black mark
against them. Speaking of the controversy between Stoics
and Peripatetics on the definition of courage (whether excitement or indignation could be spurs to bravery, properly
understood), Cicero said that the Stoics framed their definitions carefully, as the subject required; the Peripatetics,
on the other hand, defined their terms *ex rhetorum pompa*,
"with the ostentatious display of orators."[55] At one point in
the *Tusculan Disputations* Cicero remarked, "Even though
we may attack them, I fear that the Stoics may be the only
true philosophers."[56] Whereas Peripateticism was the philosophical doctrine most appropriate to oratory, therefore,
the Stoics were the philosophers who best represented philosophy itself.

These recognitions played an important part in the
Ciceronian combination of wisdom and eloquence. The
orator who joined philosophy to his own discipline of rhetoric would speak sometimes in his own proper voice, sometimes in that of the philosophers. In the first case his opinions and maxims would be drawn most often from the
Peripatetics, in the second from the more remote and rigorous Stoics. In neither instance, however, would he cease to
be an orator. The whole structure of Cicero's philosophical
culture was shaped by the rhetorical foundation of his

[54] *Tusc. Disp.* V, x, 30-31, and elsewhere.
[55] *Ibid.*, IV, xxi, 47-48 (my translation).
[56] *Ibid.*, IV, xxiv, 53 (my translation). It is true that Cicero sometimes had equally high praise for some other philosophers, notably Plato, whose teaching on the immortality of the soul he specifically preferred to the Stoics' in Bk. I of the *Tusc. Disp.* But in moral philosophy
he seldom discussed Platonic teaching (except insofar as he may have
thought it included in the "Peripatetic" system of Antiochus), and he
did not refer to Plato in *De oratore* when discussing the suitability
of various philosophical doctrines to the orator. In the *Paradoxa
Stoicorum* he transferred some of the prestige of Socratic philosophy
to the Stoics; see below.

thought. In the treatise called the *Paradoxes of the Stoics,* Cicero affirmed that "the doctrines styled *paradoxa* by the Stoics appear to me to be in the highest degree Socratic, and far and away the truest." But he prefaced this by saying that he was attempting to defend the Stoics in order to show that "nothing is so difficult to believe that oratory cannot make it acceptable, nothing so rough and uncultured as not to gain brilliance and refinement from eloquence."[57] Even in his most purely philosophical voice Cicero retained the accents of rhetoric. He never committed himself to any one of the dogmatic philosophical schools. His ideal orator would be a Stoic in his most philosophical moments, a Peripatetic in his ordinary, common-sense moments, but fundamentally a skeptic all the time. He spoke as a philosopher to philosophers, as an everyday man to everyday men, but always with an eloquence that was properly and uniquely his. The philosophy he joined to rhetoric was free in some moments to range wherever the demands of rational consistency took it; at other times it would return within the boundaries of the everyday world. In whatever way its positions might be justified in strictly philosophical terms, however, its relationship to rhetoric was controlled by the man of eloquence himself. Standing thus firmly on his own ground, the orator could confidently survey the neighboring terrain, and in this way combine philosophy and rhetoric.

The Ciceronian combination of rhetoric and philosophy was complex and intricate. As a philosophical position it was weak and inconsistent, but it was also humane. It allowed the intellectual to waver between a position based on the standards of thought and one based on those of action; it celebrated philosophy, but it recognized that men cannot be philosophers all the time.[58] Cicero has some-

[57] *Paradoxa Stoicorum,* 3-4; Loeb edn., p. 255-57.

[58] In the *Tusc. Disp.* (V, ii, 5), Cicero wrote: "O philosophy, guide of life, you who discover the way to virtue and banish vices, what should we have been, and not only we, but the very life of man, without you?" In a letter to his son, however, he declared that "One should know the precepts of philosophy, but live like a member of

times been criticized for his lack of both originality and consistency, and in general terms one hesitates to claim either for him. From his own particular point of view, however—that of the orator seeking to benefit his community and ennoble his art—he achieved something of both. His philosophical eclecticism was not entirely random, but had a certain structure and order, at least in its main lines. He was conscious of his contradictions and able to provide a justification for them, both on philosophical grounds and on the basis of his fundamental commitment to rhetoric.

In the Middle Ages and the Renaissance, Cicero's writings provided more information about ancient culture than practically any other classical source, but they did not often engender as much excitement as Aristotle's or Plato's works. This was true because later thinkers more often shared the ideals of the great philosophers than the particular purposes of the Roman orator. In the Middle Ages Cicero was valued as a mine of information, but it was Aristotle who inspired the most vigorous intellectual effort. In the latter part of the fifteenth century, attention began to shift toward Plato. For a short time between these two moments, however, during the fourteenth and fifteenth centuries, Cicero did become the object of the kind of enthusiasm directed earlier toward Aristotle and later toward Plato. The reason for this awakening of interest was that only at this point in time were Cicero's writings taken up by men who shared his commitment to rhetoric and his concern for protecting it from and relating it to philosophy. These men belonged to the first generations of the Renaissance humanists. To understand their cultural program, the Ciceronian background of their thought must be kept in mind.

---

civilized society." ("Philosophiae quidem praecepta noscenda, vivendum autem civiliter"—quoted by Lactantius, *The Divine Institutes,* III, 14, 17, and by Clarke, *The Roman Mind,* p. 64.)

CHAPTER II

IDEALS OF ELOQUENCE
AND SILENCE IN PETRARCH

WHILE Cicero was the classical figure of greatest import to the humanists of the Quattrocento, the man of their own age to whom they most often looked for intellectual guidance was Petrarch. Other writers were sometimes given credit for having begun the revival of learning (to praise someone for having done so was even a fairly commonplace compliment), but no one carried off this prize more consistently than Petrarch.[1] The description of his importance given by Leonardo Bruni, and in similar terms by Giovanni Boccaccio and Poggio Bracciolini, is suggestive: Petrarch "opened the way for us to show in what manner we could acquire learning."[2] This was anything but a restrictive statement; it could and did mean several things. The meaning which we shall try to illustrate here should help to define at least one part of Petrarch's contribution to the humanist movement with some precision. He showed his followers how to acquire learning in the sense that he rediscovered the Ciceronian model for the relations between rhetoric and philosophy, and thus made it possible for rhetoric to become once again the

[1] See Herbert Weisinger, "Who Began the Revival of Learning? The Renaissance Point of View," *Papers of the Michigan Academy,* XXIX (1944), 561-67.

[2] Bruni, *Ad Petrum Paulum Histrum Dialogus,* ed. Eugenio Garin, in *Prosatori Latini del Quattrocento* (Milan and Naples, 1952), p. 94; Boccaccio, *Opere latine minori,* ed. A. F. Massèra (Bari, 1928), p. 195; for the passage from Poggio, see the quotation from his letter (now lost) in Salutati, *Epistolario,* ed. Novati, IV, 161. On this point, see Hans Baron, *The Crisis of the Early Italian Renaissance* (2 vols., Princeton, 1955), I, 232ff., and the criticisms of Baron in my article, " 'Civic Humanism' or Ciceronian Rhetoric? The Culture of Petrarch and Bruni," *Past and Present,* No. 34 (1966). Baron's work has been reissued in a revised edition (Princeton, 1966). All references here are to the first edition.

doorway to general culture, and especially to learning in moral philosophy, that it had been in Cicero's time.

For the sake of presenting here a coherent and uncluttered analysis of the thought of Petrarch and his followers, the reasons for their profound interest in Ciceronian rhetoric must be left aside for the moment. That they had such an interest has been emphasized by a number of recent writers. It is now a matter of general knowledge that the ideal of eloquence was a fundamental feature of humanist culture, and that the humanists drew on and extended an earlier medieval rhetorical tradition.[3] We shall try to relate the humanists to this medieval background in Part Two. There we shall attempt to place the movement of ideas described in the rest of these pages in several relevant contexts. For now, our purpose will be to show that Petrarch's thought on the problem of the relationship between rhetoric and philosophy was closely patterned on Cicero's. Not only did he share Cicero's desire that the two arts be combined; he also recognized nearly identical obstacles to their union, which he sought to surmount in similar ways. Petrarch's revival of these elements of Ciceronian culture, and their development and transformation by his succes-

---

[3] Paul Oskar Kristeller, "Humanism and Scholasticism in the Italian Renaissance," *Byzantion*, XVII (1944), reprinted in Kristeller's *Studies in Renaissance Thought and Letters* (Rome, 1956) and in his paperback, *Renaissance Thought* (New York, 1961). See also the other studies in these two volumes, as well as those collected in *Renaissance Thought II* (New York, 1965), and *Eight Philosophers of the Italian Renaissance* (Stanford, 1964). In addition to Kristeller's work, the following studies also show the importance of rhetoric to humanist culture: Hanna H. Gray, "Renaissance Humanism: The Pursuit of Eloquence," *Journal of the History of Ideas*, XXIV (1963); Charles Trinkaus, "A Humanist's Image of Humanism: The Inaugural Orations of Bartolommeo della Fonte," *Studies in the Renaissance*, VII (1960), 90-147. An older work with a somewhat similar point of view, but which has had little influence, is Ciro Trabalza, *La Critica Letteraria* (Milan, 1915), Chap. I. For the influence of rhetorical ideals on the history of art, see John R. Spencer, "Ut Rhetorica Pictura," *Journal of the Warburg and Courtauld Institutes*, XX (1957), 26-44, which discusses Alberti's theory of painting. However, Spencer does not deal with other important sources of Alberti's art theory that lie outside the rhetorical tradition.

sors, will be the subject of the main body of our study. We shall attempt to understand how Petrarch's study and use of Cicero prepared the way for the humanists who followed him, and then go on to examine the directions in which they struck out for themselves.

(1)

PETRARCH's devotion to Cicero is well known. He tells us that he was drawn to the Roman's writings from his early youth, even before he could fully understand their meaning.[4] Later on he seems to have modeled his own role as an eloquent teacher of philosophical maxims upon the example of Cicero, "adapting it to the needs of his century."[5] Like St. Jerome, Petrarch feared lest his love of the Roman orator be excessive.[6] Sometimes the facts of Petrarch's biography are difficult to determine, so closely does his own account of them follow some passage in Cicero.[7] None of this prevented him from criticizing the pagan Roman for his moral failings, but even when he did so he described Cicero as "the man whom I had always loved beyond all others."[8] Of course there were vast differences between the two men; nearly fourteen centuries and the faith of Christianity separated them from each other. Petrarch's culture was far from being a mere copy of Cicero's. Had it been so, his thought would interest the historian much less than it does. But Petrarch's intelligence penetrated deeply into the structure of Cicero's mental world. He made certain features of Cicero's thought his own, and made it possible

[4] Petrarch, *Senilium rerum libri*, XV, 1; in *Opera* (Basel, 1554), II, 1046.

[5] Pierre de Nolhac, *Pétrarque et l'humanisme* (Paris, 1907), I, 215. De Nolhac's discussion of Petrarch's use of Cicero is still the most useful. See also G. Billanovich, "Petrarca e Cicerone," *Misc. Giovanni Mercati* (Vatican City, 1946), IV, 88-106; and Attilio Hortis, *M. T. Cicerone nelle opere del Petrarca e del Boccaccio* (Trieste, 1878).

[6] Petrarch, *Fam.*, XXI, 10.

[7] Umberto Bosco, *Francesco Petrarca* (Bari, 1961), pp. 113ff. Petrarch took similar inspiration from other classical figures, but he drew from Cicero most of all.

[8] *Fam.*, XXIV, 2. See also Petrarch's second letter to Cicero, *Fam.*, XXIV, 4.

for others to adapt them to serve as a basis of their literary and philosophical activity.

The ideal of eloquence occupied a central position in Petrarch's culture. The content of the ideal varied from time to time, but for the most part what Petrarch meant by eloquent speech was not harmony and beauty of language, but persuasive power. Horace, Petrarch said, was able to move his readers despite the roughness of his style.[9] Cicero was the prince of Latin eloquence: "He held the hearts of men in his hands; he ruled his listeners as a king."[10] Petrarch praised eloquence not as formal perfection, satisfying in an aesthetic sense, but as an active force in men's lives: "How much eloquence can accomplish in the shaping of human life is known both from reading in many authors and from the experience of everyday life. How great is the number of those we recognize in our own day, to whom even examples [of virtue] were of no help, who have been aroused and turned suddenly from a most wicked manner of life to a perfectly ordered one simply by the sound of others' voices!"[11] Such a conception of eloquence immediately raised the question of the relationship between the orator's art and the philosopher's. If rhetoric has this role to play in the moral reform of individuals, then what part is left for philosophy?

Petrarch answered this question, sometimes at least, in the traditional way: No true eloquence could exist apart from wisdom. He gave this response most clearly in the chapter of *De remediis utriusque fortunae* called "De elo-

[9] *On His Own Ignorance and That of Many Others*, trans. Hans Nachod, in *The Renaissance Philosophy of Man*, ed. E. Cassirer, P. O. Kristeller, and J. H. Randall, Jr. (Chicago, 1948), pp. 103-04. (All page references are to this translation.)

[10] *Rerum memorandarum libri*, ed. G. Billanovich (Florence, 1945), II, 17, 6. (Cited below, in this edition, as *Rerum mem.*)

[11] *Fam.*, I, 9, 6: "Veruntamen quantum quoque ad informationem humane vite possit eloquentia, et apud multos auctores lectum et quotidiana experientia monstrante compertum est. Quam multos, quibus nichil omnino loquentium exempla contulerant, etate nostra velut experrectos agnovimus et a sceleratissime vite cursu ad summam repente modestiam alienis tantum vocibus fuisse conversos." Cf. Cicero, *De inventione* I, ii, 3.

quentia." There he invoked both Cicero and another Roman statesman, Cato, in support of the proposition that true oratory required virtue and wisdom. Cato had defined the orator as "a good man skilled in speaking," and Cicero once described eloquence as nothing more than "wisdom speaking fluently." Mere skill in speech by itself produced only foolish talk. "If therefore," Petrarch concluded, "you are seeking the title of orator and the true honor of eloquence, give your attention first of all to virtue and wisdom."[12]

This passage reminds us that, for Petrarch as for Cicero, the ideal of wisdom was more exalted than the ideal of eloquence, and was likely in any union of the two to claim the higher place. Yet, as we have just seen, Petrarch was quite capable of praising the power of eloquence in a way that cast doubt on its inferiority to wisdom. In fact, he sometimes described true philosophy in a way which suggested that it was dependent on genuine eloquence, rather than the other way around.

> The true moral philosophers and useful teachers of the virtues are those whose first and last intention is to make hearer and reader good, those who do not merely teach what virtue and vice are and hammer into our ears the brilliant name of the one and the grim name of the other, but sow into our hearts love of the best and eager desire for it, and at the same time hatred of the worst and how to flee it.[13]

Thus philosophy required the persuasive power of eloquence quite as much as oratory needed wisdom. Petrarch criticized Aristotle's writings in moral philosophy because they failed to move their readers (perhaps he meant to place the blame on medieval Latin translations). "His lesson lacks the words that sting and set afire and urge toward love of virtue and hatred of vice, or, at any rate, does not

---

[12] *De remediis utriusque fortunae*, I, ix, in *Opera* (Basel, 1581), pp. 6-7.
[13] *On His Own Ignorance*, p. 105.

have enough of such power."[14] Placing as much emphasis as he did on the philosopher's obligation to make his teaching active, Petrarch sometimes pictured rhetoric and philosophy in ways which nearly caused the two disciplines to merge into one.

Petrarch seems never to have called himself an orator. The title that he favored, of course, and which he often coupled with that of "moral philosopher," was "poet." In his "Letter to Posterity" he said that his mind was especially adept at poetry and moral philosophy, adding that with the passage of time he had neglected the first for the second.[15] An official Venetian document relating to Petrarch's proposal to leave his library to the republic of San Marco referred to him as "moral philosopher and poet," titles which he may well have suggested himself.[16] For Petrarch, however, poetry was also closely related to rhetoric. Poetry was a branch of the tree of eloquence, and Virgil was an exemplar of eloquence in verse, as Cicero was in prose.[17] This coupling of poetry and rhetoric had been common in earlier writers. Cicero spoke of the close ties between the two arts, and a medieval tradition which drew especially on Horace attributed to rhetoric and poetry the same aims and methods.[18] Petrarch's closest followers described his own work in the same terms. Referring to his proficiency in both verse and prose, Coluccio Salutati said that Petrarch

[14] *Ibid.*, p. 103.
[15] "Posteritati," in Francesco Petrarca, *Prose*, ed. G. Martellotti, P. G. Ricci, E. Carrara, E. Bianchi (Milan and Naples, 1955), p. 6.
[16] *Petrarch's Testament*, ed. T. E. Mommsen (Ithaca, 1957), pp. 45-46.
[17] *Fam.*, VI, 4; *Rerum mem.*, II, 17, 7.
[18] On the earliest stages of this tradition, see P. O. Kristeller, "The Modern System of the Arts," *Renaissance Thought II*, p. 168; for Cicero, see *De oratore* I, xv, 70; on the tradition of Horace, see C. S. Baldwin, *Ancient Rhetoric and Poetic* (New York, 1924), pp. 224ff., esp. 246. Ernst Robert Curtius calls the transfer of rhetoric to Roman poetry "Ovid's accomplishment": *European Literature and the Latin Middle Ages*, trans. W. R. Trask (New York, 1953), p. 66. On Petrarch's conception of poetry as including the other liberal arts, see Francesco Tateo, *"Retorica" e "Poetica" fra Medioevo e Rinascimento* (Bari, 1960), pp. 221-29, and Kristeller, "Il Petrarca, l'umanesimo e la scolastica," *Lettere Italiane*, VII (1955).

IN PETRARCH

had been "the one man . . . in whom eloquence demonstrated all its powers."[19] Moreover, Petrarch's description of
his own development, from an interest in poetry in his early
years to a concern for moral philosophy later on, paralleled
similar changes he observed in the careers of both Cicero
and another of his most respected models, St. Augustine.
But in these two the first stage had been not poetry but
rhetoric. Petrarch sometimes described Cicero's career as
a movement from rhetoric to philosophy.[20] He was aware
that St. Augustine's intellectual development began with
the study and teaching of rhetoric, and he sometimes spoke
of the great Father's movement to philosophy, in which
Augustine was helped by the reading of Cicero's lost treatise *Hortensius*.[21] Thus Petrarch's description of himself as
"moral philosopher and poet" linked him in his own opinion
to the art of the orator.

Petrarch's place in the intellectual controversies of his
time also reflected his devotion to rhetoric. His long dispute
with the physicians largely turned on the relationship between eloquence and the study of medicine. Carried on in
the *Invective Against a Certain Physician* of 1352-53 and in
a series of later letters, this polemic was part of Petrarch's
advocacy of what was coming to be humanistic culture. His
defense of poetry, especially as set out in Book III of the
Invective, is better known than his championing of rhetoric,
but the cause of the latter is taken up no less vigorously
in the treatise. Petrarch described the physicians' attempt
to make rhetoric subservient to their own art of medicine
as "an unheard-of sacrilege." "I ask you, O lord of philosophy and the arts, with what mind would Cicero have discussed rhetoric in so many books and with so much zeal,
had he known that it would become the slave of such a
talent [as yours]?" Indeed, the place of rhetoric was the
crucial point at issue between Petrarch and his opponent.

[19] *Epistolario*, I, 183.
[20] *Fam.*, IV, 15, 7; *Rerum mem.*, I, 15, 2 (where Cicero's study of
philosophy in his youth is also mentioned).
[21] *On his Own Ignorance*, p. 116.

Not to tarry in details, I come to the crux of our dispute. Even if you make all of the arts, however noble and ingenious, the servants of your low and mercenary craft, by the fact of their being useful or necessary to your end (and I know not by what right this should be permitted to you), rhetoric will never thus be made your servant; for not only is it of no use toward the end to which you would turn it, but it is even of great harm....

Petrarch went on to say that physicians ought to cure their sick patients in silence, not make long-winded speeches to them. Arousing or calming emotions was the work of the orator, not the medical doctor.[22]

The penchant of physicians for meddling with eloquence had been a sore point with Petrarch from the beginning of his dispute with them, and in his later letters the position of rhetoric was still the central point at issue. The controversy from which the *Invective* resulted arose from a letter Petrarch had written to Clement VI when the Pontiff was ill, urging him to beware of the crowd of physicians that surrounded him, and to choose one "outstanding not for his eloquence but for his knowledge and faith."[23] Here Petrarch's tone seemed almost disparaging toward eloquence, as it did when, referring to the letter in the *Invective*, he said he had warned the Pope against any doctor who was "interested not in knowledge, but in empty eloquence."[24] But it was not eloquence itself against which Petrarch cautioned; it was the physicians' approach to it. This is clear from the later letters, particularly one to a well-known fourteenth-century physician, William of Ra-

---

[22] *Invective contra medicum*, ed. P. G. Ricci (Rome, 1950), pp. 29-30, 40-41, 77-78. (Page references are to this edition.) "Ne enim in singulis immorer, ad litis nostre summam venio. Si omnes, inquam, artes, quamvis nobiles, quamvis ingenuas, tuo humili et mercennario artificio servas facis, eo ipso quod utiles aut necessarie proposito tuo sunt—idque tibi nescio quo iure permittitur—nunquam profecto vel sic tibi rethorica serva fiet, quam constat ad id, quo te intendere oportet, non modo nil prodesse, sed obesse quam plurimum" (pp. 77-78).

[23] *Fam.*, V, 19, 5.   [24] *Invective*, p. 29.

venna. Here Petrarch's tone was friendlier than in his earlier writings, and his argument clearer: "No one will call in a physician who seeks eloquence, but one who seeks health. To this end drugs are useful, not words; medicinal scents, not rhetorical colors; the arguments of physics, not those of rhetoric. It is the care of the body which is entrusted to you. To care for souls and move them should be left to true philosophers and orators."[25] The coupling of "true philosophers and orators" shows Petrarch's real attitude. It had not been his intention to depreciate oratory or to say that eloquence was always "empty." Only the oratory of the physicians was *inanis*. Physicians ought not to meddle with rhetoric, not because it was itself unworthy, but, on the contrary, because eloquence was associated with true philosophy in a way that the learning of the physicians was not.

The study of medicine in the fourteenth century was closely tied to scholastic philosophy. In fact the physicians were one of the most important forces in the philosophical culture of the latter part of the Middle Ages, especially in Italy. Petrarch made a number of objections to their learning, some of which are well known. In addition to condemning their attempts to intrude on the study of rhetoric, Petrarch criticized them for their excessive attention to the details of natural philosophy, and for their immoderate devotion to dialectic. Instead of indulging in disputation for its own sake and wasting their talents in fruitless curiosity about plants and animals, he insisted, men who seek wisdom should turn their attention to the study of man's own life, to moral philosophy.[26] Yet Petrarch did not consistently claim that the physicians neglected ethics. Sometimes he objected to attempts on their part to link its study with their own brand of learning. The physician against whom he

[25] *Sen. rerum libri*, III, 8; in *Opera*, II, 861: "Nemo medicum conducit eloquentiae appetens, sed salutis, ad hanc herbis non verbis opus est, odoribus non coloribus, physicis demum non rhetoricis argumentis; cura corporum vobis imposita est, curare animos aut movere, Philosophis veris atque oratoribus linquere."

[26] See especially, in addition to the *Invective*, the treatise *On His Own Ignorance*.

wrote the *Invective* had claimed that the teaching of moral philosophy was related to the study of medicine. Petrarch replied that "Medicine has nothing in common with ethics, and much that is contrary to it."[27] This resembles his later assertion that "To care for souls and move them should be left to true philosophers and orators." Like other medieval intellectual groups, the physicians claimed a central place for their discipline in the overall curriculum, as Petrarch recognized when he attacked them: "You want to speak on every subject, forgetful of your profession, which is, if you don't know, to contemplate urine and other things that modesty forbids me to name." Rejecting his adversary's suggestion that he himself should study medicine, Petrarch said, "You tell me to violate the boundaries of others, I warn you to return within your own."[28]

The general issue between Petrarch and his opponents was not simply which disciplines should be studied, but rather which ones should be allowed to define and shape the exalted ideal of philosophy. Petrarch objected to the culture of the physicians because it reduced the importance of rhetoric in relation to philosophy (especially moral philosophy), and associated the pursuit of wisdom instead with natural philosophy and dialectic. The ideal of philosophy that he thought Cicero and St. Augustine embodied was one based on a profound respect for the power of eloquence.[29] Led by certain statements in Cicero, Petrarch even tried sometimes to claim that Aristotle had shared this regard for rhetoric too, so that the whole of antiquity could be called on to support him against his opponents. "From Aristotle's ways they swerve," he asserted in *On His Own Ignorance and That of Many Others*, "taking eloquence to be an obstacle and a disgrace to philosophy, while he considered it a mighty adornment and tried to combine it with philosophy, 'prevailed upon,' it is asserted, 'by the fame of the orator

[27] *Invective*, p. 76. On the general subject of the relations between emerging humanist culture and scholastic philosophy, see Chap. VI.
[28] *Invective*, pp. 34, 80.
[29] *On His Own Ignorance*, p. 105.

40

Isocrates.' "[30] Like Cicero, however, whom he quoted in this passage, Petrarch was not altogether certain about Aristotle's regard for eloquence. He denied in this same treatise that Aristotle's moral writings actually possessed the necessary persuasive power.[31] In an earlier work he had seemed to resolve this contradiction, blaming the corruption of Aristotle's style on the men who had translated him into Latin.[32] In *On His Own Ignorance*, however, his uncertainty about Aristotle's eloquence returned. This reveals how pervasive was Petrarch's desire to argue in favor of the need for eloquence in philosophy: he called on Aristotle for support despite his uncertainty that the Stagirite offered it.

Petrarch repeated his demand that rhetoric occupy a central place in the culture of his day when he wrote of the study of law. Writing in 1356 to a friend who had begun to study law, Petrarch pointed to the example of antiquity, when lawyers and orators had been one and the same, and he expressed a hope that his friend would pursue his career with their achievements in mind. Among the Romans, Petrarch had special praise for Cicero and the two interlocutors of *De oratore*, Crassus and Antonius. Since their day legal studies had become separated from rhetoric, and had declined as a result. "Just as the first step [in the decline of legal studies] was from the manifold learning and heavenly citadel of eloquence to the single subject of equity and civic knowledge, so assuredly the second step was from that to a loquacious ignorance." The proper pursuit of law, like that of philosophy, required that it be joined with rhetoric.[33]

[30] *Ibid.*, pp. 53-54; cf. Cicero, *Tusc. Disp.* I, iv, 7, and *De oratore* III, xxxv, 141.

[31] *On His Own Ignorance*, p. 103. Cf. above, Chap. I, and *De oratore* II, xxxviii, 160.

[32] *Rerum mem.*, II, 31, 8. Part of this confusion can probably be attributed to the fact that the treatises referred to by Cicero were the lost youthful works of Aristotle, whereas the works Petrarch could read—the ones which have survived—were unknown to Cicero. See Werner Jaeger, *Aristotile* (Ital. edn., Florence, 1935), pp. 38-39, 341.

[33] *Fam.*, XX, 4, 23: "Certe ut primus a doctrine multiplicis et

Thus much of Petrarch's writing shows his high regard for the art of oratory and his concern that it be given its rightful place among other intellectual pursuits. In this his basic cultural orientation reflected Cicero's. Yet Cicero's discussions of this question had by no means been circumscribed by an uncritical celebration of rhetoric. The Roman orator had recognized that the greatest thinkers of ancient Greece had often been suspicious of the oratory of professional rhetoricians, and in creating his image of the ideal orator he had taken account of their criticisms. Petrarch too was aware that the power of eloquence could be harmful if used unwisely, as the chapter "De eloquentia" in the *De remediis* makes clear. In some of Petrarch's writings, moreover, one finds an attitude toward the cultivation of eloquence which was not merely cautious, but suspicious and even hostile. Only when we combine the statements we have already examined with these conflicting ones do we become aware how rich and profound was Petrarch's understanding of Ciceronian rhetorical culture.

(2)

PETRARCH was not a professional rhetorician. Thanks to his enjoyment of certain church benefices, and to the patronage of the Colonna and other important families, he did not have to support himself by teaching grammar and rhetoric or by serving regularly in the chancery of a prince or of a free city. Yet his links to the professional rhetorical culture of his day were close and he probably did perform from time to time some of the tasks which made up the daily routine of professionals like his father and many of his friends.[34] He certainly knew what the orator's tasks were; and more important for our present purposes, he under-

---

celestis arce facundie ad unam equitatis ac civilis scientie disciplinam, sic secundus inde ad loquacem ignorantiam gradus fuit." See also the earlier part of this letter, 14ff.

[34] On these aspects of Petrarch's career see Kristeller, "Il Petrarca, l'umanesimo e la scolastica," pp. 373-74. On professional rhetoric in Italy, see below, pp. 205ff.

stood the ways in which the demands of the orator's profession shaped and limited his intellectual and moral personality. Like Cicero, Petrarch understood that the orator could not free himself from the life of the city. In the *De vita solitaria* Petrarch listed many ways in which the solitary life was superior to the busy, noisy life of the town, and he exhorted his readers to flee the city. To buttress his case, he pointed out that men of all occupations preferred the life of withdrawal to the many cares and anxieties of the active life. Even emperors and captains of armies shared this conviction. There was, however, a single exception: orators. "It is a peculiar characteristic of orators that they take pleasure in large cities and in the press of the crowd, in proportion to the greatness of their own talents. They curse solitude, and hate and oppose silence where decisions are to be made."[35] Petrarch referred especially to Cicero in this passage, and to his belief (which we have already encountered) that while other activities might find excellence through a flight from everyday life and common sense, rhetoric could seek its glory only among these things. For Petrarch, even more than for Cicero, this restricted the orator to a level of life which did not allow the development of man's highest capacities. "The crowd" was for him the symbol of human error and weakness. In at least two places in his writings, he adapted a statement from Cicero to say that the crowd "is not able to see anything with the mind; it judges all things according to the testimony of its eyes. It is the task of a higher spirit to recall his mind from his senses, and to remove his thoughts from the common practice."[36] The orator looked outward, Petrarch felt, involving himself with the errors of the ma-

[35] *De vita solitaria*, ed. G. Martellotti, in Petrarca, *Prose*, p. 534: "Est illud oratoribus singulare et proprium ut pro magnitudine ingenii magnis urbibus ac populorum frequentia delectentur, solitudines execrentur, iudiciorumque silentium adversentur atque oderint." (Page references are to this edition.)

[36] *Ibid.*, p. 352, and *De secreto conflictu curarum mearum*, ed. E. Carrara, in Petrarca, *Prose*, p. 66 (cited below, with page references to this edition, as *Secret*). Cf. *Tusc. Disp.* I, xvi, 37-38. Petrarch misquoted the passage slightly.

43

jority of men. Man's condition, however, required that he make use of a different standard. As Petrarch had St. Augustine remind him in the *Secret*:

What does it matter that your listeners perhaps have approved the things you say, if those things are condemned by yourself as judge? Even though the approval of one's listeners appears to be a fruit of eloquence which ought not to be spurned, if the inner approval of the orator is missing, how little pleasure the noise of the crowd can offer![37]

Or, as Petrarch wrote in the *De vita solitaria*:

The doctor who helps a sick man by his advice is not necessarily a well man himself; often he dies of the same sickness which he has cured in many others. I do not reject speech that is carefully elaborated and artfully composed to be of help to the many, and I approve of a useful work, whoever is its author. But truly this is for us a school of life, not of rhetoric; nor should we seek the empty glory of the tongue, but the lasting quiet of the mind.[38]

Despite Petrarch's many statements praising the art of oratory and his championing of it in the culture of his time, he recognized that the pursuit of eloquence did not always lead man where the fulfillment of his deepest needs should take him.

In this anti-rhetorical mood Petrarch could still profit from his reading of Cicero; indeed, many of his criticisms

[37] *Secret*, p. 72: "Quid autem attinet audientes forsitan approbasse que diceres, si te iudice damnabantur? Quamvis enim audientium plausus non spernendus eloquentie fructus esse videatur, si tamen ipsius oratoris [plausus] interior desit, quantulum voluptatis prestare potest strepitus ille vulgaris?"

[38] *De vita solitaria*, p. 324: "Sed non statim sanus est medicus, qui consilio egrum iuvat, quin eodem sepe morbo, quo multos liberaverat, interiit. Verba studio elaborata atque arte composita pro multorum salute non respuo et, quicunque sit opifex, utile opus amplector; verum hec nobis non rethorice scola sed vite est, nec inanem lingue gloriam, sed solidam quietem mentis intendimus."

44

of rhetoric are simply taken over from the Roman orator.
Yet there is something more in Petrarch's description of
the limitations of rhetoric. As a Christian, Petrarch was
more deeply concerned than Cicero had been with the differences between the needs of the inner man and the im-
pulses of his worldly companion. His worry lest the pursuit
of eloquence and its glories turn him from a higher path
was more intense than Cicero's. Moreover, Cicero was not
the only writer who contributed to Petrarch's understanding of the weaknesses of rhetoric. The most important of
the others was another professional rhetorician with a profound desire to find true philosophy: St. Augustine. Augustine began his intellectual career as a teacher of rhetoric,
and his *De doctrina christiana* passed along much of ancient rhetorical doctrine to medieval Christian learning and
preaching. But his conversion led him to a concern for truth
above all else, which turned him against the sophistic rhetoric of the fourth century and toward a recreation of the
reformed rhetoric of Plato's *Phaedrus*. This is the rhetoric
of the *De doctrina christiana*. For Augustine, spiritual
progress could be represented by a movement from speech
to silence, from outer appearance to inner truth.[39] Petrarch
sometimes spoke in the same terms. "Truly then, unless we
care more about what we seem than about what we are, the
applause of the foolish crowd will not please us so much as
truth in silence."[40] *Veritas in silentio* represented for Petrarch an ideal of life on a higher plane than the one the
orator occupied. One of his objections to city life was its
noise. The rubric of one of his letters reads: "Even those

[39] See J. A. Mazzeo, "St. Augustine's Rhetoric of Silence," *Journal
of the History of Ideas*, XXIII (1962). On the general question of
Petrarch's relationship to St. Augustine, see P. P. Gerosa, "L'umanesimo Agostiniano del Petrarca," *Didaskaleion*, N. S., III (1925), fasc.
2, 63-113 and fasc. 3, 13-29; IV (1926), fasc. 1, 107-37; V (1927),
fasc. 1, 69-127; VII (1929), fasc. 1, 125-48. Gerosa's view of the
distinction between Christian and pagan psychology with reference to
Petrarch's development seems to me somewhat exaggerated, however.

[40] *Fam.*, I, 8, 20: "Profecto itaque, nisi videri magis quam esse
propositum nobis est, non tam plausus insane multitudinis quam veritas
in silentio placebit."

who follow the public life may live innocently and piously, and from that clatter they may aspire to the silence of a higher life."[41]

The Christian and Augustinian coloration of Petrarch's view of moral philosophy is clear. The study of ethics was for him a consideration not only of virtue and vice, but also of sin and redemption. In the *Secret* he described true human self-knowledge as the attainment of an engrossing and moving meditation on man's death. Augustine's first address to Petrarch in their dialogue was a reproach ending, "Do you not remember that you are mortal?"[42] In the *Invective Against a Certain Physician,* Petrarch concluded that "true philosophy is that which some have said to be nothing other than thinking upon death."[43] Death was the ultimate silence, and to contemplate it was to look upon the ultimate truth.

Even here, however, Petrarch had not departed very far from Cicero. The source of the definition of philosophy as *cogitatio mortis* was the *Tusculan Disputations.* In the *Secret,* Petrarch was careful to have Augustine remind him of the Father's dependence on Platonic philosophy and on Cicero, particularly the latter's description of the delusions of the crowd.[44] Petrarch's basic understanding of the problems of moral philosophy, and of the limitations of rhetoric in relation to it, certainly derived from Cicero. Petrarch's Christian consciousness may have been responsible for his stating explicitly what was only implicit in Cicero's descriptions of the main concerns of the orator and the philosopher, but the terms of the comparison were Cicero's own. This appears from Petrarch's clearest declaration of the opposition of rhetoric to philosophy: "Both the di-

[41] *Fam.,* III, 12, rubric: "Ad Marcum Ianuensem, posse etiam qui reipublice student innocenter et pie vivere, posse et ex eo strepitu ad altioris vite silentium aspirare." Cf. *De vita solitaria,* p. 326: "Si solicita vita strepitum amat, multiloquio delectatur, contemplatio autem omnis amica silentio est."

[42] *Secret,* p. 28; cf. *De vita solitaria,* p. 356.

[43] *Invective,* p. 54; cf. *Tusc. Disp.* I, xxx, 74, and see above, Chap. I.

[44] *Secret,* p. 66.

versity of their ways of life and the wholly opposed ends
for which they have worked make me believe that philosophers have always thought differently from orators. For the
latter's efforts are directed toward gaining the applause of
the crowd, while the former strive—if their declarations
are not false—to know themselves, to return the soul to itself, and to despise empty glory."[45] This striking statement,
contradicting as it does so many of Petrarch's other descriptions of the relationship between rhetoric and philosophy,
shows how completely he recognized the tensions and am-
biguities involved in the ideal of a combination of the two
arts. This does not mean that he, any more than Cicero,
ever considered abandoning the ideal. It does mean, however, that Petrarch's attempt to join together rhetoric and
philosophy had to overcome difficulties which closely resembled those encountered by Cicero.

Petrarch's awareness of these difficulties appears in a
letter of 1350-51 entitled "De studio eloquentie."[46] Here
Petrarch attempted to distinguish the benefits of the pursuit of eloquence from those of the love of wisdom. "The
care of the soul requires the philosopher," he began, "the
learning of the tongue is proper to the orator. Neither
should be neglected. . . ." What each provided is explained
in this passage:

> What will be the result of your immersing yourself
> totally in the Ciceronian fount, that none of the writings
> either of the Latins or the Greeks pass you by? You will
> surely be able to speak ornately, clearly, sweetly, high-
> soundingly; but you will not yet be able to speak weight-
> ily, strictly, wisely, and what is most important, consist-
> ently. Since unless first all our desires accord one with
> another, which surely can befall only the man of wis-
> dom, just as we have divergent cares, so necessarily will

[45] *De vita solitaria*, p. 540: "Ut tamen ab oratoribus diversum semper sensisse philosophos credam, et diversitas morum facit et omnino
alius intentionum finis. Illis enim plausum populi captare animus,
horum labor, ni falsa professio est, circa notitiam sui reflectendumque
ad se animum et circa contemptum inanis glorie versatur."
[46] *Fam.*, I, 9.

our speech and our character diverge. The well-disposed mind is capable of unmoved serenity, is always placid and tranquil; it knows what it desires, and what it has once desired it does not cease to will. Therefore, even though the ornaments of the art of oratory do not aid it, it elicits from itself magnificent and weighty speech, which is surely self-consistent.[47]

Petrarch did not mean to suggest here that philosophy could do the work of rhetoric. He went on to make a place for oratory by the side of philosophy and even to describe eloquence in terms which (as we have seen above) made its task almost identical with that of moral philosophy.[48] There is much that is ambiguous in this letter; the provinces of rhetoric and of philosophy are by no means clearly separated in it. But whereas Petrarch gave the task of moral suasion sometimes to philosophy and sometimes to rhetoric, the characteristics he ascribed to the philosophic mind in the passage just quoted seem to be those which the humanist associated only with philosophy and never with rhetoric. The chief of these characteristics was consistency. This was the quality which only the study of philosophy could bring, and which Petrarch found to be the most important fruit of such study. In the treatise *On His Own Ignorance*, Petrarch remarked that "Philosophers must not be judged from isolated words but from their uninterrupted coherence and consistency."[49]

[47] *Fam.*, I, 9, 3: "Quid enim attinet quod ciceronianis te fontibus prorsus immerseris, quod nulla te neque Grecorum neque nostrorum scripta pretereant? ornate quidem, lepide, dulciter, altisone loqui poteris; graviter, severe, sapienterque, et, quod super omnia est, uniformiter certe non poteris. Quoniam nisi primum desideria invicem nostra conveniant, quod preter sapientem scito nemini posse contingere, illud necesse est ut, dissidentibus curis, et mores et verba dissideant. At bene disposita mens instar immote serenitatis placida semper ac tranquilla est: scit quid velit, et quod semel voluit, velle non desinit; itaque tametsi oratorie artis ornamenta non suppetant, ex se ipsa magnificentissimas voces atque gravissimas et certe sibi consonas elicit."
[48] See above, p. 34.
[49] *On His Own Ignorance*, p. 87. Quoted from Cicero, *Tusc. Disp.* V, x, 31.

The ideal of consistency appears many times in Petrarch's work. In a sense he regarded it as the highest ideal, both in philosophy and in life. It was essential to the spiritual state for which he was striving in the *Secret*. In that dialogue, Augustine attributed Petrarch's failure to arrive at his goal to his inability to give a consistent direction to his quest. The malady to which Petrarch had succumbed was one in which his mind, weakened by its entrance into his body, was deceived by a crowd of worldly phantasies. "Invaded by these phantasy impressions and oppressed by many differing preoccupations ceaselessly at war among themselves, it cannot determine to which of these to turn first, which to cultivate, which to suppress, or which to repel. . . . You are turned about with a marvellous inconstancy, partly here and partly there, and never anywhere wholly and completely."[50] In the *De vita solitaria* Petrarch censured those who wavered continually between various ends, and he listed consistency as one of the chief aims of the search for wisdom in solitude. "To wish always for a single and well-defined thing is a sign of wisdom. Inconstancy of purpose is the best argument for a person's foolishness." In the words of Seneca, no wind was favorable for the man who knew not what port to seek.[51]

Thus consistency was a prized fruit of the search for wisdom. But why should Petrarch have thought that the pursuit of eloquence would interfere with the attainment of consistency? There were several reasons for this. The first was that a basic rhetorical principle directed the orator to fit his speech not only to his subject, but also to his audience and circumstances. As these changed, so must the orator's message. Petrarch followed this practice. Seeking to justify the many contradictions in his letters, Petrarch listed the different categories of people to whom he had written, and concluded that "the writer has a double task: to envisage the person to whom he is writing, and also the state

[50] *Secret*, pp. 66-68. Cf. St. Augustine, *De ordine*, II, xvi, 44.

[51] *De vita solitaria*, pp. 384-86. For similar themes in Petrarch's verse, see Bosco, *Francesco Petrarca*, esp. pp. 62-67.

of mind in which the recipient will read what he proposes
to write. In the face of these difficulties, I have been forced
into many contradictions with myself."[52] A second rhetorical
principle which led to inconsistency was the principle of
imitation. The imitation of models was one of the basic
methods recommended by writers on rhetoric for developing a good style. More than that, much writing on ethics by
rhetoricians like Cicero—and much of Petrarch's own moral
doctrine—recommended the imitation of exemplars of virtue. A chief purpose of the study of history as Petrarch and
his followers conceived it was to encourage the imitation
of great men. Many of Petrarch's major writings presented
the reader with models to be imitated: the *De viris illustribus,* as well as parts of the *De remediis utriusque fortunae,* the *Rerum memorandarum,* and the *De vita solitaria.*
In the latter work, however, he criticized the principle of
imitation for introducing errors into men's lives and for
leading them in the direction of inconsistency. Quintilian
had counseled that the orator ought to try not only to imitate his literary model but to surpass him. Commenting
on this, Petrarch asserted: "What is usefully applied to oratory, the art of speaking ornately and well, is ruinously
transferred to the art of living evilly and shamefully." Men
had surpassed their models of living, but in the direction of
evil rather than good. Since the models themselves were
not perfect, their conduct contained something of evil as
well as of good; unable to distinguish perfectly between the
two, men had followed the first instead of the second. Moreover, those who make imitation the principle of their actions cannot achieve a constant tenor of life. "They must
change their goal every time they find something to
admire. There will be no limit to their changes, because
there is no limit to imitation."[53] The rhetorical principle of

[52] *Fam.,* I, 1, 29-31: "ut geminus sit labor: cogitare quisnam ille
sit cui scribere propositum est, qualiter ve tunc affectus, cum ea que
scribere instituis lecturus est. Quibus ego difficultatibus multum a me
ipso differre compulsus sum."

[53] *De vita solitaria,* pp. 386-88: "Ceterum quod utiliter in oratoria,
hoc est bene ornateque loquendi arte, precipitur, ad artem male turpi-

50

imitation thus involved the orator and those who listened
to him in inconsistencies which the philosopher should try
to shun. In addition, Petrarch described "the crowd" as
especially subject to inconstancy and changes of opinion.[54]
If the orator tried to please them, he would once again be
turning his back on the philosopher's quest.

These statements help to explain the point of view from
which Petrarch regarded rhetoric and philosophy as contradictory pursuits. They also imply that he found definite
weaknesses and limitations in his own work, since so much
of it embodied the orator's methods and purposes. Sometimes this self-criticism was quite explicit. In the *De vita
solitaria* Petrarch spoke disparagingly of those "who go
around the cities, harangue the crowds, speak much of
vices and virtues." It was to them that he addressed the
reminder that "this is for us a school of life, not of rhetoric."[55] But of whom was Petrarch speaking here if not of
himself? Though he did not literally travel about harangu-
ing crowds in public squares, his purpose as a moral philosopher was precisely to address men in eloquent language
about virtue and vice. When the physician against whom
he wrote the *Invective* referred to the humanist's writings
as homilies, Petrarch did not object. He only replied that
this was a genre "which is known to have pleased the most
holy and most learned men."[56] In the *Secret*, however, he
had Augustine reproach him: "If you had studied for yourself and not for others, and if you had turned the reading
of so many books into a rule for your own life, instead of
toward the windy approval of the crowd and empty show,
you wouldn't now say such silly and stupid things."[57] Pe-

---

terque vivendi damnabiliter est translatum, et quod ille iussit implevi-
mus: contendimus, equavimus, vicimus; iam de sequacibus duces
sumus . . ." (p. 386). "Nullus itaque mutandi, quia nullus imitandi
modus" (p. 388). On the importance of imitation for humanist historical theory, see Myron Gilmore, "The Renaissance Conception of the
Lessons of History," *Humanists and Jurists* (Cambridge, Mass., 1963),
pp. 14ff.

[54] *Fam.*, II, 4, 3; XXI, 13, 11; XIV, 4, 3; *Secret*, p. 202.
[55] *De vita solitaria*, p. 324.   [56] *Invective*, p. 75.
[57] *Secret*, p. 32.

trarch's criticism of his own work is one of the most striking evidences of his awareness of the tensions which separated the pursuit of eloquence from the search for wisdom. How, then, was he able to continue to pursue the ideal of the union of rhetoric and philosophy?

(3)

PETRARCH's solution to this dilemma followed lines traced out by Cicero. His understanding of "philosophy," like Cicero's, embraced not only the abstract ideal of the love of wisdom, but also the concrete doctrines of several ancient philosophical schools. Following Cicero, Petrarch regarded the Academics, the Peripatetics, and the Stoics as each of interest to the ideal orator, though not all in the same way. Cicero had shown that taken together the three schools—each in a different fashion—allowed the orator both to involve himself in philosophy and to protect his art from it.[58] Petrarch's union of wisdom and eloquence was not a simple copy of Cicero's, but it was based on the Ciceronian model.

Petrarch's writings offer support for quite different philosophic opinions at different times. A recent study of Petrarch's moral philosophy has found his discussions of ethics to be a chaos of contradictions. Following now one ancient source, now another, Petrarch several times reversed himself on the question of whether fortune, of which he often spoke, actually existed or not. Moreover, on a whole range of issues which can be identified in the *De finibus* and other of Cicero's works as subjects debated between Stoics and Peripatetics, the humanist expressed by turns the view of first one side and then the other. This was true on such basic questions as whether moral philosophy sought to extinguish human passions or only to temper them, whether prosperity was a real good or only a seeming one, and conversely whether adversity was a true evil or only apparently harmful.[59]

[58] See above, Chap. I.
[59] Klaus Heitmann, *Fortuna und Virtus, Eine Studie zu Petrarcas*

52

The Stoics and Peripatetics were the two groups of nonskeptical philosophers whose opinions Cicero had found most interesting in his attempt to provide the orator with a philosophic culture which suited his needs. The first were perhaps "the only true philosophers," and their teachings were suited to the ears of a philosophic audience. The doctrine of the Peripatetics was closer to everyday life, and more intelligible to the men with whom the orator had to deal in the performance of his everyday tasks. Petrarch found similar differences between the two schools. The Stoics were the more "philosophical" of the two. The ideal of consistency, which we have seen Petrarch associate with the pursuit of wisdom in general, on closer inspection turns out to be the special property of the Stoics. In the letter "De studio eloquentie," from which we earlier quoted at length, the attainment of a consistent pattern of life and thought was associated with a mind which was "capable of unmoved serenity," and which was "always placid and tranquil." Petrarch regarded these characteristics as the special property of the Stoic sage. In the *Secret*, where Petrarch had St. Augustine criticize his inability to give a consistent direction to his life, Petrarch replied to Augustine's exhortation: "You recall me to the teaching of the Stoics, far removed from popular opinion, and nearer to truth than to custom."[60]

If the Stoics were the guardians of the philosophical virtues of truth and consistency, the Peripatetics were the philosophers whose teachings were most relevant to the lives of ordinary men. Except where he was specifically engaged in advocating a Stoic point of view, Petrarch pictured himself as such a man. He could not quell the passions he felt, especially his love of Laura and his desire for the fame which accompanies the poet's crown. In the *Secret* he excused himself for not following more resolutely

---

Lebensweisheit (Cologne, 1958). See especially the conclusion and the tabular view of contradictory maxims, p. 251.

[60] *Secret*, p. 34: "ad stoicorum precepta me revocas, populorum opinionibus aversa et veritati proprinquiora quam usui."

the path toward the higher life, on the grounds that he was subject to "the necessity of human nature."[61] "Just as my reason is often Stoic," he confessed in one of his letters, "so are my feelings always Peripatetic."[62] Thus he was unable to put into effect the Stoic counsels he directed to himself in the *Secret*. This did not mean that his life was totally devoid of virtue, but only that he could not achieve it on the highest level. Augustine exhorted Petrarch to rise above this barrier, but at one point he agreed to let Petrarch limit his dampening of passion to "the attenuation offered by the Peripatetics."[63]

Petrarch was not proud of the limits he set to his own moral progress, but he insisted that he could not go beyond them. His picture of himself, both in the *Secret* and elsewhere, was deeply colored by his sense of always striving to reach a moral level which his natural weakness did not allow him to attain. This feature of Petrarch's personality has often been noted. It is his famous *dissidio*, the internal psychological conflict between the poet's human nature and his divine vision.[64] While Petrarch yearned intensely for a higher plane of existence, he never ceased to admit that he was destined to remain on a lower, fully human one. In one passage of the *Secret*, St. Augustine pictured to Petrarch the fully rational man, one who lives in total conformity to the reason which separates him from the beasts: "He will be conscious of his own mortality, so that he has it before his eyes every day; he will regulate his life according to this vision, and scorning mortal things will aspire to that life where, still more intensely rational, he will cease to be mortal. Then finally will he have true and useful knowledge of the definition of man."[65] More openly, in another

[61] *Ibid.*, p. 90.
[62] *Fam.*, XXIII, 12, 11, quoted by Heitmann, *Fortuna und Virtus*, pp. 256-57: "Ad summam sic me invenio, ut sepe ratio stoica, sensus michi perypatheticus semper sit."
[63] *Secret*, p. 98.
[64] On the *dissidio*, see esp. Bosco, *Francesco Petrarca*, pp. 83-100, and Gerosa, "L'umanesimo Agostiniano del Petrarca," Part I.
[65] *Secret*, pp. 52-54.

place in the dialogue, Augustine tells Petrarch that in order
to arrive at some of the goals he must set for himself, "it
would be necessary for you to divest yourself of your humanity and become a god."[66] The notion that the study of
philosophy raised man to—or at least towards—the level
of divinity was a common one in ancient writers, and it
was to reappear in several well-known Renaissance thinkers. As Petrarch used it here, however, it was less a call to
the study of wisdom than a denial that the philosophic
ideal was fully relevant to man's condition. Petrarch suggested precisely this in one of his letters: "You will act differently as a philosopher than you do as a man. No one is so
given to wisdom that he does not, when he returns to
the common human state, condescend also to public ways
of acting."[67] Petrarch himself lived and wrote sometimes as
a philosopher and sometimes as a man. This meant that he
wavered between encouraging himself and others to take
the path which led to consistency, solitude, and silent contemplation, and admitting that men could only attain the
level of virtue permitted by human weakness and by the
noisy confusions of ordinary human life. His own moral
limitations held him to the level of everyday life, but from
within them he reached out toward a higher plane of
existence.[68]

[66] *Ibid.*, p. 92.
[67] *Fam.*, XXI, 13, 1: "Alterum ut philosophus facis, alterum ut
homo; nemo tam sapientie deditus, qui non quandoque ad humanitatem redeat comunem et publicis moribus condescendat." Sometimes
Petrarch regarded this dichotomy in different terms, as when he said
"Let us speak in the crowd's way, but not think as they do." ("Loquamur ut vulgus, non sentiamus ut vulgus"; *Fam.*, II, 1, 6. Cf. *Sen. rerum
libri*, VIII, 3.) This sort of statement should however be regarded in
one of two ways: either as a commonplace which Petrarch took over
from classical writers, but which did not really describe his own state
of mind as it appears in the *Secret* or in an important letter to his
brother (*Fam.*, X, 5); or else as a manner of speaking *ut philosophus*
which differed from Petrarch's own situation *ut homo*. The contradictions in Petrarch's writing, in other words, must be regarded as genuine parts of his personality and his culture, not as the result of simple
concessions to a popular audience.
[68] Thus the comment quoted above: "Even those who follow the

These considerations form the basis for Petrarch's combination of rhetoric and philosophy. The philosophical school which Petrarch regarded as most in harmony with rhetoric was Peripateticism. The virtue which the Peripatetics urged was a kind of excellence man could achieve while living among his fellows and accepting the burdens of everyday life. This, as Petrarch observed in the *De vita solitaria*, was the career to which the orator, more than any other man, was committed.[69] Although Petrarch seems never to have quoted Cicero's direct statements on the harmony of Peripatetic ethics with the tasks of the orator, he must have felt the connection. Oratory and Peripatetic philosophy shared a common moral and intellectual perspective; their union was natural and uncontested.

With Stoicism this ideal union was much more problematical. Stoic virtue met the highest standards of truth and consistency, but man could only achieve it if he could free himself from the ordinary limitations of human nature. To live as a Stoic sage meant to flee the city and take up the life of solitude. Petrarch recognized that this vision clashed with the natural position of the orator. Because the Stoics were the most rigorously philosophical of all the lovers of wisdom, the opposition between Stoicism and oratory sometimes led Petrarch to describe philosophy and rhetoric as fundamentally opposed. Yet Petrarch did not therefore turn his back on the Stoics. Like Cicero, he often defended Stoic positions and included Stoic maxims in his works. To do so was to recognize the claims of philosophy on rhetorical culture and on human life, as well as to show that (as Cicero had insisted in the *Paradoxa Stoicorum*) eloquence could add luster to any philosophical doctrine. Moreover, Petrarch's espousal of a Stoic viewpoint conformed to the principles of rhetoric in another sense. Like Cicero, he directed his truly "philosophical" writings to a philosophic

---

public life may live innocently and piously, and from that clatter they may aspire to the silence of a higher life" (*Fam.*, III, 12, rubric).

[69] See above, pp. 42-43.

56

audience: men of wisdom could be expected to listen to Stoic teachings in a way that ordinary men would not.[70] Thus Petrarch showed himself to be a true Ciceronian orator, one who knew how to speak as a philosopher on behalf of the Stoics with as much force as he employed in speaking as an orator on behalf of the Peripatetics.

Cicero also taught Petrarch that there was one school of philosophers which joined the rhetorician in his refusal to accept any philosophical doctrine as true: the Academic skeptics. As a Christian, Petrarch could not fully accept Cicero's assertion that men possessed no light to lead them to the truth. But he agreed that no pagan philosopher had been able to distinguish truth from mere opinion; indeed, the conviction that Christian teachings were superior to those of any philosophical school encouraged such a view. Petrarch several times spoke with approval of the attitude of the Academics toward philosophical knowledge, and at least once he described himself as one of their number.[71] This fits perfectly with the free use he made of the diverse opinions of Stoics and Peripatetics. Petrarch does not seem to have commented directly on the harmony of oratory and skepticism, as Cicero did; nonetheless, the two played cooperative roles in his writings.

Despite some clear statements of the opposition between rhetoric and philosophy, therefore, Petrarch continued to pursue the ideal of their union in his work. Indeed, his view of human nature and human needs demanded that he proclaim both the ideal and the contradictions within it. Men were sometimes able to think and act as philosophers, sometimes not; the true moral philosopher, who was also the perfect orator, spoke to both conditions. To men in their capacity as rational creatures he announced the vision of a life fully in accord with wisdom; this vision demanded a

---

[70] For Petrarch's awareness of the need to address different philosophical doctrines to different audiences, see, among many other passages, *De vita solitaria*, p. 294; *Fam.*, I, 1, 26ff.

[71] E.g., *On His Own Ignorance*, pp. 125-26; and *Sen. rerum libri*, I, 6, also trans. H. Nachod in *The Renaissance Philosophy of Man*, pp. 34-35.

recognition of the moral and intellectual inadequacy of rhetoric itself. To men in their everyday capacities, however, his message was more moderate. Philosophy made smaller claims on their lives, and it did not demand that they banish the glory of eloquence from them. Since no man could be a philosopher all the time, Stoic counsels could appear at particular moments within a moral prescription whose general import was Peripatetic. Such a procedure recognized both man's striving for consistency and his inability to achieve it, both the nobility of his vision and the necessary imperfections of his life. These are the reasons for the many inconsistencies in Petrarch's writings. Petrarch could justify them either as a skeptic or as an orator, but it is the second identity which best describes his overall understanding of himself. While he often described consistency as a major goal of the philosopher, he regarded its opposite as inescapable for the man of eloquence.

Because these two conflicting attitudes toward philosophy and its relationship with oratory each had a necessary role to play in Petrarch's intellectual and moral outlook, we should not expect to be able to organize his contrasting statements according to any developing chronological pattern. An examination of the succession of the major Petrarchian writings considered here reveals a seesaw allegiance to the divergent ideals of moral philosophy we have encountered.[72] The first of Petrarch's major works was the *De viris illustribus*, on which he worked between 1338 and 1343. This was an historical treatise whose purpose was to encourage the imitation of virtuous examples, a procedure which Petrarch later criticized in the *De vita solitaria*. In 1342 and 1343 Petrarch produced the first version of the *Secret*, with its devotion to St. Augustine and the Stoics, and its criticism of Petrarch's desire to achieve fame through

[72] On the chronology of Petrarch's Latin writings, see the critical notes in the volume cited above, Petrarca, *Prose*, pp. 1161-79, and the literature noted there; also the helpful list given by Bosco, *Francesco Petrarca*, pp. 293-302. For the dates of the letters, see the invaluable manual of E. H. Wilkins, *The Prose Letters of Petrarch* (rev. ed., New York, 1951), and the literature given for each letter.

eloquence. Immediately afterwards, from 1343 to 1345, Petrarch was at work on the *Rerum memorandarum*, a book whose organization was based on Cicero's *De inventione rhetorica*; it contained a celebration of everyday life and common speech, and like the *De viris* embodied the notion of moral philosophy as the imitation of virtuous examples.[73] This work was never completed, but in 1346, soon after he stopped work on it, Petrarch began to write the *De vita solitaria*. This was the most anti-rhetorical of all his writings, in which imitation as a principle of ethics was sharply criticized and in which the ideals of rhetoric and philosophy were plainly said to be at odds. Petrarch continued to work on this book for the next ten years. During that period he wrote the letter "De studio eloquentie," in which both attitudes are affirmed: on the one hand the insistence that only philosophy leads man to the high goal of consistency, and on the other the conviction that eloquent speech can move man to a life of virtue. In the years immediately following the writing of this letter (1352-53), Petrarch wrote the books making up the *Invective Against a Certain Physician*, where the defense of rhetoric was a leading motif, but in which the definition of philosophy as a *cognitio mortis* also had a place. From 1351 to 1353 Petrarch worked on a second version of the *De viris*, more Christian than the first, but no less inspired by the ideal of imitation. From 1354 to 1360 Petrarch was at work on his most extensive treatise of moral philosophy, the *De remediis utriusque fortunae* (*On the Remedies for Both Kinds of Fortune*). This work is largely Stoic in conception and tone, but it contains both Stoic and Peripatetic maxims, as Klaus Heitmann has pointed out.[74] In 1367 Petrarch composed his last major prose treatise, *On His Own Ignorance and That of Many Others*. This was a defense of his own classical and rhetorical culture against the attacks of some partisans of scholastic Aristotelianism. It contained some of Petrarch's

---

[73] See Part X of G. Billanovich's introduction to his edition of *Rerum Memorandarum*, cited above.
[74] Heitmann, *Fortuna und Virtus, passim.*

clearest statements of the need for eloquence in moral philosophy, but it also quoted with approval the classical definition of philosophy as "a thinking upon death." Our study of Petrarch thus leads us to agree fully with Umberto Bosco that the poet was *senza storia*, "without a history," if by "history" is meant any development in a consistent direction.[75] There is a different kind of consistency in Petrarch: the constant affirmation of his humanity, with all its inescapable contradictions.

Petrarch conceived of and described these contradictions in Ciceronian terms. Cicero's influence on Petrarch does not make itself felt only—or even mainly—in specific quotations. Rather, it appears in Petrarch's broader concern for many of the same basic questions that Cicero had faced, particularly the question of the relationship between rhetorical and philosophical ideals in man's intellectual and moral life. One of the chief reasons why Cicero became the central figure of classical culture for Petrarch was that he provided such an extensive discussion of this problem and suggested a solution to it which both admitted the claims of wisdom and preserved an exalted place for eloquence. Petrarch was not able to read every word of all of Cicero's works; even the text of the *De oratore* available to him suffered from serious lacunae.[76] Yet this did not prevent him from achieving a good understanding of the Ciceronian combination of rhetoric and philosophy. Doubtless he was aided in this understanding by other writers, notably Seneca and St. Augustine.

Petrarch was two things that Cicero was not: a poet (though Cicero had written some inconsequential verses) and a Christian. Both identities encouraged a degree of self-

---

[75] Bosco, *op. cit.*, p. 7. This view of Petrarch contrasts with that of Hans Baron, "The Evolution of Petrarch's Thought: Reflections on the State of Petrarch Studies," *Bibliothèque d'Humanisme et Renaissance*, XXIV (1962), 7-41.

[76] For an account of the discovery of the full text of the *De oratore* in 1421, and a list of the passages missing from earlier manuscripts, see R. Sabbadini, *Le Scoperte dei Codici Latini e Greci ne' secoli XIV e XV* (Florence, 1905), p. 100 and note 59.

preoccupation which distinguished the first humanist from the practicing politician of pagan Rome. Yet even Petrarch's brooding and seemingly modern self-consciousness found expression, at least in his Latin prose writings, largely in Ciceronian terms. As Petrarch presented his conflicting psychological states in the *Secret*, they corresponded very well to the traditional debate between Stoic and Peripatetic ideals of ethics, viewed at times through certain medieval traditions and amplified by the psychological insights of Augustine's *Confessions*. Though the chief figure in the dialogue was Augustine, Petrarch defined the issues in terms of Cicero's distinction between the rigorous Stoics and the common-sense Peripatetics.

Petrarch's work was to be of great importance to the humanists who followed him. In the words quoted at the beginning of this chapter, they felt he had "opened the way for us to show in what manner we could acquire learning." The meaning of this statement in the context of the present study should by now have begun to emerge, and should become clearer in the chapters which follow. Petrarch provided later humanists with a view of ancient philosophic culture which opened its riches to men who were fundamentally rhetoricians. Thus rhetoric could claim to be what it had been in Cicero's day, the central cultural discipline, the doorway to learning in philosophy. The votaries of eloquence could defend their culture in the name of the rediscovered philosophy of antiquity, which for them meant philosophy as Cicero had presented it. This was true philosophy, not the corrupt and barbarous mouthings of the scholastics.[77]

Yet there was a problem here for the humanists. Petrarch seldom admitted that the scholastic philosophy of his own day had much in common with the great tradition of philosophy in antiquity, but we can learn from his writings

---

[77] See Bruni, *Ad Petrum Paulum Histrum Dialogus*, ed. Garin, in *Prosatori Latini*, p. 54: "Fuit philosophia olim ex Graecia in Italiam a Cicerone traducta, atque aureo illo eloquentiae flumine irrigata; erat in eius libris cum omnis philosophiae exposita ratio, tum singulae philosophorum scholae diligenter explicatae."

that, on one point at least, it did: both harbored suspicions of rhetoric. Petrarch belittled the scholastics for believing that Aristotle "in the way of one who would understand the highest things, held all eloquence in contempt, as if there were no place in the high reaches of knowledge for splendor of language."[78] As we have seen, however, Petrarch sometimes attributed very similar ideas both to himself and to St. Augustine; he was certainly acquainted with the current of suspicion of rhetoric which flowed through classical philosophy. Most humanists were slow to admit to the existence of this or any other similarity between the admired ancients and the corrupt scholastics. But the recognition that the scholastics were, after all, philosophers in a sense in which the humanists were not, could not always be avoided. Leonardo Bruni would later try to fend off this admission by adding new substance to the Petrarchian combination of rhetoric and philosophy. At times, however, both Bruni's elder friend and guide Coluccio Salutati and his younger associate Lorenzo Valla would acknowledge that basic similarities existed between ancient and medieval philosophic ideals. The two men would respond to the challenge of this admission in very different ways.

[78] *Rerum mem.*, II, 31, 8.

CHAPTER III

WISDOM AND ELOQUENCE
IN SALUTATI, AND THE
"PETRARCH CONTROVERSY"
OF 1405-1406

(1)

T HE MOST famous and influential representative of humanist culture in the generation after Petrarch was Coluccio Salutati.[1] In his three decades as chancellor of the Florentine republic his name became known and respected all over Italy. Within Florence he gathered around himself a group of younger men which included several who would be among the most eminent humanists of the fifteenth century: Pier Paolo Vergerio, Niccolò Niccoli, Leonardo Bruni, and Poggio Bracciolini. He defended the humanist program, the *studia humanitatis*, from the attacks of writers who either objected to all forms of pagan learning or who preferred the scholastic disciplines of medicine and natural philosophy to literary and rhetorical pursuits.[2] In this activity he was inspired and aided by the work of Petrarch.

[1] On Salutati's life and career, see B. L. Ullman, *The Humanism of Coluccio Salutati* (Padua, 1963); F. Novati, *La Giovinezza di Coluccio Salutati* (Turin, 1888); Vittorio Rossi, *Il Quattrocento* (Rome, 1933; rev. ed. 1956), pp. 17-19; Eugenio Garin, "I cancellieri umanisti della Repubblica fiorentina da Coluccio Salutati a Bartolomeo Scala," in *La Cultura Filosofica del Rinascimento Italiano* (Florence, 1961), pp. 3-18; Lauro Martines, *The Social World of the Florentine Humanists, 1390-1460* (Princeton, 1963), esp. pp. 147-54. A basic source for information on Salutati's life and thought is the magisterial *Epistolario di Coluccio Salutati*, ed. Francesco Novati (4 vols., Rome, 1891-1911), which includes Salutati's private letters. This work is cited here as *Epistolario*. The public letters which Salutati wrote as chancellor of Florence are preserved in the Archivio di Stato at Florence, and have been the basis of important recent work on his career. See Peter Herde, "Politik und Rhetorik in Florenz am Vorabend der Renaissance," *Archiv für Kulturgeschichte*, XLVII (1965), 141-220.

[2] On the humanists' use of the phrase *studia humanitatis*, or *studia*

Salutati was deeply concerned with the problem of the relation between rhetoric and philosophy. His treatment of this question followed the main lines laid down by Cicero and Petrarch, as did his discussions of the ancient philosophical schools. Like Cicero and Petrarch, Salutati sought to approach the world of learning along a path which had its beginning in the regions of oratory, and which could be most easily traveled by one whose intellectual bearings were given by the art of rhetoric. As we have seen, however, a course plotted in this way would not avoid areas of opposition to the orator. What is of special interest about Salutati is that while he sometimes attempted to neutralize this hostility, at other times he took it much more seriously than Petrarch did. In the last years of his life he stated the anti-rhetorical position more completely than Petrarch had, and he openly pointed out implications in it which Petrarch had never allowed to come to the surface. In doing so he showed what dangers, for the humanists, lurked in the philosophical suspicion of rhetoric, and how important the defense of oratory was for the *studia humanitatis.* Salutati's writings tell us much about the problems of humanism after Petrarch, and help us to understand some important features of the humanist movement in the fifteenth century.

Salutati's career differed from Petrarch's in a number of ways, two of which are significant here. First of all, unlike Petrarch, Salutati was a professional rhetorician.[3] He was

---

humanitatis et eloquentiae (*eloquentie* in Salutati's spelling), see P. O. Kristeller, "Humanism and Scholasticism in the Italian Renaissance," *Studies in Renaissance Thought and Letters* (Rome, 1956), pp. 572-74. For Salutati's use of the phrase, see, e.g., *Epistolario*, I, 229-30. On Salutati's defense of humanistic studies, see Ullman, Chap. IV.

[3] For Salutati's early training, see Novati, *La Giovinezza di Coluccio Salutati*; Ullman, Chap. I; L. Frati, "Pietro da Muglio e il suo commento a Boezio," *Studi e memorie per la storia dell' università di Bologna*, V (1920); on Salutati's connection with the earlier rhetorical tradition in Italy, see below, Chap. VII; also, on a collection of Salutati's letters to serve as models of style, see *Epistolario di Pellegrino Zambeccari*, ed. Carlo Frati (Rome, 1929), preface, p. xvii. The col-

trained in *ars notaria* by one of the most famous teachers of rhetoric of the day, Pietro da Muglio. Pietro, who was also called Petrus de Rethorica, had been a friend and admirer of Petrarch, and he was probably responsible for introducing Salutati to the first humanist's writings. Salutati spent all his life as a rhetorician. For a time he worked in the chancery of Lucca. In 1374 he went to Florence; the next year he was elected chancellor of that city, a post he held until his death in 1406. His duties, like those of other *dictatores* of the day, consisted primarily of writing letters, both for the government of the city and for important citizens. His day-to-day concern was with the production of clear and persuasive prose, with practical rhetoric. This accounts for the interest which questions about the nature and purpose of rhetoric held for him. It also helps to explain a slight difference between the questions he asked about rhetoric and those Petrarch had posed. Petrarch, free from the practical concerns which occupied Salutati, had usually examined wisdom and eloquence as moral and intellectual ideals, considering the claims each made on man's life. Salutati was concerned about these questions, but he more often asked himself about the place of wisdom in the production of true eloquence itself.

The second notable difference between the lives and perspectives of the two men had to do with their respective relations to scholastic philosophy. Petrarch had at times been friendly with certain scholastics, but the overwhelming impression one receives from his writings is one of hostility to scholastic culture. Salutati, despite his own clearer association with professional rhetoric, was rather more moderate toward scholasticism than Petrarch had been. The contrast should not be too sharply drawn, since the representative of scholastic learning with whom Salutati had the closest relationship, namely the Augustinian friar

---

lection was titled *Magistri Petri De Vineis, Colucii Fiorentini et Peregrini de Zambecariis epistolae.* It placed Salutati's letters together with those of Pier delle Vigne, chancellor of Frederick II, and Pellegrino Zambeccari, Salutati's contemporary and chancellor of Bologna.

Luigi Marsili, had also been Petrarch's friend. A Florentine, Marsili studied theology at the University of Paris but spent most of his later life in Florence. Petrarch once sent him a copy of St. Augustine's *Confessions* and asked him to take up the fight against the followers of that enemy of true religion, Averroës. Salutati was much closer to Marsili than Petrarch had been. In one of his letters he described the Augustinian friar as an "angelic intellect." In the *Dialogues* inscribed to Pier Paolo Vergerio (*Ad Petrum Histrum*), Leonardo Bruni had Salutati tell of his great admiration for Marsili, and of how the Chancellor would often cross the Arno to visit his friend and hold discussions on a wide variety of questions.[4] Salutati knew and respected many other scholastics as well. In the second half of the fourteenth century the University of Florence (*Studio Fiorentino*) began to operate with some regularity, and Salutati, as a man of respected learning who was a high official of the government, naturally had a good deal to do with university affairs. Since a large proportion of instruction in the *Studio* was in scholastic disciplines, this brought him into contact with the men who taught them. He is known to have written letters full of praise for scholastics whom the Florentines wished to have as teachers.[5] In *Il Paradiso degli Alberti*, Giovanni da Prato pictures Salutati as host to some of the leading scholastic philosophers of the day on their visits to Florence, and indicates that his admiration for these men was shared by other prominent Florentines as well.[6]

[4] On Salutati and Marsili, see Bruni, *Ad Petrum Paulum Histrum Dialogus*, ed. Garin, in *Prosatori Latini*, p. 50. Salutati's own most extensive reference to Marsili is found in a letter of 1393, *Epistolario*, II, 469. On Marsili himself, see Rossi, *Il Quattrocento*, pp. 20-21; F. Del Secolo, *Un teologo dell' ultimo Trecento: Luigi Marsili* (Trani, 1898); C. Casari, *Notizie intorno a L. Marsili* (Lovere, 1900).

[5] C. Vasoli, "Pietro Alboini da Mantova 'scolastico' della fine del Trecento e un' epistola di Coluccio Salutati," *Rinascimento*, 2nd series, III (1963), 3-22; Eugenio Garin, "La cultura fiorentina nella seconda metà del 300 e i 'barbari britanni,'" *Rassegna della Letteratura Italiana*, LXIV (1960), 181-95.

[6] Giovanni da Prato, *Il Paradiso degli Alberti*, ed. A. Wesselofsky,

A number of other indications of Salutati's respect for scholastic learning appear in his writings. He sometimes asked scholastics to explain to him natural phenomena (like the images produced by mirrors) or the meaning of certain logical terms. At one point he expressed his pleasure on hearing of the existence of a philosopher, Peter of Mantua, who had brought recent techniques of English scholasticism to Italy. To be sure, he described Peter as eminent in "that which we today call philosophy," but he clearly respected him, and at other times he declared that his scholastic correspondents deserved "the glorious name of philosopher."[7] Reversing Petrarch's stand, Salutati encouraged a physician to study rhetoric, and he tried to suggest that Petrarch's comments on the physicians had been made in jest.[8] Moreover, Salutati sometimes referred to Aristotle as "the Philosopher," a habit which he certainly took over from the schoolmen.[9] On occasion he adopted scholastic procedures of argument and composition. This last point is especially noteworthy. In one letter to a physician, Salutati thanked his correspondent for having written "in the manner of oratory, not in that of logic"; for aiming, that is, at persuasion rather than demonstrative proof.[10] This was the

---

in *Scelta di curiosità letterarie*, Vols. 86-88 (Bologna, 1867), III, 3-5. The philosophers included Marsilio of Santa Sofia, Blaise of Parma, and Francesco Landino, as well as Luigi Marsili.

[7] See the letter to Iacopo da Uzzano, *Epistolario*, I, 127-29; Salutati asks him to explain the mirror, and comments: "harum enim rerum studia ab ipsius iuventutis recentiorisque etatis temporibus domestica tibi familiariaque fuere, ex quo philosophi nomen, nomen siquidem gloriosum, promeruisti." For the letter to Peter of Mantua, see *Epistolario*, III, 318-22. On Peter of Mantua, see above, note 5, and Kristeller, *Studies in Renaissance Thought and Letters*, p. 577n. On Salutati's desire to have recent scholastic logic explained to him, see *Epistolario*, II, 345.

[8] Salutati, *Magistro Anthonio de Baruffaldis physico faventino tractatus quod medici eloquentie studeant et de verecundia, an sit virtus aut vitium*, ed. Eugenio Garin (Florence, 1947), p. 280.

[9] Salutati, *De nobilitate legum et medicinae*, ed. Eugenio Garin (Florence, 1947), pp. 132, 138, 186. (Page references are to this edition.)

[10] *Epistolario*, IV, 36-37; on this letter, addressed to Francesco Casini, see below, Sec. 4 of this chapter.

procedure Salutati preferred, and the one that he most
often used. But in the treatise *De nobilitate legum et medicinae* (*On the Excellence of Law and Medicine*) he wrote
precisely in the other manner, seeking to demonstrate a
series of propositions, which he even numbered in characteristic scholastic fashion as he established them. None of
this means that Salutati should be regarded as partially a
scholastic. In the *De nobilitate* he confessed his unfamil-
iarity with the subjects of logic and metaphysics, and shied
away from discussing them.[11] But when an occasion seemed
to call for it, he would adopt procedures similar to those
the scholastics used. Salutati's relationship to scholastic
culture shows that humanism and scholasticism were not
always hostile to one another. Despite the well-known instances of conflict between the two, they could sometimes
coexist peacefully.[12]

This harmony was not permanent, however, even for single individuals. Salutati also engaged in polemic with the
professional philosophers of his day. His most extensive debates with them took the form of defending poetry and
of attempting to demonstrate the superiority of legal studies
to medicine. The link the humanists found between poetry
and the art of oratory has already been suggested in our
discussion of Petrarch. For Salutati the tie appears to have
been even closer than it had been for his predecessor. Especially in discussions of the place of poetry in relation to
other arts, Salutati regarded poetry and oratory as equivalent or interchangeable terms. He referred to Cicero's statements of the close kinship between the two, and he freely
applied descriptions of one to the other. In his hands, as in
Petrarch's the defense of poetry was a defense of rhetoric
too.[13]

The same may be said in large part about Salutati's

[11] *De nobilitate,* Chap. XVI.
[12] On this general problem of the relations between humanism and
scholasticism, see Kristeller, "Humanism and Scholasticism in the
Italian Renaissance," and below, Chap. VIII.
[13] On the close kinship of oratory to poetry in Salutati's thinking,
see, for example, *Epistolario,* III, 69-70, 493; IV, 182, 202.

championing of law. Petrarch had regarded a close connection between law and rhetoric, like the one he discovered in ancient Rome, as a necessary condition for the proper development of legal studies. This connection was not wholly absent in the fourteenth century. The greatest center of legal study in medieval Europe, the law faculty of the University of Bologna, had developed out of an earlier school of rhetoric. The teachers of law in the time of Irnerius had made legal study independent of rhetoric, but some ties between the two remained. Since notaries were responsible for drawing up contracts, and often for keeping records which would be suitable for use in law courts, they had to have some knowledge of law. Jurists inserted counsels for notaries in their works, and teachers of *ars notaria* sometimes taught law as well. *Giudici* and *notai* usually belonged to the same guild.[14] Salutati himself seems to have hesitated between the two careers of *notaria* and law, choosing the first because the course was shorter and therefore less expensive. Several of his good friends were lawyers. Some of the most prominent early enthusiasts for ancient literature had been lawyers, as Salutati was himself aware.[15] He also noted that jurists had taken over some tasks which had once belonged to orators, including representing clients in court. Thus he thought it legitimate to defend the dignity of law with arguments drawn from the tradition of rhetoric. "Is it not true that both Cicero and Quintilian hold and teach that the perfection of the orator—whose task it is to defend in law courts, which lawyers do today—requires knowledge of and familiarity with all sciences and subjects?"[16] At the beginning of his *De nobilitate*, Salutati asked why it was that the physicians failed to persuade other men of the things their arguments tried to demonstrate. "Is

[14] On these matters, see Novati, *La Giovinezza di Coluccio Salutati*; also H. Wieruszowski, "Arezzo as a Center of Learning and Letters in the Thirteenth Century," *Traditio*, IX (1953), 321-91, where the connections between rhetoric and poetry are also discussed.

[15] Roberto Weiss, *The Dawn of Humanism in Italy* (Inaugural Lecture, University College, London, 1947); and *idem, Il Primo Secolo dell' Umanesimo* (Rome, 1949).

[16] *De nobilitate*, p. 224. Cf. *Epistolario*, I, 79-80.

69

it because persuasion is a greater thing than demonstrative proof? Should it be admitted that logic is a lesser science than rhetoric? I don't believe you think so."[17] Yet this was one of the things that Salutati's defense of legal studies implied.

The study of law as Salutati described it was more than an art of speech. It included the whole realm of politics, and sometimes seemed to include ethics as well. But it should be remembered that Cicero had declared this part of philosophy to be the province of the orator.[18] Salutati does not seem to have repeated this statement exactly, but he did emphasize the importance of human speech and of the power of eloquence in maintaining social life and effecting moral reform.[19] The praise of law did not lead Salutati any further from the pursuit of eloquence than the defense of poetry did. One way to describe the perfect orator of Cicero's *De oratore* is to say that he was partly a prose poet and partly a lawyer. This description fits Coluccio Salutati very well.

(2)

HOWEVER, such a description of Salutati, as of Cicero, is incomplete. The main element that it neglects is the interest in moral philosophy displayed by both men. Before going on to examine Salutati's discussions of the relationship between oratory and philosophy, it will be useful to look first at his treatment of moral philosophy itself. In its main lines it closely resembled that of Petrarch, save that Salutati's use of philosophical opinions and maxims was even more marked by contradictions than Petrarch's had been. Like Petrarch, Salutati sometimes followed the Stoics. He often remarked on the folly of putting one's trust in such deceptive things as riches, health, and fame. He noted the changeability of all earthly things. He saw in Virgil's *Aeneid* an allegory of man seeking a quiet resting place for

---

[17] *De nobilitate*, p. 4.
[18] *Ibid.*, pp. 36, 168-70. Cf. Cicero, *De oratore* I, xv, 68.
[19] See his eulogy of Petrarch (*Epistolario*, I, 179-80), discussed below.

his mind, symbolized by the home Aeneas found in Latium. Coluccio wrote of the quiet of the cloister in his treatise *De seculo et religione*, applying Stoic maxims to the life of Christian withdrawal from the world.[20] Yet against all this one must place Salutati's many exhortations to the life of action, his declaration that the greatest of the Christian virtues was active charity, his often-cited argument upholding the superiority of the will over the intellect, and his assertion that God would not have created man as a social and political animal if He had not wished him to find blessedness through a life together with his fellows. In this mood Salutati was as likely to use Peripatetic maxims as Stoic ones.[21]

How easily he could turn from one doctrine to the other is shown by three letters that he wrote between August of 1400 and February of 1401. The first and third are both to a jurist, Francesco Zabarella. Zabarella had written to console Salutati after two of his sons had been carried off by the plague.[22] Grateful and impressed, Salutati praised his friend in return as the most eloquent lawyer of the age, and lauded eloquence itself as "that power which adorns, hon-

[20] E.g., *Epistolario*, I, 207-08; on the changeability of all earthly things, *ibid.*, I, 265; on the allegory of the *Aeneid*, *ibid.*, I, 208; the *De seculo et religione* has been edited by B. L. Ullman (Florence, 1957). See also Alfred von Martin, *Mittelalterliche Welt- und Lebensanschauung im Spiegel der Schriften Coluccio Salutatis* (Munich and Berlin, 1913).

[21] See *Epistolario*, II, 303-07; Eugenio Garin, *L'Umanesimo Italiano* (Bari, 1958), pp. 31ff., or in the Eng. trans. (Oxford and New York, 1965), pp. 27ff. Also: L. Borghi, "La dottrina morale di Coluccio Salutati," *Annali della R. Scuola Normale Superiore di Pisa*, III (1934), 75ff. and 469ff.; A. von Martin, *Coluccio Salutati und das Humanistische Lebensideal* (Leipzig, 1916). The argument for the superiority of the will over the intellect is in the *De nobilitate*, Chap. XXIII. But see below for evidence that Salutati could contradict this position also. The view that Salutati's contradictions derive from his being a transitional figure between the Middle Ages and the Renaissance has recently been restated by Ullman, *The Humanism of Coluccio Salutati*, Chap. III. This view is inadequate, however, since it does not take account of the Ciceronian basis of Salutati's use of moral philosophy.

[22] Zabarella's letters are printed in *Epistolario*, IV, 347-49, 350-61; for Salutati's letters, see *ibid.*, III, 408-22, 456-79.

71

ors, and exalts all the other sciences, both speculative and practical; to whose perfection a knowledge even of all the highest things, both human and divine, is necessary; in whose praise it is rash to speak after Cicero."[23] But Zabarella's eloquence had not really caused Salutati to accept the Stoical arguments against mourning which the jurist had employed. To say that death was not an evil, that it was common to all men, and that mourning was of no use seemed to Salutati neither true nor consoling. The first argument was over-scrupulous and sophistical. Even if death was not an evil in the moral sense of an act contrary to the good, it was nonetheless evil according to man's nature, just as blindness from birth was. Both human and divine law regard death as evil, Salutati asserted: why else impose punishments for murder? "There can be no greater evil for man," he concluded, "than that which deprives him of his being." Though the soul and the elements of the body remained after death, man himself, who is a combination of body and soul, ceased to be.[24] As for the argument that death is common to all men, to make this a consolatory maxim was simply to vaunt the misfortunes of others. And if mourning did no good, neither was it of any use to say so. Such an assertion was exasperating, not comforting. None of these rigidly philosophical maxims could console men. The only consolation was in God, and in the acceptance of His decrees.[25]

Salutati wrote these things on August 30, 1400. Zabarella replied with a defense of the Stoic position, and in February 1401 Salutati took up the subject again. He repeated his previous arguments and added some new ones.[26] He cited Cicero in the orator's treatise *On Friendship* as an opponent of the Stoic notion of a "hard and almost iron virtue."

[23] *Ibid.*, III, 411.
[24] *Ibid.*, III, 418: "maius enim homini malum esse non potest, quam quod hominem redigit ad non esse." This was not a radical or anti-Christian statement for a man of Salutati's time. For similar notions in late medieval thought, see Lucien Febvre, *Le Problème de l'incroyance au 16ᵉ siècle: la religion de Rabelais* (Paris, 1942), p. 209.
[25] *Epistolario*, III, 418-20.   [26] *Ibid.*, III, 462ff.

He doubted that meditation on death could ever be of use to man. Not even Cicero had been able to "drive all the power of human feeling" from his mind thereby. Christ's meditation on His own death had caused Him to sweat blood.[27] Those ancient pagans who had despised death had done so not from philosophical conviction, but from a desire for glory.[28]

These two letters might make Salutati seem constant in his opposition to the rigidly philosophical attitude represented by the Stoics, were it not that he took precisely the opposite position in a letter he wrote on September 9, 1400—that is, between the two letters to Zabarella.[29] Here he tried to console the notary Pietro di ser Mino for a recent loss. In total contradiction to what he had written ten days earlier, and would repeat five months later, Salutati now said that to mourn for the dead was worse than foolish. "Death is not an evil, except to men who are evil and base."[30] Pagans were not the only ones to say so. Christianity taught that "the souls of the righteous are in the hand of God." Death is not destruction for man, but salvation; it is the best of things, not the worst.[31] Salutati could embrace or reject philosophical doctrines as the occasion demanded.

One other instance of Salutati's philosophical inconsistency should be noted here. He is well known for his argument in the *De nobilitate legum et medicinae* that the will was superior to the intellect. Since the object of the will was the good, while that of the intellect was the true, the will was superior to the intellect just as the good surpassed the true, and as virtue was a greater thing than knowledge.[32] On this basis, Salutati also argued for the superiority of the active life to the contemplative, and his

---

[27] *Ibid.*, III, 470.   [28] *Ibid.*, III, 472.   [29] *Ibid.*, III, 422-33.

[30] *Ibid.*, III, 426: "mala quidem non est mors, nisi sceleratis et malis."

[31] *Ibid.*, III, 430: "licet enim mortem timendam non esse probavero, quoniam malum non sit, sed exoptandam potius, quoniam bonum bonumque, sicut multi philosophorum voluerunt, dici debeat, quin imo cum mors optima rerum, ut inquit poeta noster, potius sit dicenda quam mala, nescio si tibi metum mortis excussero."

[32] *De nobilitate*, Chap. XXIII.

73

attitude has often been cited as typical of the humanists. Yet he did not always hold to this position. The *De nobilitate* was completed in 1399. In a letter probably written in 1401, Salutati said flatly that "the mind is the highest part of man."[33] Several years before the *De nobilitate*, he had described the intellect in similar terms as "the real and greatest difference between man and the other animals," the means through which one man surpasses another, and the basis of man's kinship with the angels.[34] Later, in 1405, he described men of wisdom as those who "do not follow the will, but who subject the will to the reason."[35] Thus it is hard to believe that Salutati was genuinely committed to his famous argument for the superiority of the will. He made his stand as convincing as he could, but he abandoned it when the occasion required, just as he did other philosophical positions. Like Petrarch's contradictions, Salutati's inconsistencies were not the result of a development from one set of attitudes to another, but of a willingness to affirm conflicting points of view as the need arose.[36]

Salutati was aware of the philosophic importance of consistency. In November of 1400 he wrote: "I do not think that anything can be said which would be both true and false at the same time of the same thing and in the same respect; so much do things which are contrary and opposite repel each other."[37] At the same time, however, Salutati recognized the force of the Academic skeptic's point of view. "Every truth which is grasped by reason can be made doubtful by a contrary reason," he asserted in *De nobilitate*. "The more you know," he added some years later, "the more true you will know it to be that you know nothing at all. For to speak properly, what to us is knowledge is really only a kind of reasonable uncertainty." St. Augustine had

[33] *Epistolario*, III, 488: "cumque mens optima pars hominis sit eiusque vigor hominem super hominem evehat."
[34] *Ibid.*, II, 204.   [35] *Ibid.*, IV, 117-18.
[36] For a striking demonstration of the same phenomenon in Salutati's official correspondence, see Herde, "Politik und Rhetorik in Florenz . . ." (cited in note 1, above).
[37] *Epistolario*, III, 439.

contended against this Academic view, but to hold to it still seemed a good idea to Salutati. It was the first step in the study of wisdom.[38]

Skepticism was not only a useful philosophic position. Salutati explicitly described the recognition of ignorance as necessary not only to learning in philosophy but also to the pursuit of eloquence.[39] Like Cicero, he recognized that the Academic position was appropriate to the orator, who would support different points of view in different situations. He also shared Cicero's belief that the moral perspective of the orator should not differ too sharply from that of his audience. He quoted Cicero's dictum that "in oratory the very cardinal sin is to depart from the language of everyday life and the usage approved by the sense of the community," and he added that the man of eloquence will say and write nothing which is "not in keeping with custom, and nothing which does not have a wholly virtuous ring."[40] Salutati appears not to have concluded explicitly from this that the most appropriate doctrine for the orator was Peripateticism. But he contrasted Stoic and Peripatetic morality, calling the first "hard and nowhere to be found," the second humane and "filed down to the mean." In another place he remarked that "the latter spoke in accord with the ordinary condition and course of mortal life, the former, however, came closer to the truth of the matter."[41]

Salutati's discussions of moral philosophy thus followed the main lines of those of Cicero and Petrarch. Like them

[38] De nobilitate, pp. 136-38; Epistolario, III, 603, and also II, 319.
[39] Epistolario, III, 602: ". . . primo sapientie, moxque dicendi viam ostendam. premittam tamen unum, quod ambobus commune est quodque verissimum esse cum in me tum in aliis sum expertus. velim igitur tibi persuadeas, quicquid didiceris quantumcunqueve tibi videaris in eloquentia profecisse, te penitus nichil scire, quod quanto plus sciveris, tanto verius esse cognosces."
[40] Ibid., III, 606-07.
[41] Ibid., II, 292: "rigida stoicorum et nunquam reperienda profectio . . . humanitas et ad mediocritatem peripateticorum limata traditio." Ibid., II, 311: "unde dicere possumus secundum communem mortalium condicionem et cursum hos [scil. Peripateticos] locutos; illos [Stoicos] autem ad rei veritatem propius accessisse."

he moved freely from rigidly philosophical, Stoic opinions to milder, Peripatetic ones, and he recognized this procedure as characteristic of both the Academic and the orator. Like Cicero and Petrarch, too, he saw that Peripatetic teaching was closer to the needs of everyday life and hence to the world of the orator, while Stoic doctrine approached nearer to the truth of philosophers. Employing these various elements, he sought to join together wisdom and eloquence.

(3)

THE QUESTION of the relationship between these two ideals often concerned Salutati. The occasion for his first extensive discussion of this problem was the death of Petrarch in 1374.[42] In praising the poet for his many literary accomplishments, he listed each of the arts in turn, telling what its purpose was and how Petrarch had excelled in it. He described philosophy as "in Cicero's words, the governess of the virtues, scourge of the vices, and queen and mistress of all the arts and sciences." The philosophy in which Petrarch had been eminent was not the windy wordiness of the modern sophists, but "that which ennobles men's souls, establishes the virtues, washes away the filth of the vices, and leaving behind the obscurities of disputation, brings to light the truth about all things." Salutati followed this description of philosophy with a praise of theology, "priestess of all knowledge," in which Petrarch had also excelled. Salutati's accounts of these disciplines easily lead one to believe that he thought them to be the most important ones. Yet this conclusion would be false, for his celebration of Petrarch reached its climax in the following statement:

> But let us leave these things aside, and consider his eloquence, through which he showed how much he excelled in the other humanistic studies, and whose praise I have reserved for last because in my judgment it is the greatest. For what could be more important than to control the motions of the mind, to turn your hearer where

42 See the letter in *Epistolario*, I, 176-87.

you will, and to lead him back to the place from which you moved him, pleasantly and with love. These, unless I am mistaken, are the powers of eloquence; this is its work. All the force and power of rhetoricians strains to attain it. To be sure, it is a great thing to adorn writing with words and maxims, but the greatest and most difficult—however embellished and dignified be the language —is to move the minds of the listeners. Only eloquence accomplishes all these things.[43]

Only by means of eloquence, Salutati went on to say, could one man aid another by applying the force of his reason against his fellow's passions. It was through the power of speech—unique to man—that men were able to realize their God-given capacity for helping one another. Thus it was eloquence which was to be thanked for the benefits of human society.[44]

Salutati's statements contain a number of features already familiar to us. First, although he described philosophy in terms which would seem to make it clearly superior to rhetoric ("queen and mistress of all the arts and sciences"), he rejected the implications of his own description and called rhetoric after all the greatest of the arts. Second, he regarded the most important characteristic of eloquence to be not formal perfection in an aesthetic sense, but the power to persuade and move a listener.[45] Both these things mark him as a follower of Cicero and Petrarch.

[43] *Ibid.*, I, 179: "sed omittamus ista, et eloquentiam, si placet, ipsius contemplemur, qua quantum in ceteris humanitatis prevaluerit studiis manifeste monstravit, cuiusque laudes in ultimis reservavi, quia iudicio meo maxima quidem est. quid enim maius quam animorum motibus dominari, quo volueris audientem inflectere, et unde flexeris cum gratia et amore reducere? he, ni fallor, eloquentie vires sunt; hic labor, huc omnis rhetorum vis potentiaque desudat. magnum est equidem tum verbis tum sententiis exornare dictamen; maximum autem, imo et difficillimum est, quanvis ornata quanvisque gravi oratione, auditorum animos incurvare. hec omnia una perficit eloquentia."

[44] *Ibid.*, I, 179-80.

[45] This was recognized by R. P. Oliver, "Salutati's Criticism of Petrarch," *Italica*, XVI (1939), 52. Oliver provides a skeleton account

Especially in his early letters do we find Salutati's enthusiasm for eloquence unbounded. "I have always been an admirer of virtue, and of that which is an adornment of virtue, eloquence," he wrote in 1369.[46] Sometimes he seems to have wanted to praise eloquence more unrestrainedly than caution allowed. "Let others esteem riches, honors, power, the rewards of the virtues, offices," he once exclaimed. "As for me I shall always admire virtue, and among the others which nature with the aid of art excellently forms in man, let the celebration of eloquence have first place." Eloquence was connected with intelligence and reason, Salutati indicated, but it was the power of speech itself which gave man his excellence and which allowed some men to excel others.[47]

In these passages eloquence at times appears to be worthy of the highest praise by itself, regardless of its relationship to wisdom. Yet this was not Salutati's only attitude toward this problem. In a letter of 1393 he quoted from *De inventione* Cicero's statement that eloquence without wisdom was often of great harm to men, and never of any benefit.[48] At roughly the same time he declared himself unworthy of the title of perfect orator because he lacked the knowledge which true eloquence required. Referring to Cicero's *De oratore*, he insisted that "It is from knowledge that oratory must derive its beauty and fullness, and unless there is such knowledge, well-grasped and comprehended by the speaker, there must be something empty and almost childish in the utterance."[49] Poetry, too, required such knowledge. Writing to a young friend about his first efforts at verse writing, Salutati advised him to seek knowledge as well as literary art, "so that the things you write will be not only

---

of Salutati's changing attitudes toward Petrarch, but he does not discuss these attitudes in the terms employed here.

[46] *Epistolario*, I, 76-77. [47] *Ibid.*, I, 79.

[48] *Ibid.*, II, 479.

[49] *Ibid.*, III, 84-85: "ex rerum cognitione florescat et redundet oportet oratio, que nisi sit ab oratore percepta et cognita, inanem quandam habet elocutionem et pene puerilem." Cf. *De oratore* I, vi, 21; Loeb edn., I, p. 21.

sweet-sounding, but weighty as well, not only handsome, but earnest, such that they edify as much as they delight. For mere melodious trifles pass through the ears, and like musical instruments, when they cease to resound leave nothing remaining. Therefore let the things you write produce something in your readers which not only charms them, but does them good."[50] In another letter he cited Horace's opinion that "Knowledge is the beginning and source of writing well, as the Socratic writings demonstrate." From this it followed that: "It is true of rhetoric as well as of poetry that they proceed along the right track when they do not lack the teachings of philosophy, that is, wisdom. Just as a poem should be censured which does not give forth the precepts of philosophy, and 'an ignorant verse and melodic trifles,' so should one be praised which has been composed according to the doctrine of philosophy."[51] Thus, while eloquence alone sometimes seemed admirable in Salutati's eyes, at other times it required the presence of wisdom. Clearly the two had to be joined. "One thing has always carried me away beyond measure," he wrote in 1401: "fullness of knowledge together with elegance and power in speaking."[52]

We have already discovered, however, that the meaning of the ideal of a union of rhetoric and philosophy was by no means constant. To call for such a combination did not make clear what the relation between the two arts would be within it. How great should the dependence of eloquence on wisdom be? Some philosophers, such as Plato, had sought to make it absolute. Few professional rhetoricians accepted such a view, but Salutati took the Platonic attitude more seriously than most. "In what way," he asked in a letter, "can we rightly say what we do not

[50] *Epistolario*, III, 69.
[51] *Ibid.*, III, 484: "comune quidem est tam rethorice quam poesi, ut tunc tantum recto calle procedant, cum philosophie, hoc est sapientie, instituta non deserunt; ut sicut vituperandum est poema, quod philosophie precepta non redolet, et 'versus inopes rerum nugeque canore,' sic laudandum quod iuxta philosophie rationem carmen compositum est." (The quotation is from Horace, *Ars Poetica*, 322.)
[52] *Epistolario*, III, 506.

know? As Cicero said, the thing Socrates used to say—that everyone is eloquent enough in those matters which they know—is quite credible, even if not true. It is more true that no one could be eloquent in matters which he does not understand."[53] To endorse the Platonic attitude that eloquence was dependent on wisdom, even with reservations, raised problems for a man like Salutati, who was primarily a master of the art of rhetoric. If the chief component of eloquence was wisdom, then should we not expect to find more men of eloquence among philosophers than among those whose chief concern was oratory? A humanist who accepted this line of reasoning weakened many of the humanists' best arguments against their rivals the scholastic philosophers. Few of the humanists were willing to rob their own arsenal, but, as we have seen, Salutati's relations with scholastics were not always hostile. Thus he did not always refuse to grant them the rewards of their dedication to philosophic knowledge. Replying in 1404 to a letter from Francesco Casini, a well-known Sienese physician, Salutati thanked his correspondent for having written "in the manner of oratory, not in that of logic"—seeking to persuade rather than to prove logically—and he praised him for having argued "so subtly and copiously that nothing relevant is lacking or could be desired even by experts."

And indeed Socrates said truly, or to speak more properly, credibly, that everyone is eloquent enough in those matters they know, as did Ovid when he wrote "Everyone is eloquent in his own cause." You know the matter, and the cause is yours. And because of this, even though, as I suppose, you have never concerned yourself with the art of rhetoric, you spoke most artfully. I can bear witness

[53] *Ibid.*, III, 494: "nunc autem quomodo possumus recte dicere que nescimus? probabilius autem, neque tamen verum, ut Tullius inquit, quod Socrates dicere solebat, omnes in eo quod scirent satis esse eloquentes; illud verius neque quenquam in eo disertum esse posse quod nesciat." Cf. *De oratore* I, xiv, 63.

that you persuade rhetorically as forcefully as you dispute dialectically.[54]

Scholastics could be eloquent too. To speak as Salutati did here was to make the dependence of eloquence on wisdom so great that it raised basic questions about the value of the independent pursuit of eloquence.

To be sure, the humanists usually claimed that their desire was not to give eloquence free rein, but to keep it closely tied to philosophy. Yet an attitude like Salutati's, which found eloquence in the writings of the schoolmen, might also question the validity of the philosophy which the humanists claimed to possess. Indeed, Salutati did sometimes find his colleagues too careless about the content of their rhetoric. In September of 1400 he cautioned the notary Pietro di ser Mino against praising any man by calling him a "divine spirit" (Pietro had used the phrase about Coluccio himself), and warned against the bad example set by Pietro's teacher, Giovanni Malpaghini of Ravenna.

Don't follow too closely that excessive and tendrilous style of your teacher, which he counts as flowery. According to him all things are divine, superb, and in brief such, that when you come to examine the truth of the matter, none of the things he says stands up. Swim through the sea of eloquence in such a way that you don't desert truth. For the ocean of eloquence becomes infinite and impassable if you lose sight of truth. True things are

[54] *Epistolario*, IV, 37: "sed vere Socrates inquit vel, ut rectius loquar, probabiliter, omnes in eo quod scirent satis esse eloquentes; et Naso noster: 'Proque sua causa quisque disertus erat.' scis materiam tuaque causa est; et ob id, licet artem nunquam, ut reor, attigeris, artificiosissime locutus es. ego vero tibi possum attestari te non minore vehementia persuadere rethorice, quam dialectice disputare." Salutati went on to praise Casini's commentary on Aristotle's *Ethics*, saying that he preferred it to those of Albertus Magnus, Giraldus Odonis, Walter Burley, Buridan, Thomas Aquinas, and Aegidius Romanus. After instructing the physician on the proper spelling of *logica*, Salutati concluded: "physicus es, imo philosophus" (IV, 40). He seems to have regarded Casini as a genuine philosopher.

firm, clearly bounded, such that he who follows them is always on solid ground.[55]

Thus Salutati regarded the necessity of truthfulness more seriously than he thought some other humanists did. He cautioned lest the seekers of high-sounding words close their ears to simple truths.

Salutati often insisted that man's life required wisdom. The theme appears more often in his later writings than in his earlier ones, for a reason that he himself explained. Following a widespread classical and medieval commonplace, he pointed out that a man's concerns should not be the same in old age as they had been in youth. The different ages of man required different kinds of conduct.[56] The desire to gain glory through literary effort might be unavoidable in one's youth, but in old age men should have other concerns. "After we have attained that age at which we must gather up our burdens, and sigh for Him who is at once the creator and goal of all things, let us put aside that nonsense and these trifles."[57] As old age approached, Salutati wrote, one must leave behind the pleasures of youth, and give oneself faithfully to learning. Salutati now regarded man's characteristic excellence to be not speech,

[55] *Ibid.*, III, 424: "noli magistri tui stilum illum redundantem et pampineum, quem floridum reputat, nimis sequi. omnia sunt apud ipsum divina, superlativa et denique talia, quod, cum at veritatis examen veneris, nichil eorum, que dixerit, sibi constet. tu sic enata per eloquentie pelagus, quod veritatem non deseras. infinitum et intranabile mare fit eloquentie si dimiseris veritatem. vera quidem fixa sunt, determinata sunt, que qui sequitur in solido semper est." (On the identification of Giovanni Malpaghini as Pietro di ser Mino's teacher, see *ibid.*, III, 424n., and Salutati's letters to Malpaghini, discussed below. For a similar caution against the use of language for rhetorical effect, see *ibid.*, II, 170.

[56] For a general discussion of the use of this theme in medieval literature, see Philippe Ariès, *Centuries of Childhood*, trans. Robert Baldick (New York, 1962), Part One, Chap. I. For a classical example, see Cicero, *De senectute*. The theme appears often in Petrarch. See, for example, *Fam.*, VIII, 3.

[57] *Epistolario*, II, 426; cf. also II, 226. For a possible parallel to this in Salutati's political attitudes, see Baron, *Crisis*, I, 94. But see also the criticism of Baron's views in Ullman, *The Humanism of Coluccio Salutati*, pp. 47-48.

as he had held elsewhere, but reason. It was man's intellect which raised him above the other animals, and which allowed some men to surpass others.[58] In the terms of the quotation from Petrarch with which we began this study, he spoke now not as an orator, but as a philosopher.

It was not simply wisdom to which Salutati now turned, but a specifically Christian wisdom. Truth, as he more than once affirmed, was Christian truth. "As Christ is truth, to be Christian is the same thing as to be truthful."[59] God was the source of that wisdom on which true eloquence depended. Replying to the praise of his own learning addressed to him by contemporaries, Salutati several times repeated that man was a weak creature, wholly dependent on God for any worthwhile accomplishment. "Therefore, whatever I spoke about well, comes from God and His wisdom; if I spoke poorly in some respect, however, that I spoke by myself."[60] When Salutati questioned the independent value of eloquence and insisted on its dependence on wisdom, he breathed a spirit which he thought appropriate to a Christian old age.

None of the statements of rhetoric's limitations which we have noted so far, however, should be interpreted as indications that Salutati was ready to desert the *studia humanitatis et eloquentiae*. In his view, such affirmations of the dependence of eloquence on wisdom could still be reconciled with a program of learning which gave first place to rhetoric. But it was a tortuous reconciliation, as the extraordinary passage which follows, probably written in 1402, makes clear:

The best thing is for wisdom and eloquence to join together, so that the second expounds what the first comprehends. In a contest over which was to be preferred, give the palm to wisdom. Never think it is useless, how-

---

[58] *Epistolario*, II, 204.
[59] *Ibid.*, II, 164. Cf. also II, 424.
[60] *Ibid.*, I, 300. This letter was written in 1378. Salutati used the same reply more often as he grew older. Cf. *ibid.*, II, 111ff.; II, 474-79; III, 455-56.

ever, to give individual, especial and continued attention to eloquence. For the pursuit of eloquence is itself a duty of wisdom. Eloquence is placed under wisdom, and contained in it as in the sum of all things which can be known, so that whoever pursues wisdom necessarily pursues eloquence at the same time. Accordingly as the two can be separated by the intellect, however, eloquence is more rare than wisdom. Thus we can suitably conclude that it is more difficult than wisdom, since rarity is a most certain evidence of difficulty in those attainments which are the products of study and industry, and which we obtain through effort. Let it be added that the intention, zeal, and opportunity for speaking well spurs us on in the desire to know; so that the pursuit of eloquence is a means to the end of seeking wisdom. For nothing can be well said which is not most perfectly known. We can know many things, however, which we do not know how to say clearly and with the required ornament or grandeur of speech. Therefore eloquence, with its connection to the pursuit of wisdom, ought especially to be studied.[61]

That is, while eloquence was a smaller good than wisdom, and dependent on it, the separate pursuit of eloquence

[61] *Ibid.*, III, 602: "optime quidem simul coalescunt sapientia et eloquentia, ut quantum illa capit tantum et ista pertractet. quod si certamen utriusque fiat, que cui preoptanda sit, sapientie palmam dato. non tamen inutile puta semper eloquentie singularem, precipuam et continuam operam dare. non enim eloquentie studium non etiam sapientie munus est. subicitur eloquentia sapientie et in ipsa, quasi toto quodam, quod cuncta scibilia possideat, continetur, ut qui sapientie studium profitetur, simul et eloquentie profiteatur necesse sit. quia tamen ea ratione, qua duo hec per intellectum ab invicem separantur, eloquentia rarior sapientia est, difficiliorem eam esse sapientia non inconvenienter possumus arbitrari, quoniam quidem in his habitibus, qui studio industriaque parantur quosque laboribus adipiscimur, raritas argumentum est certissimum difficultatis. accedit ad hec, quod intentio, studium facultasque bene dicendi calcar est ut sapere concupiscamus; ut huius eloquentie studium capessende sapientie sit etiam instrumentum. neque etiam aliquid bene dicitur quod perfectissime non sciatur. possumus multa scire, que tamen eloqui distincte debitoque cum ornatu sermonisve maiestate nescimus; ut maxime studendum sit eloquentie, cui et sapientie studium annexum est."

should still be recommended because (or perhaps provided that) it led in the end to wisdom itself. But if it was
true that "whoever pursues wisdom necessarily pursues
eloquence at the same time," then why not recommend
the single-minded pursuit of wisdom itself? Why was eloquence, rather than wisdom, "especially" (*maxime*) to be
studied? Salutati remained committed to eloquence for
reasons quite apart from the ones he could advance in this
sort of justification of it. His devotion to rhetoric could not
be diminished by any kind of abstract analysis of the superiority of philosophy. His assertion of the superiority of
philosophy still left rhetoric as "the finest [*pulcerrima*] of
the sciences."[62] He recognized that other rhetoricians,
notably St. Jerome, had sometimes used their rhetorical
skills to criticize rhetoric.[63] It was from within the camp
of oratory that Salutati cautioned against the excesses of
eloquence. When Giovanni Malpaghini defended himself against the attack Salutati had made on his style
and terminology, Salutati simply backed down. He wrote
a long letter of praise to Malpaghini, carefully lauding
his knowledge as well as his eloquence. Malpaghini
accepted the apology, and Salutati wrote again, more briefly.
"One thing I want you to know most certainly," he assured
his friend, "and that is that I have always sung the praises
of your knowledge and eloquence, in which, among other
things, you marvellously excel." He said that while he found
Giovanni's statement that Coluccio's erudition would win
eternal glory for him to be in error and carelessly made, he
would try to make the best of it by attempting to be worthy
of his friend's esteem.[64] Even at this point, in 1404, Salutati was no more willing than Cicero or Petrarch had been
to accept the full implications of the admitted superiority
of philosophy to rhetoric.

[62] *Ibid.*, II, 295.   [63] *Ibid.*, I, 305.
[64] *Ibid.*, III, 517: "unum tamen certissime scias velim, me semper
tuam scientiam et eloquentiam, quibus ceteris mirabiliter emines, celebrasse" (from Salutati's second letter to Malpaghini; for the first, see
III, 501-11).

In 1404 Coluccio Salutati was over seventy years old. He seems to have worked regularly at his job in the Florentine chancery until his death in 1406. During the last two years of his life he engaged in a debate with his young friend, Poggio Bracciolini, in the course of which Salutati went much further than he had before in affirming the dependence of eloquence on wisdom. The subject of the debate was the achievement of Petrarch in comparison with that of the ancients, and it has come to be known as the "Petrarch Controversy." Before we examine this discussion, we must sketch in the history of Salutati's judgment of Petrarch.[65]

We have already noted the high regard in which Salutati held Petrarch. In his eulogy of 1374 he praised the poet for his achievement in philosophy and for his eloquence. The second was the greater accomplishment, Salutati said; moreover, it was here that Petrarch showed his superiority to the ancients. For whereas Cicero, the greatest of orators, grew weak when he turned to verse writing ("the other type of eloquence"), and Virgil, the best of ancient poets, was a poor orator, Petrarch had excelled in both. He was "the one man . . . in whom eloquence demonstrated all its powers."[66]

This picture of Petrarch as having excelled both in poetry and in prose always remained a part of Salutati's view of him. Even after he had seen and been disappointed by Petrarch's much-vaunted Latin epic *Africa* (which dealt with the story of Scipio Africanus), Salutati still argued that Petrarch's versatility made him greater than any of the ancients. In a letter of 1379 he admitted that Virgil was a better poet than Petrarch (only the humanist's Latin verse was thought relevant in the comparison), but he asserted that poetry was a lesser accomplishment than prose eloquence. Prose excelled poetry, just as the sea was greater

---

[65] For an outline of Salutati's attitudes; see Oliver, "Salutati's Criticism of Petrarch."

[66] *Epistolario*, I, 183. Cf. above, pp. 76-77.

than any of the rivers which flowed into it. Petrarch had provided maxims for prose composition which surpassed even Cicero's. If he had not shone in the practical eloquence for which Cicero was so famous, the reason was that law cases were no longer handled by orators, as they once had been, but by jurists. Without explicitly comparing Petrarch as an orator to Cicero, Salutati said that all agreed he was a better poet. Since, then, he surpassed Cicero in poetry, and Virgil in prose, what reason was there for preferring any of the ancients to him?[67] This was not as confident a conclusion as Salutati had reached in 1374, but it still maintained Petrarch's preeminence.

Perhaps from a reluctance to retreat any further, however, Salutati seems not to have spoken of the matter of Petrarch's achievement again for many years. When he next touched on the question, in 1395, he no longer asserted Petrarch's superiority. Instead he described literary studies as having reached a height in the time of Cicero which had not been sustained thereafter. "Believe me," he wrote, "antiquity surpasses us in wisdom and in eloquence." Petrarch and Boccaccio were fine writers, but they had not been in the same class with the ancients.[68] It is hard to say whether Salutati had really changed his mind. The context of this declaration of the superiority of the ancients was a reply to a friend who had placed Salutati himself above Cassiodorus. Salutati often went to great lengths to refute such claims on his own behalf, and it is possible that he exaggerated his esteem for the ancients here in order to emphasize his own inferiority to them. By establishing the superiority of antiquity to Petrarch and Boccaccio, it was

[67] *Ibid.*, I, 337-42.
[68] *Ibid.*, III, 79-80: "tenet gradum suum insuperata vetustas et in campo remanet signis immobilibus atque fixis. et quicquid sibi de subtilitate sophistica blandiatur modernitas, sapientia nos, crede michi, et eloquentia vincit; nec in aliquo videmus nostri temporis tantarum totque rerum esse noticiam, quot et quantarum fuisse decrevimus in antiquis." It has been incorrectly asserted that in this letter Salutati referred only to the "rise and fall of classical Latin and rhetoric (the 'facultas dicendi')": Baron, *Crisis*, I, 230. The terms were "wisdom and eloquence," just as they were to be in 1405-06.

easy to argue his own inferiority to Cassiodorus. Salutati pointed out that true eloquence required knowledge of all things; without it, one's utterance was childish and empty. He could not claim such knowledge for himself, but he thought the ancients had possessed it.[69]

Such a sentiment may seem ordinary enough for a humanist of the Renaissance, given the enthusiasm of all humanists for the revival of antiquity. Yet it was a difficult position to maintain for a man like Salutati, who often insisted that true wisdom was to be found in Christianity, and who attributed whatever eloquence he himself possessed to "God and His wisdom." When he next returned to the question of Petrarch's accomplishments, in 1405, he was to view the matter of the wisdom of the ancients quite differently from the way he had looked at it ten years earlier.

The so-called Petrarch Controversy should be seen against two different backgrounds. First, the question of Petrarch's achievement and worth was a lively topic of discussion in the years around 1400. The most famous example of a debate about him is the one pictured by Leonardo Bruni in his *Dialogues* inscribed to Pier Paolo Vergerio ("ad Petrum Histrum"). There Niccolò Niccoli bitterly attacked Petrarch, together with Dante and Boccaccio, in the first book, insisting that all three of the great Trecento poets had remained mired in the darkness of their age. In the second book, however, he retracted this, and praised each of the poets in turn. Bruni's *Dialogues* are a rhetorical exercise in more than one sense, and it may be doubted that anyone with close ties to Salutati's circle in Florence (such as Niccoli) ever really regarded Petrarch with such disdain as Niccoli heaped on the poet's head in Book I.[70] Yet it is clear that the question of Petrarch's reputation was debated at the time. Salutati was once asked to reply to the poet's detractors, probably in 1402.[71]

[69] *Epistolario*, III, 84-85.
[70] See my discussion of Bruni's *Dialogi*, in *Past and Present*, No. 34 (1966), pp. 10ff.
[71] *Epistolario*, III, 614. See Cino Rinuccini, "Invettiva contro a

The second development which led to Salutati's debate with Poggio Bracciolini concerned the Chancellor's relations with the younger group of humanists in Florence. There is no doubt that Salutati was the center of humanist learning in Florence in the first years of the fifteenth century. Poggio and Bruni looked to Salutati for help, encouragement, and the recommendations which would launch them successfully on their careers. Yet certain tensions had begun to build up between the man of seventy and his young friends. Bruni and Poggio had begun to apply a much closer and more imitative approach to ancient literature than the earlier humanists had practiced. They censured any deviation from classical forms of address, such as the commonly used "de" indicating the author's place of birth (thus Bruni called himself Leonardus Aretinus, not Leonardus de Aretio), and the addition of a patronymic (so that Bruni did not wish to be called Leonardus Cecchus, and Poggio objected to the form Poggius Guccius). Salutati found all this rather silly. At one point he asked Poggio to give his greeting to "Leonardus Aretinus, if that is what he wishes to be called, as if there were no other Leonardus from Arezzo, or he detested his father's first name." Writing to Bruni, Salutati said that it was not the meaning of the contemporary practice which offended his young colleague but the mere sound of it.[72] Salutati's fear that the younger humanists were becoming too concerned with "sound, not

cierti calumniatori di Dante e di messer Francesco Petrarca e di messer Giovanni Boccaccio," summarized by C. Vasoli, "Polemiche Occamiste," *Rinascimento*, III (1952), 133-36.

[72] See Salutati's letters to Bruni, *Epistolario*, IV, 147ff., and to Poggio, IV, 158ff. For the passage about Bruni's name, see IV, 169-70; for the comment about "sound, not sense," IV, 153. The similarity of Salutati's strictures on both his young friends suggests that Bruni can be identified as the friend who joined Poggio in his criticism of Petrarch in 1405, despite Hans Baron's attempt to show that he was not (*Crisis*, I, 228). Although Salutati felt a close bond with Bruni (see *Crisis*, I, 213), it remains true that he found fault with both young men for the same excesses. Salutati's disagreement with Bruni was serious enough to cause Bruni to fear that his friend might retract the praises which had helped him to win a post as papal secretary. See *Epistolario*, IV, 156.

sense" recalls his criticism of Giovanni Malpaghini. It also inspired some of the statements he made in his last defenses of Petrarch.

The letter which Poggio wrote to Salutati opening the debate has been lost, but Salutati in reply quoted his friend's assertion that "no comparison, or only a very slight one, can be made between the most learned ancients and the men who have been famous in these times." This closely resembled what Salutati himself had asserted in 1395, but now he rejected it.[73] Did Poggio mean by the ancients the old pagans, or the early Christians? If the latter, Salutati observed, and especially if Poggio meant the incomparable Augustine, then it was true that none of the moderns could contend with them. But it seemed that Poggio referred to the most ancient writers, that is, to the pagans. Coluccio asked his friend to put aside the "authority, shadow, and opinion" of ancient superiority, and to allow the contest to be one of knowledge, not mere age. Cicero had not hesitated to affirm the superiority of Latin culture over the older Greeks, and Aristotle had sternly criticized earlier writers on physics and metaphysics.[74]

From this beginning Salutati proceeded to what he called the "real matters" (*solida*). There are two things in which *eruditio nostra* can be seen, he declared: wisdom and eloquence. As for the first, there could be no question about the superiority of the moderns; their Christian faith assures it. Were Plato or Aristotle reborn today, neither would dare prefer his own learning even to that of an uncultured Christian, for God makes foolish the wisdom of this world.[75] Since this was so, the ancients could not have surpassed the moderns in eloquence either. "For whatever we say is made up of words and things. And the worth of things is such, that a weighty and knowledgeable utterance even without any adornment of language must be preferred to the most eloquent and ornate style." Salutati cited

[73] *Epistolario*, IV, 131; cf. III, 84. For the full text of Salutati's letter to Poggio, see IV, 126-45.
[74] *Ibid.*, IV, 131-33.   [75] *Ibid.*, IV, 135.

Horace's dictum that "Knowledge is the beginning and source of writing well," and the testimony of Cicero that the perfect orator required knowledge of all things. A speech must be distinguished by knowledge or it will be empty and childish. Salutati had given voice to such ideas before, but he had not accepted all their implications. Now he did: "it is necessary to admit that all those who excel others in wisdom, similarly surpass them in eloquence."[76] Eloquence was not the property of those who pursued it for its own sake, but of those who acquired it through the search for wisdom.

For the humanists this immediately raised the question of what was to be said about their intellectual rivals, the scholastic philosophers. That this question did immediately present itself to Salutati at this point is in itself significant, for it shows how deeply the humanists' attitude toward the scholastics was tied up with the valuation of rhetoric in relation to philosophy. Salutati met the problem head-on, and he did not shrink from the implications of his position:

> But you will say: "Would you drive me to madness? Would you compel me to admit that the theologians of our time and of the last three centuries are eloquent, when they belong to that class of whom St. Augustine says that they relate true things in such a way that 'it bores one to listen, interferes with understanding, and worst of all, is not pleasing to believe?'" I know, my dearest Poggio, that just as our theologians surpass the pagans in knowledge of the truth, so do the latter surpass them, not in skill and majesty of speech, which without the knowledge of truth is childish, but in those things which Horace called "ignorant verses and melodic trifles."[77]

[76] *Ibid.*, IV, 136-37: "quicquid enim dicimus rebus constat et verbis; tantaque rerum dignitas est, quod sine verborum ornatu gravis et scientifica oratio eloquentissimo et ornatissimo stilo debeat anteferri. . . . ut fateri necessarium sit omnes qui sapientia cuiquam antecellunt, eloquentia pariter antistari."

[77] *Ibid.*, IV, 137: "sed dices: tune me rediges ad insaniam? cogesne me fateri theologos nostri temporis quive iam ferme tribus seculis

Salutati's position in this passage more resembles the stand of the scholastic opponents of classical literature than it does the usual statements of the humanists. Having asserted the full dependence of eloquence on wisdom, Salutati found himself reversing many of his own declarations on the value of ancient literature. We have seen above that his attitude toward the schoolmen was not wholly negative, but nowhere else does he seem to have accepted their standards to the extent that he did here. Once the primacy of wisdom was fully admitted, the major humanist criticism of scholasticism was dissipated. It is true that Salutati granted eloquence only to theologians here, not to scholastic philosophers, but we have seen that he was willing to apply the principle that eloquence derived from wisdom to the latter as well, as he did in the letter to Francesco Casini discussed above. The argument was stronger when it was clear that wisdom meant the truth of faith, but it did not really depend on this. What called into question the usual humanist criticism of the scholastics was not the identification of wisdom with Christianity, but the unconditional affirmation of the primacy of wisdom over eloquence.

Salutati's statement also raised the question of what in fact the ancients whom the humanists so admired had achieved, if they had been blind to the light of true wisdom. Salutati's comments on this may seem forced and artificial, but they are also revealing. The pagans, he suggested, had sought eloquence by itself because they discovered that all their efforts to gain real knowledge were in vain. Giving a new turn to an important sentence from Cicero's *De oratore*, he reminded Poggio that oratory was not an abstruse or esoteric art, but one closely tied to the com-

claruerunt, eloquentes esse, cum de illorum numero sint, de quibus divus inquit Aurelius quod vera sic narrent, ut audire tedeat, intelligere non pateat, credere postremo non libeat? scio, carissime Poggi, quod quantum nostri theologi vincunt veritatis eruditione Gentiles, tantum nostros illi superant non peritia maiestateque dicendi, que sine veritatis scientia puerilis est, sed illa, de qua Flaccus ait: 'versus inopes rerum nugeque canore.'" Cf. Horace, *Ars Poetica*, 322; St. Augustine, *De doctrina christiana*, IV, 3.

mon sense of all men.[78] Thus it resembled all of the subjects in which the ancient pagans had made some progress, in that it could be known by unaided nature. This was true of arithmetic, geometry, music, grammar, and logic, as well as rhetoric. In astronomy, the pagans had gone as far as conjecture could take them. But the higher subjects of natural philosophy, metaphysics, and—above all—theology had remained beyond their ability. Acknowledging the difficulty of these things, Socrates, the wisest of the ancients, had directed his attention to moral philosophy. But in this too the pagans had failed: How could they have discovered the end of life, since God is its end?

> When they saw that they could not even attain this knowledge, they tried by every means to obtain the method and faculty of speech; for they judged to be false, I think, what Socrates, nearly their own god, was wont to say, that everyone is eloquent enough in those matters they know. Which statement, even though Cicero said it was credible but denied it was true, I judge to be most true and certain. For although a man who knows the rules of speech is not necessarily eloquent, anyone must be eloquent enough on a subject he knows, unless he is completely inexperienced and a fool.[79]

What did Salutati mean by his implication that ancient thinkers after Socrates had given up the search for knowledge and limited themselves to the attempt to speak well? The humanists admired ancient writers more often for their eloquence than for anything else, but they seldom went as far as to claim that the ancients had sought eloquence

[78] *Epistolario*, IV, 137. Cf. *De oratore* I, iii, 12.
[79] *Epistolario*, IV, 138: "quod cum viderent se nondum assecutos esse, dicendi rationem facultatemque conati sunt modis omnibus adipisci; credo falsum arbitrantes, quod Socrates, ipsorum ferme deus, dicere solitus erat, omnes scilicet in eo quod scirent satis esse eloquentes. quod quidem, licet Cicero probabile dicat, verum autem neget; ego tamen verissimum arbitror atque certum. quanvis enim qui dicenda novit, simpliciter et absolute non sit eloquens, satis tamen eloquens in eo quod scit quilibet esse debet, nisi penitus desipiat et ignarus sit."

alone. It may be, however, that when Salutati related the ancients' cultivation of eloquence to their recognition of their own ignorance, he did not seriously mean to assert that ancient thinkers possessed no knowledge, but only to remind his correspondent that skepticism was popular among ancient thinkers and that a number of classical orators had espoused it. Salutati himself sometimes praised the Academics, and regarded their point of view as appropriate to the cultivation of fluent speech.[80] Here, however, Salutati rejected the Academic position; the wisdom on which eloquence depended was founded on real, existing knowledge. In affirming this, Salutati found himself opposing Cicero's view of the relationship between knowledge and speaking well, and supporting instead that of Plato. Previously he had accepted the Platonic standpoint only to the limited extent that Cicero had; now he embraced it wholly. To do so was to deny that the ancients had been able to achieve "true" eloquence, however single-mindedly they had striven for it.

Salutati proceeded to show what he meant by true learning through the example of a man who had achieved it: his old friend Luigi Marsili. In him, he said, nothing had been lacking of eloquence (Marsili had been a good preacher) or of any important branch of knowledge. While it is true that Marsili was not associated with any of the currents in scholasticism to which the humanists most strongly objected, and that he had been admired by Petrarch as well as by Salutati, nevertheless his learning was not of the kind embodied in the program of the *studia humanitatis*. Salutati's attitude toward humanistic studies certainly seems ambiguous at this point. After repeating his agreement with Socrates about the dependence of eloquence on knowledge, he went on to praise Petrarch. But he also reaffirmed that, since Christians must excel pagans in knowledge, the ancient writers had not achieved true eloquence, but only "melodic trifles." This was the fate of "those who pursue only eloquence."[81]

[80] Cf. above, p. 75.   [81] *Epistolario*, IV, 141-42.

Yet this letter was not Coluccio Salutati's declaration of independence from the *studia humanitatis et eloquentiae.* He had spent a long and fruitful life in the pursuit of these studies, and he wrote now to defend the reputation of the man from whom he had learned more about them than from anyone else, Petrarch. It is likely that he was suspicious of the direction humanism was taking in the hands of Poggio and Bruni. He criticized their desire to write in a style which imitated classical models so closely that it seemed strange and unusual to the men they addressed.[82] But his final argument for Petrarch's superiority was the familiar and curious formulation of 1379: Petrarch had excelled Virgil in prose, and Cicero in poetry. Each of the great ancients had remained within a single sphere. Both surpassed Petrarch in certain ways, but he excelled each in one field. Moreover, in knowledge of the truth Petrarch was superior not only to Virgil and Cicero, but to all of pagan antiquity. Cicero had known nothing, as he frankly admitted himself.[83] What is striking about this final argument for Petrarch's preeminence is that it contradicts the main lines of the case Salutati had been developing all along. If greater wisdom meant greater eloquence, and if Petrarch excelled both Virgil and Cicero in knowledge of the truth, why was it necessary to say that Petrarch surpassed each of the two Romans in only one kind of writing? Why not in both? One explanation for this contradiction might be that Salutati had rather unthinkingly recalled his earlier praise of Petrarch and used it again, not seeing that it did not fit with what he had already said. But it is more likely that Salutati, whose many contradictions, waverings, and arguments for the sake of argument we have already noted, was simply not committed to his own declaration of the subjection of eloquence to wisdom.

Salutati's position may be illuminated by a letter which is roughly contemporary with the Petrarch Controversy, one in which he defended poetry against a scholastic's strictures on it. Here Salutati argued that poetry was superior

[82] *Ibid.*, IV, 142.   [83] *Ibid.*, IV, 142-45.

to philosophy precisely because philosophy was necessary to poetry, while the reverse was not the case.[84] In this context Salutati regarded the necessity of philosophy to poetry as evidence that the first was tributary, and hence subordinate, to the second. Since he referred to poetry as "the other type of eloquence" and was fond of quoting Cicero on the close kinship of poetry and oratory, this letter certainly gives reason to doubt that he held firmly to the arguments he used in defending Petrarch to Poggio. Like the good orator he was, Salutati knew both how to reason persuasively and how to turn his reasons upside down.

Even if Salutati regarded his defense of Petrarch as nothing more than a rhetorical exercise, however, this controversy remains a revealing incident in the early development of Renaissance humanism. It shows how important the defense of rhetoric was in the humanists' attempt to secure their position from scholastic attacks. Petrarch too had criticized rhetoric, and in doing so had taken a position similar to the one he attributed to the scholastics, but he had not admitted that this constituted a rapprochement with them. Salutati made the implications of engaging in a philosophic critique of the pursuit of eloquence more explicit. To find a humanist bringing out these implications is surprising. Perhaps Salutati would not have discussed them had he not been affected by his age and his view of what was appropriate to it, as well as by his suspicion of the innovations of younger men. Yet his statements certainly demonstrate that a follower of Petrarch and Cicero might harbor genuine suspicions about the pursuit of eloquence.

It would be useful to know more than we do about the way in which Poggio replied. His letter is lost, but we have those parts of it which Salutati quoted when he wrote again to his young friend. The most important passage is the following:

> Let us listen to our Poggio miraculously rebutting this statement [that Plato and Aristotle, if alive today, would

[84] *Ibid.*, IV, 201-02.

96

not dare to contradict Christian truth]: "As if," you say, "one does not find even Christians who oppose the truth every day; or else you call that truth which, if you want to prove it, you cannot adduce anything beyond faith, in which no reason is sought, but only credulity. For such is this statement: whoever excels in wisdom equally prevails in eloquence. And to do away first with this, can anyone excel in wisdom, which is defined as the knowledge of human and divine things, who does not know how to give literary expression to his thoughts?"[85]

Poggio has sometimes been described as a pagan rationalist on the basis of this passage, and one would not wish to deny entirely the revolutionary possibilities inherent in his statement. Whatever one may think of Poggio's religious position, however, his target here was not religious faith or even credulity, but the belief defended by Salutati: that superior wisdom always carried with it a better style. Poggio refuted this contention as Salutati himself had sometimes done. "It can be the case that someone understands a thing rightly and yet cannot speak well of what he knows," Salutati had once written, quoting Cicero.[86] Poggio's position (at least as it appears in this brief quotation) did not differ significantly from Salutati's formulation of 1402: Eloquence is a part of wisdom, but it can only be attained by those who give attention to it for itself.[87] Neither man questioned the desirability of joining these two things together. Where Salutati's views seemed to have changed, and where they differed from Poggio's, was in the interpretation of this union of philosophy and rhetoric. Salutati revealed that this slogan could be turned against

[85] Ibid., IV, 165: "audiamus Poggium nostrum dictum hoc mirabiliter refellentem: quasi non reperiantur, inquis, qui quotidie etiam Christiani contradicunt, aut veritatem appelles id quod si velles probare nil possis adducere preter fidem, in qua nulla ratio queritur, sed credulitas sola. ut est eciam illud: quicumque sapientia excellunt eloquentia pariter antistari. et ut hoc prius expediam, excellitne sapientia, que rerum divinarum et humanarum scientia diffinitur, qui nesciat mandare litteris cogitationes suas?"
[86] Ibid., II, 77-78 (a letter of 1383).
[87] See above, pp. 83-85.

those who approved and encouraged the independent pursuit of eloquence. This was the lesson of the Petrarch Controversy of 1405-06.

It cannot be shown that this exchange of letters between Coluccio Salutati and Poggio Bracciolini had any real effect on the subsequent development of the humanist movement. There is no need, however, to insist that it did. The main point of our examination of the Petrarch Controversy has been to show that, even in the hands of the humanists themselves, the slogan of a combination of rhetoric and philosophy could be turned against the culture of professional rhetoricians. Once wisdom was admitted to be a higher ideal than eloquence, a call for the combination of the two no longer served to exalt the followers of rhetoric. The humanists of the Quattrocento would be aware of this. The challenge it posed to their place in the intellectual life of their times could be met either by enhancing their own claims to be men of wisdom as well as of eloquence, or by rejecting the ideal of an equal combination of rhetoric and philosophy in favor of a frank subordination of philosophy to their own art. Leonardo Bruni responded in the first way. Lorenzo Valla in the second.

CHAPTER IV

LEONARDO BRUNI AND THE NEW ARISTOTLE

(1)

ONE OF the most talented and versatile of the young men who belonged to Coluccio Salutati's circle in the years around 1400 was Leonardo Bruni. A successor to Salutati as chancellor of Florence, Bruni carried on and deepened the ties between the humanist movement and the increasingly powerful and famous Tuscan city. A diligent historian, he produced a history of Florence which claims a place in the early development of modern historical writing. One of the first of Petrarch's followers to possess a real knowledge of Greek, he helped to turn the humanist movement toward that interest in Hellenism which was to have such important effects on the evolution of European thought.[1]

Like Petrarch, Bruni had been born in Arezzo, but he was

---

[1] Among the works to be consulted on Bruni's career are the following: F. Beck, *Studien zu Leonardo Bruni* (Leipzig and Berlin, 1912); Lauro Martines, *The Social World of the Florentine Humanists, 1390-1460* (Princeton, 1963), esp. pp. 117-23, 165-76; Hans Baron, *The Crisis of the Early Italian Renaissance* (Princeton, 1955). See also Vittorio Rossi, *Il Quattrocento* (Rome, 1933; rev. ed. 1956), pp. 31ff.; on Bruni as a historian, B. L. Ullman, "Leonardo Bruni and Humanistic Historiography," *Medievalia et Humanistica*, IV (1946), 45-61; Emilio Santini, "Leonardo Bruni Aretino," *Annali della R. Scuola Normale Superiore di Pisa*, XXII (1910); on Bruni's *De militia*, C. C. Bayley, *War and Society in Renaissance Florence: The De militia of Leonardo Bruni* (Toronto, 1961). The text of Bruni's *Historiarum Florentini populi Libri XII*, is edited by E. Santini and C. di Pierro, in *Rerum Italicarum Scriptores*, XIX, Part 3. A number of Bruni's works are printed in Leonardo Bruni Aretino, *Humanistisch-Philosophische Schriften, Mit einer Chronologie seiner Werke und Briefe*, ed. Hans Baron (Leipzig and Berlin, 1928). On this edition, however, see L. Bertalot, "Forschungen über Leonardo Bruni Aretino," *Archivum Romanicum*, XV (1931), 284-323, and the reply by Baron, *Archiv f. Kulturgeschichte*, XXII (1932); also a review by Walter L. Bullock in *Speculum*, IV (1929), 476-83. Baron's edition of Bruni's works will be cited below as *Schriften*.

connected with Florence for much of his life. He first lived there in the 1390's, at which time he became associated with the group of enthusiasts of ancient learning gathered around Coluccio Salutati. In 1405 he left Florence to work in the papal curia (a source of employment for many humanists), but he returned briefly in 1410, acting for a few months as chancellor. He soon left again, but returned to live permanently in the city on the Arno in 1415. In 1416, on the completion of the first volume of his *History of Florence*, he was granted Florentine citizenship. In 1427 he became chancellor of the republic again, this time to remain in the post until his death in 1444.

Bruni learned his Greek from Manuel Chrysoloras, a Byzantine scholar who arrived in Florence in 1397, and who taught the language to a number of men who later made noteworthy use of it. Chrysoloras was the first teacher of Greek to have a significant influence on the development of humanism.[2] The main results of his teaching were evident in the impressive number of translations from Greek which began to appear in Italy in the early Quattrocento. Bruni was one of the most prominent of the translators. Like the others, he devoted his efforts both to works which were not available in Latin and to those whose existing versions were thought to be inadequate. Bruni translated works of Greek oratory, patristic literature, history, and philosophy. Of these, it is his new versions of Aristotle which will concern us here. His translations of Peripatetic writings included the *Nicomachean Ethics*, the *Politics*, and the pseudo-Aristotelian *Economics*.[3] In connection with

[2] On Chrysoloras, see Giuseppe Cammelli, *I Dotti Bizantini e le origini dell' Umanesimo, I: Manuele Crisolora* (Florence, 1941).

[3] See L. Bertalot, "Zur Bibliographie der Uebersetzungen des Leonardo Bruni Aretino," *Quellen und Forschungen aus Italienischen Archiven und Bibliotheken*, XXVII (1937); Eugenio Garin, "Le traduzioni umanistiche di Aristotele nel secolo XV," *Atti dell' Accademia Fiorentina di Scienze Morali: La Columbaria*, XVI (Florence, 1951; covering the years 1947-50), 62-88; Hans Baron, *Humanistic and Political Literature in Florence and Venice at the Beginning of the Quattrocento* (Cambridge, Mass., 1955), pp. 114-25, 166-73; Josef Soudek, "The Genesis and Tradition of Leonardo Bruni's Anno-

this work, he also wrote a short *Life of Aristotle,* and an *Introduction to Moral Philosophy* which drew heavily on Aristotelian teaching.[4] He often mentioned Aristotle in his letters, too. Bruni's approach to Aristotle gives an excellent point of departure for our consideration of the way in which he confronted the problem of relating rhetoric and philosophy. Like Salutati, Bruni was a professional rhetorician. His concern with Aristotle was the attempt of an orator to come to terms with the Philosopher.

Like the other thinkers we have examined, Bruni made the combination of rhetoric and philosophy the keystone of his cultural program. "By learning," he wrote in a treatise on education, "I understand not that vulgar and confused sort which those who now profess theology practice, but the fitting and honorable kind which joins literary skill with the knowledge of things."[5] As usual, we must be cautious in our attempt to define this ideal. Sometimes Bruni insisted on the independent place reserved for philosophic knowledge in his program, naming Aristotle as the source of this knowledge. In one of his letters Bruni described his literary course as the combination of Aristotelian doctrine with Ciceronian style.[6] Similarly, he once insisted that the content of his teaching was Aristotelian, and that it was wrong to attribute it only to Cicero.[7] These comments were characteristic of Bruni's view of his own learning in the period when his new versions of Aristotle were completed or well begun. Earlier, however, Leonardo's understanding of

---

tated Latin Version of the (Pseudo-) Aristotelian *Economics,*" *Scriptorium,* XII (1958). See also E. Garin, "La fortuna dell' etica aristotelica nel Quattrocento," *La Cultura Filosofica del Rinascimento Italiano* (Florence, 1961), pp. 60-71.

[4] The *Vita Aristotelis* has never been printed in its entirety, but large sections of it are available in *Schriften,* pp. 41-49; the *Isagogicon moralis disciplinae* also appears there.

[5] *De studiis et litteris,* in *Schriften,* p. 6.

[6] Leonardo Bruni Arretini, *Epistolarum Libri VIII,* ed. Laurentius Mehus (Florence, 1741), II, 49. (This is still the only edition of Bruni's letters; it will be cited below as "Mehus.") This same letter appears in *La Disputa Delle Arti nel Quattrocento,* ed. E. Garin (Florence, 1947), pp. 7-8.

[7] Mehus, I, 135.

the true union of oratory and philosophy had been somewhat different. In the first of his works to consider any philosophical issues, the *Dialogues* inscribed to Pier Paolo Vergerio, Bruni (speaking through Niccolò Niccoli) gave much
greater importance to Cicero as a source of learning in
philosophy:

> At a certain time philosophy was brought from Greece
> into Italy by Cicero, and it was nourished by the golden
> stream of his eloquence. In his books not only was the
> rational basis of all philosophy carefully set forth, but
> also the positions of each of the philosophic schools.
> Which, it seems to me, was very useful for inciting men
> to learning; for whoever came to the study of philosophy
> had immediately before him the authors he should fol-
> low, and he learned both to defend his own opinions, and
> to refute those of others. Here were the Stoics, the Aca-
> demics, the Peripatetics, the Epicureans, with all their
> arguments and differences of opinion. . . . But now that a
> great part of these books has been lost, and those which
> remain are so corrupt that they are nearly lost, how do
> you expect us to be able to learn philosophy?[8]

The last sentence of this passage exaggerates both the number of Cicero's works which were unavailable in 1401 when
Bruni wrote, and Bruni's own pessimism about the possibil-

[8] *Ad Petrum Paulum Histrum dialogus*, ed. Garin, in *Prosatori
Latini*, p. 54: "Fuit philosophia olim ex Graecia in Italiam a Cicerone
traducta, atque aureo illo eloquentiae flumine irrigata: erat in eius
libris cum omnis philosophiae exposita ratio, tum singulae philosophorum scholae diligenter explicatae. Quae res, ut michi quidem
videtur, plurimum valebat ad studia hominum incendenda; ut enim
quisque ad philosophiam accedebat, continuo sibi quos sequeretur
proponebat, discebatque non solum sua tueri, sed etiam aliena refellere. Hinc Stoici, Academici, Peripatetici, Epicurei; hinc omnes inter
eos contentiones dissensionesque nascebantur. Qui libri utinam nunc
extarent, nec maiorum nostrorum tanta fuisset ignavia! . . . Sed cum
illorum librorum magna pars interierit, hi vero, qui supersunt, adeo
mendosi sint ut paulo ab interitu distent, quemadmodum nobis philosophiam hoc tempore discendam putas?" (There is also a good edition
of the *Dialogues* by Theodor Klette, in *Beiträge zur Geschichte und
Literatur der Italienischen Gelehrtenrenaissance* [Greifswald, 1889],
pp. 39-83.)

102

ity of gaining knowledge of philosophy at that time. In the second book of the *Dialogues* the speaker Niccoli dispelled much of this pessimism, and said that Petrarch had "opened the way for us to show in what manner we could acquire learning." Niccoli did not retract his statement of the fundamental importance of Cicero to the kind of learning the humanists approved, however. One of the works he had most in mind when he praised Cicero was the *De oratore*. The version of that dialogue available to Bruni in 1401 was marred by a number of lacunae, but Bruni knew enough of it to make it the basis for his own *Dialogues*. The themes he discussed there, as well as some of the language he used, were modeled on Cicero.[9] The main source of learning as Bruni conceived it here, in matters of philosophical content as well as of rhetorical form, was Cicero. Though he later made a place for Aristotle as a source of philosophical knowledge, it should be remembered that his earliest loyalty was to the Roman orator.

Aristotle and Cicero were the authors on whom Bruni relied most in his attempt to combine rhetoric and philosophy. He was much influenced by the earlier humanists, but in one very important way Bruni's version of this ideal union differed from that of Petrarch or Salutati. We have seen that both of these men, speaking "as philosophers," sometimes voiced criticisms of rhetoric or doubts about the harmony of its purposes with those of philosophy. It appears that Bruni never did. He sometimes granted to philosophical learning, separate from rhetoric, a greater degree of independence than he did in the youthful *Dialogues*; but he neither made wisdom the ruler of eloquence, in the way Salutati did at the end of his life, nor described the philosophic ideal as too exalted to be touched by rhetoric, as Petrarch several times had done. Throughout his career his attitude toward the pursuit of eloquence remained strongly positive, and his faith in the union of eloquence and wisdom was unimpaired.

[9] On the *Dialogues*, see my discussion in *Past and Present*, No. 34 (1966), pp. 10ff.

This was possible first of all because Bruni took a position with regard to the ancient philosophic schools which was different from the one Petrarch and Salutati had absorbed from Cicero. Like his predecessors, Bruni learned of the issues which divided ancient philosophers mainly through Cicero, and he described the differences between Stoics and Peripatetics much as the Roman orator had. But he chose a philosophic perspective which highlighted the common elements in their teachings rather than the contrasts between them. In his *Introduction to Moral Philosophy*, Bruni attempted what he called a "conciliation of philosophers." The differences between the various schools, he asserted, were only a matter of words; in substance all agreed. The point of agreement that Bruni stressed derived from the high praise all the philosophers had given to virtue. Since Stoics and Peripatetics agreed that the "queen and cause" of a happy life was virtue, none of their lesser disagreements were of any importance. It did not matter that the Peripatetics, using the term "good" in the common way, called bodily health and favorable circumstances "good," while the Stoics, rejecting common usage, termed these things in their own fashion "preferred." The relative value each school attached to virtue, health, and wealth was the same; the superiority of virtue to the others was admitted by both.[10] In making this argument, Bruni built his case almost word for word on Cicero. Especially in the *De finibus*, Cicero had several times given such an account of the relationships between the two groups.[11] For Cicero, however, this assertion had been a Peripatetic criticism of the Stoics, who were thereby accused of having simply taken over their rivals' teachings and clothed them in a new terminology. Cicero also gave attention to the Stoic argu-

[10] *Isagogicon moralis disciplinae*, in *Schriften*, pp. 27-28.

[11] E.g., *De finibus* IV, xxii, 61; IV, xxxi, 72; V, xxvi, 74; but especially (as pointed out by Baron) IV, ix, 23: "Quid enim interest, divitias, opes, valetudinem bona dicas, anne praeposita, cum ille, que ista bona dicit, nihilo plus iis tribuat quam tu, qui eadem illa praeposita nominas?"

ment for the reality of the differences between the doctrines, both in the *De finibus* and elsewhere. Petrarch's position had been quite close to Cicero's: he sometimes declared the differences between the philosophers to be
merely a matter of words, but more often he accepted them
as substantial and important.[12] Salutati had also been aware
of the view that the two schools were harmonious, but he
rejected it. "To harmonize Aristotle with Cicero and Seneca,
that is the Peripatetics with the Stoics, is a great deal more
difficult than you think," he wrote once to a friend.[13] Bruni,
on the other hand, found this harmony quite to his taste.
He does not seem to have questioned it after he wrote his
Introduction to Moral Philosophy. Moreover, he included
other philosophers in it. He wrote that the Epicureans also
joined in the praise of virtue, once again relying on Cicero's
words while going beyond his intention. Cicero had allowed a partisan of Epicurus to state in the *De finibus* that
the life of pleasure was impossible apart from virtue, but
Cicero himself was not willing to overlook the differences
between this school and the other two, which he respected
a great deal more. Bruni echoed Cicero almost exactly, but
he gave much greater credence than Cicero had to the
harmony of Epicurean teachings with the tenets of the
other philosophers.[14] In other places Bruni extended the
area of philosophic concord to include the similarity of
Platonic and Aristotelian opinions (once again echoing

[12] *Fam.*, VIII, 3, 7: "magno ac perpetuo apud doctos philosophi
poeticique dogmatis consensu rerum, sed verborum varietate multi-
plici"; cf. also *Fam.*, X, 5, 9. On Petrarch's acceptance of the reality
of these differences, see above, Chap. II.

[13] *Epistolario*, II, 310: "concordare autem Aristotelem cum Cicerone
et Seneca, imo peripatheticos cum stoicis, magis operosum est omnino
quam credas."

[14] *Schriften*, p. 28: "Clamat enim Epicurus ipse: non posse cum
voluptate vivi, nisi juste, temperate, prudenterque vivatur, neque
rursus iuste, temperate, prudenter, nisi cum voluptate." Cf. *De finibus*
I, xxvi, 57: "Clamat Epicurus, is quem vos nimis voluptatibus esse
deditum dicitis, non posse jucunde vivi, nisi sapienter, honeste, juste-
que vivatur nec sapienter, honeste, juste, nisi jucunde."

statements often found in Cicero), and the proximity of pagan moral doctrine to Christian teaching.[15] Virtue was the concern of all moral philosophers alike.

Bruni's conciliation of philosophers seems to have had in view two noteworthy consequences. One was to disarm any possible criticism of his own emphasis on Aristotle and his relative neglect of the Stoics: since all philosophers agreed in their evaluation of virtue, it was enough to follow one school. The second effect of Bruni's procedure was to eliminate the necessity felt by Petrarch and Salutati to declare their loyalty much of the time to a notion of philosophy so rigorously committed to the life of wisdom that it could not accept the compromises demanded by ordinary life. Bruni's own position was Aristotelian; his efforts to harmonize the teachings of all philosophers had the effect of bringing the other schools closer to the Peripatetic mean. The implication of this was clear: philosophy as Bruni envisioned it never led where the orator could not follow.

Bruni's dealings with philosophy thus entailed none of the suspicion of rhetoric which we have noted in Petrarch and Salutati. While Bruni was wholehearted in his pursuit of eloquence, however, he was often uncertain in his attitude toward the search for wisdom. He often praised philosophy as the "mother of the arts" or the guide to human happiness, but he was sometimes much less enthusiastic about philosophers. Significantly, Bruni's criticism of philosophers was not limited to scholastics. It is true that most of his barbs were aimed at the schoolmen, and that he was harsher with them than Salutati or Petrarch had been. Petrarch had censured the style of the scholastics, but he had not always denied their knowledge of Aristotle.[16] Bruni found them not only barbaric and tiresome in their speech, but also bad Aristotelians. "I do not think they properly

[15] On the agreement of Plato and Aristotle, see *Vita Aristotelis*, in *Schriften*, pp. 44-45. Cf. *De finibus* IV, ii, 5; *Academics* I. On the proximity of pagan moral teaching to Christian tenets, see the letter to Eugene IV in *Schriften*, pp. 72-73. Here Bruni mentioned Socrates, Plato, and Aristotle.

[16] *Rerum mem.*, II, 31, 7. See also *On His Own Ignorance, passim.*

understand what Aristotle thought," he declared, "even about the smallest thing."[17] But Bruni's suspicions on this matter were not confined to these modern philosophers. In the *Dialogues* he used a comment that Cicero had made about the ancient philosophers as a reason for believing the modern ones to be ignorant of Aristotle. In his *Topics* Cicero had excused a certain rhetorician's ignorance of Aristotle on the grounds that the Stagirite was unknown even to the philosophers themselves, save for a very few. To Bruni, this pronouncement seemed enough to keep "that unworthy herd" in its place. No doubt he realized that Cicero had not been speaking of the men of the Middle Ages. But Bruni argued a fortiori: since Cicero had been able to say that the philosophers were ignorant of Aristotle in the days when all the arts were at their height, their ignorance must be even greater in the days of intellectual decline.[18] However curious the argument, the passage is worth noting because of what it reveals about Bruni's attitude toward philosophy. Bruni saw a continuity between the philosophers of Cicero's day and those of his own, and thought that the faults of modern philosophers had been shared in some degree by philosophers of antiquity. Here, at least, he included the scholastics among those whom Cicero called not orators but philosophers.

At other times, Bruni referred to the weaknesses of philosophers in general. One flaw was that they did not possess the true power of eloquent speech. In his treatise *On Studies and Letters* he recommended the reading of orators in these terms:

> I also exhort you not to neglect to read orators. For who is wont to extoll virtue more ardently or thunder more fiercely against vice? From them we learn to praise what is well done and to execrate villainies; from them to console, to exhort, to incite, to restrain. Granted that all these

[17] *Ad Petrum Paulum Histrum dialogus*, ed. Garin, p. 56: "Non puto illos ne minima quidem in re, quid Aristoteles senserit recte tenere."

[18] *Ibid.*, pp. 56-58. Cf. Cicero, *Topics* I, ii, 3.

things are done by philosophers, still it is true somehow that anger and pity and every excitement and restraint of the soul are in the power of the orator.[19]

Thus Bruni faulted philosophers sometimes for their lack of knowledge, and at other times for their lack of eloquence. Once he allowed his dislike of philosophy to break out in more sweeping fashion. Citing a passage from Virgil's *Aeneid* to show the value of poetry, Bruni exclaimed: "When we read these lines, what philosopher do we not despise?"[20]

Bruni did not always mean the same thing by the term philosophy. Philosophy in one sense drew forth his warmest praise, but in another it evoked his disdain. The difference was that only philosophy of the first sort joined true knowledge to practice in writing well. The true philosophers were those who joined wisdom to eloquence. Bruni had little reason to believe that all ancient writers had done so (Cicero indicated that some had not), but he claimed that they had. This assertion was not a historical discovery about the quality of ancient culture; it was a form of propaganda for the humanist program. The great philosophers of antiquity were endowed with enormous prestige in Bruni's day. Unless Bruni were to deny (as Valla sometimes did later on) that they deserved the reverence in which they were held, he had no choice but to claim them for the program of learning he sponsored. Aristotle was the most important of these ancient thinkers, both because of his domination of contemporary philosophy, and because of the special place Cicero assigned to Peripatetic moral doctrine in the culture of the orator. If the main source of philosophic knowledge was Aristotle, and if the Philosopher

[19] *De studiis*, in *Schriften*, p. 13: "Oratores quoque ut legere non negligas suadebo. Quis enim aut virtutes extollere ardentius aut vitia fulminare atrocius solet? Ab his et laudare bene facta et detestari facinora addiscemus; ab his consolari, cohortari, impellere, absterrere. Quae licet omnia a philosophis fiant, tamen nescio quomodo et ira et misericordia et omnis animi suscitatio ac repressio in potestate est oratoris."

[20] *Ibid.*, p. 15: "Quae cum legimus, quem philosophum non contemnimus?"

were himself part orator, then the kind of criticism of eloquence in the name of wisdom adumbrated by Salutati in the last years of his life could be turned aside. The purpose of Bruni's new view of Aristotle was to bring the prestige of the Stagirite's name fully behind the humanist program, and thus to give new life to the combination of rhetoric and philosophy.

(2)

IN ORDER to understand Bruni's involvement with Aristotle's treatises on moral philosophy, we shall examine four separate aspects of it. The first is the image of Aristotle which Leonardo tried to project through various descriptions of and comments about him; the second is the background which some earlier humanist attempts to get more satisfactory texts of classical writings provided for Bruni's activity as a translator; the third is the series of controversies which Bruni's new versions of Aristotle inspired; the fourth is the echo of Bruni's work which appeared in the writings of other humanists. The combination of these various perspectives should yield a reasonably accurate portrait of Leonardo Bruni's Aristotelianism.

In his youthful *Dialogues*, Bruni had denied that the scholastics' claim to follow Aristotle was a valid one: they did not understand the philosopher, even in the smallest thing. To the question of precisely what he meant by this, Bruni gave only one answer: "Cicero's opinion was that Aristotle had a zeal for eloquence, and that he wrote with a certain extraordinary sweetness. But these books of Aristotle [i.e., the translations used in the schools], if they ought indeed to be thought to be his, are, we see, troublesome and disagreeable to read, so much so that no one but Oedipus or the Sybil could understand them."[21] The scho-

---

[21] *Ad Petrum Paulum Histrum dialogus*, ed. Garin, p. 58: "Nam studiosum eloquentiae fuisse Aristotelem atque incredibili quadam cum suavitate scripsisse, Ciceronis sententia est. Nunc vero hos Aristotelis libros, si tamen eos Aristotelis esse putandum est, et molestos in legendo et absonos videmus, tantaque obscuritate perplexos, ut praeter Sybillam aut Oedipodem nemo intelligat." Cf. Petrarch, *Rerum mem.*, II, 31. For Cicero's comments on Aristotle's style, see above, Chap. I.

lastics erred in failing to recognize that Aristotle had also been a man of eloquence.

The words of Cicero to which Bruni referred had been noticed before, but they would play a larger part in Bruni's career than they had in any earlier humanist's work. For that reason, something should now be said about Cicero's knowledge of Aristotelian philosophy. Modern historians of ancient thought divide Aristotle's works into two main groups. Of these, the first is the series of rather technical discussions of philosophical problems which—in a form rather like that of lecture notes—survived the ancient world, and which make up the Aristotelian corpus as it is usually conceived of today: the logical works, the scientific and metaphysical treatises, the *Rhetoric, Politics, Ethics,* and so forth. The second group is a set of earlier writings in which Aristotle's Platonic beginnings showed more clearly, and which were written in a more finished and popular style; these writings survive today only in a few fragments. In Cicero's time it was the latter works which were usually read, and it was to them that Cicero referred when he spoke of Aristotle's "golden stream of eloquence." In mistakenly applying these words to Aristotle's more technical and less polished writings, Bruni was the victim of a complicated trick of fate. As a result, he may have been led to distort some features of the Aristotelian writings he possessed, but at the same time he entered into other aspects of Aristotle's world which few of his contemporaries approached.[22]

[22] On the various classes of Aristotle's writings, see Ueberweg and Praechter, *Die Philosophie des Altertums* (Berlin, 1926), p. 353. On Cicero's reading of Aristotle, see Werner Jaeger, *Aristotile* (Ital. edn., Florence, 1935), p. 341. Jaeger believes that Aristotle's style, even in his early works, aimed primarily at clarity rather than rhetorical ornament, even though some of his works contained myths and made use of rhetorical devices. This diffidence toward the rhetorical practice of the day was abandoned by later Peripatetics, however, beginning with Theophrastus. It may be that Cicero's references to Aristotle's style reflected later Peripatetic literary practice rather than Aristotle's own, since his notions of Peripatetic doctrine definitely relied on post-Aristotelian thinking. See *ibid.*, pp. 37-38 and note.

110

Bruni's view of Aristotle received its fullest outline in the *Life of Aristotle*, written in 1429. By this date Bruni's acquaintance with the philosopher was of long standing, and he proposed to write his life in order that men might know more about this acknowledged benefactor of humanity.[23] Bruni was less interested in the details of Aristotle's life and in the specific doctrines he taught than in giving a general picture of the philosopher's chief concerns and activities. Bruni depicted Aristotle as a thinker whose intellectual formation was in close harmony with the traditions of rhetoric. In the background was Aristotle's teacher, Plato. To him Bruni attributed wide-ranging knowledge, and "such eloquence that he appears to raise himself above the level of men by his speech. Sometimes his treatises are such that they are based more on the assent of the upright mind than on proof by logical necessity."[24] Plato spoke according to the precepts of rhetoric. To Aristotle Bruni ascribed a characteristic of the orator which Plato did not display, one whose Ciceronian roots were clearly recognizable. Bruni described him as more cautious and moderate than his teacher, and (using the terms in which Cicero had contrasted Aristotle to the Stoics) more favorable to commonly accepted ideas. "He appears to support those things which take part in ordinary life and practice, not to invent things which are strange and abhorrent and of no use to it."[25] Thus

[23] *Vita Aristotelis*, in *Schriften*, pp. 41-42.

[24] *Ibid.*, p. 45: "Fuit enim Plato, vir singularis quidem ac praecellens, multarum ac variarum rerum scientia praeditus, eloquentia vero tanta, ut supra hominem sese attollere illius eloquium videatur. Ceterum traditiones eius interdum tales sunt, ut assensu potius bonae mentis quam probationis necessitate nitantur."

[25] *Ibid.*: "Praeterea doctrina Platonis varia est et incerta. Socrates enim, ubique inductus, nullo disciplinarum ordine quasi a carcere ad calcem discurrit; sed modo hoc modo illud pro arbitrio agit et in disputando non tam, quae ipse sentiat, dicere videtur, quam aliorum sententias dictaque refellere. Aristoteles vero et cautior in tradendo fuit (nihil enim aggreditur, quod probare non possit) et moderatior in opinando, ut haec, quae in usu vitaque communi versantur, adiuvare, non aliena et abhorrentia et nunquam profutura meditari illum appareat." Bruni here stated his lack of enthusiasm for the doctrine of the transmigration of souls, and for the community of women in the *Republic*.

Aristotle was a friend to the life of men as it is actually lived; he was not merely a philosopher's philosopher. Moreover, he had not only excelled in philosophy, he had also been "most diligent" in his attention to "other arts and faculties." Of these latter, Bruni mentioned only two, rhetoric and poetry. Following the lead of Cicero and Petrarch, he told how Aristotle had been moved by the fame and success of the rhetorician Isocrates to add practice in speaking to the curriculum of his school, thus mixing wisdom with eloquence. He had also filled his own writings with figures and ornaments of speech. That all this was not appreciated at the present time was, Bruni asserted, the fault of the inept translations which the schoolmen had produced. Many ancients testified to Aristotle's eloquence. The men who called themselves philosophers in the present day were ignorant of letters, and they misrepresented the philosopher as like themselves. Aristotle had been very different from them. He knew all the poets and orators who had written until his own time, and "his rhetorical books demonstrate how precisely he held to the precepts of speaking." His concern for the rules of style extended even to the most minute matters, such as the use of meter in prose. Moreover, his treatises on rhetoric demonstrated that he not only had a zeal for eloquence himself, but also wanted to teach the art to others. No one who recognized the quality of Aristotle's genius could sensibly deny that he had in fact achieved an eloquent style, since he so clearly sought to cultivate one.[26]

In summary Bruni listed the main fields of the Stagirite's interest, giving four headings. He placed rhetoric ("eloquence and persuasion") first, followed by civic and moral philosophy, logic ("the precepts of discourse"), and natural philosophy ("the secrets of nature and the causes and reasons of the most occult things").[27] The basis of this list was the traditional division of philosophy into ethics, logic, and natural philosophy, but Bruni altered it by adding

[26] *Ibid.*, pp. 46-48.
[27] *Ibid.*, 48-49.

112

rhetoric as a separate category at the beginning. He thus implied that rhetoric was the first of Aristotle's concerns. Petrarch had also claimed that Aristotle was interested in the art of oratory, but much more moderately. "In addition to many treatises in the three divisions of philosophy," he had noted, "Aristotle also wrote some books on rhetoric."[28] Sometimes Petrarch had denied that Aristotle actually achieved the power of eloquent speech.[29] Bruni went beyond Petrarch, picturing Aristotle's attachment to rhetoric as much deeper than Petrarch had thought it to be, and never permitting this bond to be questioned.

Part of the difference between Petrarch's somewhat hesitant attitude toward Aristotle's eloquence and Bruni's confident affirmation of it might be attributed to the general development of humanism in the early fifteenth century, but much of it is due to Bruni's own activity as a translator from the Greek. Petrarch, cherishing the Greek Homer he could not read, could only groan in the face of the Latin Aristotle which so hid the "golden stream of eloquence" praised by Cicero. He hoped that Greek works could be rendered into Latin "with their ornaments of speech preserved," but as for the books of Aristotle, their infection was so far advanced that there seemed no hope of remedy for them.[30] By the time Bruni wrote his *Life of Aristotle*, he had already made Petrarch's pessimism obsolete through his new version of the *Nicomachean Ethics*, completed in 1417. In his own opinion and that of other humanists, he had made Aristotle available to Latin readers in a guise which matched the philosopher's original Greek dress.[31] The clearest indication of what this meant to Bruni himself

[28] *Rerum mem.*, II, 31, 5.
[29] *On His Own Ignorance*, p. 103.
[30] *Rerum mem.*, II, 31, 9-10.
[31] Antonio da Rho wrote: "Leonardum vobis Aretinum pro oculis pingerem, ut aiunt, Atticae eloquentiae virum quippe qui Aristotelis atque Plutarchi libros aliaque quam plurima e Graeco in Latinum traducens ita Latina Graecis, ita Graeca Latinis accomodavit, ut ex iis veluti alter Cicero videatur sese immortalitati perpetuaeque memoriae commendasse." *Reden und Briefe Italienischer Humanisten*, ed. Carl Muellner (Vienna, 1899), p. 166.

appears from a treatise he wrote to explain and justify his work: *On Correct Translation.*[32]

Here Bruni set forth his understanding of the role he had tried to fill as translator. To be able to translate properly, he declared, one must be a skilled master of both languages involved, be thoroughly familiar with all kinds of literature in each, and be practiced in the use of difficult idioms. The purpose of such literary proficiency was not only to develop one's own style. The writings of learned men were such, Bruni suggested, that a profound knowledge of the many intricate artifices of language was required in order to understand them. This was so because the best authors used many tropes and figures of speech. Plato and Aristotle, "great masters of letters, as I would say," had used such metaphorical language abundantly. As a result, their words often seemed to mean one thing, while literary custom gave them quite a different meaning. It was not enough to know the meanings of individual words; one also had to be familiar with figurative phrases. In addition, learned writers could call up a whole train of associations and meanings by the mere mention of a name or the use of a phrase: Could anyone properly understand Aristotle who failed to comprehend a reference to the grace and beauty of Helen?[33]

The translator's duty was to recreate the work of his author in the manner of an artist who copied another's picture. He must strive to make his will conform to that of the author, and thus to reproduce accurately every aspect of the original work. He must be able to adapt himself to the characteristics of different authors. To do this he must give close attention to their differing styles of writing and uses of language. The purpose of such attention, Bruni reiterated, was not merely stylistic. It was necessary in order that the sense of the original be faithfully rendered.[34]

[32] Edited by Baron in *Schriften*, pp. 81-96. On the dating of this work (1424/26), see Baron, *Crisis*, II, 615 and 618.
[33] *Schriften*, pp. 83-85; cf. *De studiis*, in *Schriften*, p. 7.
[34] *Schriften*, p. 87.

Bruni's principles of translation were admirable, but his argument made good sense only if the use of metaphor was as characteristic of Greek philosophy as it was of poetry or oratory. He devoted the last portion of his treatise to demonstrating that this was so: "In order that what I have said may be better understood, I should like to add examples of all these things, so that it may be clear that ornaments of this type are frequently used not only by orators but also by philosophers, and that the majesty of their discourse is totally lost unless their form is preserved in translation."[35] These words referred primarily to Aristotle's *Ethics*, which was the only one of the philosopher's writings that Bruni had as yet translated when he wrote *On Correct Translation*. But he was equally concerned to show Aristotle's interest in rhetoric when he turned to the *Politics*. He once wrote of this work that "Its subject is concerned with public life, and is suitable for eloquence."[36] In the prologue attached to his new version of 1435, he declared: "Surely Aristotle filled this book with such eloquence, such variety and fullness of speech, and such a wealth of narratives and examples, that it seems to be written nearly in the style of oratory."[37] How much of Bruni's purpose was to produce a more accurate Latin text of Aristotle, and how much of it was only to justify this view?

(3)

WE MAY approach this question first of all through an examination of some antecedents of Bruni's work. The emergence of Leonardo Bruni as a translator of Greek philosophy is not as simple and straightforward a story as it may seem. To be sure, Bruni shared Petrarch's longing

[35] *Ibid.*, p. 88: "De quibus omnibus, quo melius ea, quae dixi, intelligantur, exempla quaedam adscribere libuit, ut conspicuum sit non ab oratoribus modo, verum etiam a philosophis huiusmodi exornationes frequentari et maiestatem orationis totam perire, nisi servata earum figura transferantur."

[36] Mehus, II, 95: "Materia est civilis, et capax eloquentiae."

[37] *Schriften*, p. 74: "Aristoteles certe tanta facundia, tanta varietate et copia, tanta historiarum exemplorumque cumulatione hos libros refersit, ut oratorio paene stilo scripti videantur."

to know Greek, grasped the opportunity of learning Greek
offered by the arrival of Manuel Chrysoloras in 1397, and
finally turned his linguistic ability to the task of reviving
the long-buried Greek heritage. But this account leaves out
much that is significant in the early history of humanist
translation. In particular it leaves out certain evidence
which may not be flattering to the humanists, but which
should not be ignored. This evidence indicates that the
humanists did not wait for the knowledge of Greek to revive among them before beginning the work of replacing
the medieval translations with ones they found more suitable. By considering the relationship between Bruni's
efforts and these previous humanist attempts at "translation," we may be able to judge the relative impact on his
work of, on the one hand, a desire to uphold and further
humanist rhetorical culture and, on the other, the understanding of the deficiencies of the scholastic translators
which his knowledge of Greek gave him.

Our information about earlier humanist efforts along this
line comes from two letters of Coluccio Salutati.[38] Both
were written in the 1390's, in the period when Bruni arrived
in Florence and was becoming associated with Salutati's
circle. Neither Salutati nor his correspondents, Pietro Corsini and Antonio Loschi, knew Greek. Yet in the first letter
the Chancellor encouraged Loschi to proceed with his revision of a poor translation of the *Iliad* (a project which
Salutati noted had occurred to both men independently).
He observed that the version in question had been done
"word for word" (*secundum verba*), with the result that
there was "nothing pleasing in it." Salutati told his friend to
"consider things [*res*], not words." He advised him to
"adorn and ornament the matter [*res*], and making use

[38] Printed in *Epistolario*, II, 354-57 and 480-83. Perhaps it should
be explicitly stated here that the following discussion is not intended
to imply any judgment about the *quality* of the humanist efforts at
translation. For this, a collation with the Greek texts would be the
necessary starting point. What is sought is rather an understanding of
the purpose of these men as translators, and of the attitudes which
inspired them in this activity.

116

both of unchanged and of altered words, add decoration and such splendor of language that you display and echo that Homeric quality which we all have in mind, not only in the poetic imagination [*inventione*] of the work, but even in its language."[39] From this advice, it is clear that Salutati did not suppose Loschi's *Iliad* would come any closer to Homer's literal meaning than the earlier version had. The best that may be said for Salutati's intention is that he thought a concerted effort to create a style worthy of the greatest of Greek poets might cause something of the proper Homeric spirit to emerge. It was in this sense that he invoked the malleable slogan "consider things, not words." As he used it, this formula implied not a strict attention to meaning separate from style, but rather the presumption that faithfulness to meaning did not require a strict use of language. Specifically, he recommended that Loschi add conjunctions, exclamations, and interrogations, as well as "more proper, more splendid and more sonorous words." To "consider things, not words" meant to strive more for style than for meaning.

Loschi applied this freewheeling method of improving a translation to a work of poetry, but Salutati used the same principles to revise a philosophical treatise as well: Plutarch's *On Restraining Anger*. A translation of this work had been done for Pietro Corsini by Simon Attumano, the archbishop of Thebes.[40] Salutati, despite his own ignorance of Greek, thought this version unworthy of Plutarch. The reason for his conviction will be familiar to us: he could cite testimony for Plutarch's eloquence, whereas Simon Attumano's translation failed to reveal it. The testimony came not from a classical writer, but from a medieval one, John of Salisbury, who had claimed to draw on Plutarch in composing his *Policraticus*. John's Latin rendering of Plutarch demonstrated the sweetness of his style; it fol-

[39] *Epistolario*, II, 356-57.
[40] On this Byzantine scholar and his activities in Italy, see K. M. Setton, "The Byzantine Background of the Italian Renaissance," *Proceedings of the American Philosophical Society*, C (1956), esp. 50-55.

lowed that the obscurity and harshness of Simon's translation must have been the fault of the translator, and Salutati felt justified in trying to restore Plutarch's eloquence.[41] To do so he adopted the methods that he had suggested Loschi apply to Homer, changing the word order and substituting interrogative or exclamatory phrases for the declarative ones of the original, "for the sake of ornament." In all this Salutati demonstrated his usual moderation, admitting that he had sometimes hesitated to make changes lest he depart too far from the sense, and asking to be excused for any mistakes. But he thought he had produced a more readable and attractive version than the one he had started with. "In short, instead of a half-Greek translation I return to you a Latin treatise, which I judge to be intelligible and clear."[42]

Salutati's words and the comments Bruni made on his own new version of Aristotle were similar. Salutati had complained that the version of Plutarch on which he tried to improve was barbarous and "half-Greek." These are precisely the faults that Bruni charged against the older version of the *Ethics* in the preface he wrote in 1419 for his new translation.[43] Referring to the evidence of Aristotle's eloquence, upon which he would elaborate more fully in his *Life of Aristotle*, Bruni castigated the scholastic translator for causing the philosopher to appear to Romans in a guise so unlike the one in which the Greeks had known him.

[41] Actually, John of Salisbury's claim that he drew on Plutarch in the *Policraticus* was a fiction. See H. Liebeschütz, "John of Salisbury and Pseudo-Plutarch," *Journal of the Warburg and Courtauld Institutes*, VI (1943), 33-59.

[42] *Epistolario*, II, 481-83. For a discussion of these letters and of humanist translation in general, see Remigio Sabbadini, *Il Metodo degli Umanisti* (Florence, 1922), pp. 25ff. There is an interesting account of Poggio's method of translation in Ernst Walser, *Poggius Florentinus, Leben und Werke* (Leipzig, 1914), pp. 229-31.

[43] Bruni translated the *Ethics* in 1416-17, but the prefaces seem to have been written in March of 1419 or later (Baron, *Crisis*, II, 612). On the many questions about the authorship of the medieval versions of the *Ethics* and which of them Bruni referred to, see E. Francheschini, "Leonardo Bruni e il 'vetus interpres' dell' etica a Nicomaco," in *Medioevo e Rinascimento, studi in onore di Bruno Nardi* (Florence, 1955), and the literature cited there.

Bruni objected particularly to his predecessor's practice of leaving many philosophic terms in the original Greek, citing Cicero's treatises as evidence that Aristotelian philosophy could be discussed elegantly and accurately in Latin. He gave specific examples of terms which the earlier translator had misused, and he claimed that his own achievement was "to do this work into Latin for the first time, since it had not been before."[44]

Of course Bruni stated his claims in terms which emphasized his own knowledge of Greek. Yet Bruni's translation of Aristotle on the basis of his knowledge of Greek was not of an entirely different order from Salutati's rendering of Plutarch, despite Salutati's ignorance of the language. In Eugenio Garin's comparison of several humanistic versions of Aristotle with the medieval texts they were meant to replace, he concludes that, for all the humanists' insistence on their own originality, their new translations were generally mere revisions of the medieval ones. Bruni's work was typical. He seems to have had the version of his predecessor before him while working on the *Ethics*. He followed its structure faithfully, "limiting himself to certain formal embellishments and to certain variations—not always wholly happy—in terms." The result appears to be as much a systematic revision of the scholastic translation as a wholly new rendering, showing that Bruni had, in Professor Garin's words, a "strange way of conceiving of translation."[45] Such a conception was indeed strange for Bruni, who after all knew Greek. But what Professor Garin's study demonstrates is that Bruni's work as a translator followed lines marked out by Salutati. The revived knowledge of Greek was by no means the sole impulse for the human-

[44] *Schriften*, pp. 77-81. The letter is also printed by Birkenmajer in the study cited below, note 55.

[45] Garin, "Le traduzioni umanistiche di Aristotele . . . ," p. 65. Professor Garin's discussion of Bruni's version of the *Economics* should be revised in the light of the work of Baron and Soudek cited in note 3, above. These two writers successfully clear Bruni of the charge of dishonesty which has been leveled against him, but their conclusions do not substantially affect our view of what Garin calls Bruni's "curioso modo di intendere la traduzione."

ists' work as translators. Their procedures seem to have owed as much to their preconceptions as to their particular abilities.

Bruni's ideas about translation are usually traced to the man who taught him Greek, Manuel Chrysoloras.[46] Perhaps this Byzantine scholar did influence his student. He recommended that his pupils use their knowledge of Greek to translate Greek authors; in doing so they would follow the example of Cicero and other ancient Romans. He criticized the medieval translators for having worked *ad verbum*, "word for word"; this perverted the true meaning of the Greek. To preserve this meaning, translators should work *ad sententiam*, being careful that the overall meaning of a text was not lost through a too-fastidious attention to partial meanings.[47] Good as this advice was, however, it was hardly new to the members of Salutati's circle by the time Chrysoloras arrived in Florence. Salutati's suggestions to Loschi, offered five years before Chrysoloras appeared, al-already contained the substance of these ideas. Moreover, the Byzantine scholar seems actually to have approved of Salutati's revision of Plutarch, although it was done, of course, without any substantial knowledge of Greek.[48] Chrysoloras may well have been as good a teacher of Greek as his students declared, but there is little reason to conclude that his teaching produced any fundamental alteration in either the ideas or the methods of Salutati's circle in Florence. His influence on Bruni's view of the purpose of translation may have been simply to confirm the opinions Bruni had already absorbed from Salutati. Bruni's new versions of Aristotle carried on the work which Salutati and Loschi had begun with Plutarch and Homer. The aim of these two older men had been to find in classical authors what they expected to find there, regardless of the

[46] Cammelli, *I Dotti Bizantini e le origini dell' Umanesimo, I: Manuele Crisolora*, p. 91.

[47] This information about Chrysoloras' principles of translation is contained in a letter by his disciple, Cincius Romanus (Cencio de' Rustici), printed in Cammelli, pp. 90-91n.

[48] See the letter in *Epistolario*, IV, 341-44.

inadequacy of their own linguistic perception. It is more difficult to judge whether Bruni's purpose was the same, but we must at least listen to the voices of his critics, who thought that it was.

(4)

IN FACT, some of the most enlightening indications we possess about the relationship of the humanists to other participants in the intellectual life of their times come from the debates which broke out over the value of Bruni's new translations. Three of Bruni's critics are of interest to us. A fourth, the physician Ugo Benzi of Siena, has received greater attention than the other three from students of Renaissance culture. However, the point he raised was not as central to Bruni's effort as were the issues broached by the three lesser-known critics to whom we shall give our attention.[49] The earliest of these was a man of whom we know only his name, Demetrios. Even the letter he wrote to Bruni has not survived, so that we must infer his criticism from Bruni's reply to it. The main point of his objection seems to have been a simple and obvious one, namely that Bruni had been mistaken in his basic presupposition. Aristotle was not in fact an eloquent writer, Demetrios appears to have argued; indeed, he had not tried to be one. With what degree of sophistication Demetrios advanced this view, we shall probably never know. Nevertheless it is clear that he understood Bruni's purpose as a translator. Bruni replied with an argument he would later develop more fully in the *Life of Aristotle*: various kinds of evidence existed to demonstrate Aristotle's enthusiasm for eloquence. Given these indications, how are we to suppose that a man of Aristotle's genius did not succeed in attaining a pleasing and powerful style? Bruni assured his correspondent that, as far as his own powers could discern, no one could have written more sweetly, more fittingly, or

---

[49] On Ugo Benzi, see Dean P. Lockwood, *Ugo Benzi, Medieval Philosopher and Physician, 1376-1439* (Chicago, 1951). For Bruni's letter to Benzi, see Mehus, II, 3ff.

more richly about philosophical subjects than Aristotle had. The humanist added a warning to barbarians against trying to judge in matters of which they were ignorant and so the matter ended.[50]

We know more about the second of these critics, even though he was unknown to Bruni himself, for the very good reason that he wrote some forty years after the Florentine's death. He was a Dominican named Battista de' Giudici.[51] At the time Bruni's version of the *Ethics* came to his attention, he was archbishop of Ventimiglia. A student of theology, he admitted that he had never read Aristotle's *Ethics* until, finding himself with some leisure one summer, he decided to look at Bruni's translation. Having heard of Bruni and of his new version of Aristotle beforehand, he said that he was "led by the desire to see what a good rhetorician could conjure up in philosophy."[52] With this statement Battista revealed what place he thought Bruni occupied in the intellectual life of the time. Perhaps he also admitted to a prejudice against him. In any case, the Archbishop was not pleased with Leonardo's work. He found that Bruni's care for "pleasing words" had led him to err greatly, and to "depart from the truth of philosophy." Battista realized that many people regarded Bruni highly and thought "whatever he said was Gospel," but the Archbishop's own opinion was different; "Leonardo had enough of eloquence, but little of philosophy."[53] For this reason, Battista considered the older translator of Aristotle superior to the humanist. "More zealous for philosophical truth, he did not wish to speak so ornately, lest

---

[50] See Bruni's letter in Mehus, I, 137-40 (dated 1423/26? by Baron, *Schriften*, p. 207). On Demetrios, see p. 138 of Birkenmajer's study, cited in note 55.

[51] Martin Grabmann, "Eine ungedruckte Verteidigungsschrift der scholastischen Uebersetzung der Nikomachischen Ethik gegenüber dem Humanisten Leonard Bruni," *Mittelalterliches Geistesleben* (Munich, 1926), I, 440-48.

[52] *Ibid.*, p. 443n.: "ductus cupiditate videndi, quid rhetor bonus in philosophia divinare valuerit."

[53] *Ibid.*, p. 444n.: "Leonardum eloquentie quidem satis habuisse, philosophie parum."

122

he fall into the errors in which [Bruni] lapsed." One of the examples Battista gave may serve to illustrate what he meant. The older translator had properly written *nocivum*, harmful, for the opposite of *utile*, useful. Bruni, seeking harmony of language instead of precision of meaning, had replaced *novicum* with *inutile*, useless. In his search for ornament he had corrupted the sense.[54]

Though we cannot know for certain how Bruni would have replied to these criticisms, we can get quite a good idea from the answers he made to an earlier writer, Alonzo Garcia of Cartagena, who developed a similar line of argument much more fully.[55] Alonzo deserves a considerable

[54] *Ibid.*, p. 445 and note.

[55] Alonzo's treatise against Bruni has been printed, together with the longer of Bruni's two prefaces to the *Ethics* and with Bruni's replies to Alonzo, by Alexander Birkenmajer as appendices to his study, "Der Streit des Alonzo von Cartagena mit Leonardo Bruni Aretino," which is the fifth section of his *Vermischte Untersuchungen zur Geschichte der Mittelalterlichen Philosophie*, in *Beiträge zur Geschichte der Philosophie des Mittelalters*, XX, Part 5 (Münster, 1922), 129-210. Birkenmajer does not discuss the controversy in the terms used here. Paul O. Kristeller has called attention to a Vatican manuscript, Ottob. lat. 2054, which purports to be a Spanish translation of Bruni's Latin *Ethics* by Alonzo. If the Spaniard did make such a translation, then he must have changed his mind about the value of Leonardo's version. However, Ludwig Bertalot had previously examined this manuscript (which is practically illegible), and noted that the first few words of it do not correspond to the beginning of Aristotle's *Ethics*; he suggested that the Vatican manuscript might not contain the *Ethics* at all, but the medieval compendium of them found in Bk. VI of Brunetto Latini's *Tesoretto*. Thus this codex would seem to have nothing to do with Bruni, despite the rubric describing it as a Spanish rendering of his translation of the *Ethics*. (See Kristeller, "Un codice di Aristotele postillato da Francesco e Ermolao Barbaro. Il manoscritto Plimpton 17 della Columbia University Library a New York," *La Bibliofilia*, L [1948], 165n., and *Studies in Renaissance Thought and Letters*, p. 340n. Also, Bertalot, "Zur Bibliographie der Uebersetzungen . . . ," p. 185.) Professor Kristeller has kindly informed me of a second codex with a similar rubric, which identifies it as a vernacular translation of Bruni's Latin version of the *Ethics*. The first page of this manuscript was reproduced by Frances Spalding, *Mudejar Ornament in Manuscripts* (New York, 1953), figure 9; cf. p. 56, note 8. Since the publication of this book, however, the manuscript has become inaccessible. The first page of it contains a prologue which certainly does not correspond to the opening of the *Ethics*; however, we cannot exclude the possibility that the remaining pages—not now

amount of our attention. The son of a converted Jew who had become bishop of the Castillian See of Burgos, he studied at Burgos and at the University of Salamanca. He became a canon of Burgos Cathedral, and at the same time served as a diplomat for John II of Castille. In 1434 he was the Castillian king's representative at the Council of Basel. There he made a reputation as a speaker, impressing Aeneas Silvius Piccolomini (the future Pope Pius II) and other humanists with his learning and eloquence. He was appointed by Eugene IV to succeed his father as bishop of Burgos in 1435.[56]

Bruni's translation of the *Nicomachean Ethics* came to Alonzo's attention around 1430. Earlier the Spaniard had come across some of Bruni's versions of Greek oratory and patristic literature, and had been impressed by them. They caused him to "marvel at the eloquence of this age, in which these most polished orators vie with each other," and particularly to admire Bruni. Bruni's stylistic excellence was such, Alonzo said, that "I should call him in a certain sense a new Cicero."[57] But Bruni's version of the *Ethics* produced a different reaction. Alonzo recognized that Bruni's eloquence was still present, but he questioned the way in which it was used. The Florentine's unrestrained scorn for the earlier translator troubled him. Bruni had not described the older version as in need of revision, but rather as totally without value. Alonzo did not want to attack Bruni, he said, but to defend the scholastic translator against the humanist's slights.[58]

---

available to scholars—may actually contain what the rubric claims they do. Thus the question of whether Alonzo changed his mind about the value of Bruni's translation must remain open. To the present writer it does not seem likely that Alonzo had a change of heart, but the possibility should not be completely dismissed. Alonzo admired Bruni's style in his translations of Greek oratory. (See text.)

[56] On Alonzo's life, see Birkenmajer, pp. 130ff. The conversion of Alonzo's father was known to Marsilio Ficino. See Ficino, *De christ. relig.*, in *Opera* (Basel, 1576; reissued Turin, 1959), p. 39: "Alfonsus Burgensis summus metaphysicus in sexagesimo aetatis suae anno fidem Christi suscepit, pluraque adversus Iudaeos egregia scripsit."

[57] Birkenmajer, p. 164.   [58] *Ibid.*, pp. 164-65.

Alonzo lacked one qualification which may seem absolutely essential for the judge of a translation of Aristotle: he did not know Greek. He attempted to make up for this by raising questions which did not concern the accuracy of Bruni's rendering of the text, but rather the suitability of the new version as a work of philosophy. "Let us investigate whether what is written in Latin has the proper sense, and supports and agrees with the things themselves, not whether it harmonizes with the Greek." This procedure could claim to be a valid way of judging a translation of Aristotle, Alonzo believed, because the philosopher had based his treatment on "reason," which is common to all men despite their differences of language. "Since therefore Aristotle himself did not attain to reason on account of authority, but to authority on account of reason, whatever accords with reason should be thought to be what Aristotle said, and we should judge to have been written in the Greek whatever our translation [i.e., the old one] wisely expresses in Latin words."[59] Alonzo's argument may seem odd to a modern reader, but his faith in Aristotle's "reason" was hardly more abstract than Bruni's conviction that Aristotle was "eloquent."

Alonzo raised several questions along the way which we cannot pause to examine. He questioned (incorrectly) Bruni's assertion that the author of the old version had been a Franciscan (in fact the author was Robert Grosseteste). He denied that the old translator should be accused of obscurity, since texts ought to be concise. It was the task of commentators to expand at length on the sense of the text.[60] Bruni's objection to the inclusion of Greek words was also unjustified: many terms had come into Latin from Greek, as well as from the vernacular languages. "What therefore is unfitting about our translator's having left some words

[59] *Ibid.*, p. 166: "Cum igitur Aristoteles ipse non rationem ab auctoritate, sed auctoritatem a ratione consecutus est, quicquid rationi consonat, haec Aristoteles dixisse putandus est et Graece arbitremur scriptum fuisse, quicquid Latinis verbis translatio nostra sapienter depromit."

[60] *Ibid.*, pp. 166-67.

in their Greek form, especially in those places where their meaning could not be expressed with equal brevity in any other way?"[61] Moreover, the Latin equivalents that Bruni had proposed for some of Aristotle's Greek terms were unsuitable because they carried contemporary overtones which distorted the Peripatetic teaching. In praising the earlier translator for avoiding the errors into which Bruni fell, Alonzo announced one of his basic principles: "In philosophy words ought not to be allowed to run loose without restraint, since out of the improper use of words errors of substance gradually grow up."[62]

A similar concern with maintaining philosophic rigor animated much of Alonzo's criticism of Bruni. What he called the "weightier matters" (*graviora*) at issue derived from Bruni's assertion that one should always follow the "approved language" of Cicero and other respected authors, and that the scholastic translator had erred in not doing so. Alonzo replied to this by introducing a distinction between Cicero as an orator and Cicero as a philosopher. In eloquence, he said, everyone acknowledged Cicero's preeminence among the Romans, and even his superiority to the Greek orator Demosthenes. In moral philosophy, however, in defining the virtues and distinguishing them one from another, Cicero did not occupy the same high place. His discussions of these things were elegant enough, but they did not equal Aristotle's in insight. Either Cicero had never really read Aristotle's *Ethics*, Alonzo speculated, or else his purpose had been simply to speak elegantly about some matters of moral philosophy, while leaving the true philosophic study of the virtues and vices to others.[63] The same might be said of Seneca. He succeeded very well in encouraging men to be virtuous, even

---

[61] *Ibid.*, p. 169.

[62] *Ibid.*, p. 170: "Nec enim in philosophia verba sine freno laxanda sunt, cum ex improprietate verborum error ad ipsas res paulatim accrescat."

[63] *Ibid.*, pp. 172-74. Petrarch had made a somewhat similar remark about Cicero. See *On His Own Ignorance*, p. 103.

in a Christian sense, but his inquiry into the nature of the virtues was summary and inadequate.[64]

Thus the main thrust of Alonzo's assault on Bruni as a translator of Aristotle was that orators should not mix in philosophy. Cicero himself, Alonzo believed, while properly claiming the art of oratory as his own, had admitted that ethics was a higher pursuit and had left it to others. Other orators should do the same; otherwise philosophy would be corrupted by them.

Whoever would subject the highly rigorous conclusions of the sciences to the rules of eloquence does not understand that although to add and subtract words is suitable for obtaining the sweetness of persuasive speech, it is unfit for the severity of scientific knowledge. Whoever endeavors to place science under the domination of eloquence necessarily opens the way therefore for many errors. But I judge it proper for the man of wisdom to conduct an inquiry with words that are precise and used in their most proper sense; these are the terms of science. Afterwards, in urging shining examples and pure teachings, he may exclaim in eloquent language. Our translation ought not to be attacked for not having harmonized with the word usage even of the best authors; instead it should be examined to see whether it complies with the truth of the matter, and the strict propriety of language. For often if elegance of language is not guided by strict judgment, it confuses the truth of the matter, and confounds proper scientific comprehension exceedingly.[65]

[64] Birkenmajer, pp. 174-75.

[65] *Ibid.*, p. 175: "Crede enim mihi: qui scientiarum districtissimas conclusiones eloquentiae regulis subdere vult, non sapit, cum verba addere ac detrahere ad persuasionis dulcedinem pertinet, quod scientiae rigor abhorret. Multis ergo erroribus pateat oportet, qui scientiam sub eloquentia tradere nititur; sed sapienti viro illud congruum iudico sub restrictis et proprissimis verbis, quae scientifica sunt, discutere, post vero ad elimata documenta et purificatas doctrinas persuadendo verbis eloquentibus acclamare. Non ergo ex eo translatio nostra mordenda est, quod oratorum etiam summorum usitatis verbis discordet,

Alonzo gave several examples of words which Bruni, basing himself on Cicero, had used in place of those the earlier translator had chosen. In every case, the Bishop asserted, the scholastic translator had chosen better than Bruni, and had avoided some error or pitfall into which Bruni and his readers would fall. Thus he had used *delectatio* instead of *voluptas* because the first was the more general term and could be applied in either a spiritual or a material sense without allowing the discussion to be inconvenienced by the overtones of *voluptas.* Similarly, the older version had made the proper use of *tristitia* and *dolor,* indicating that it was sadness and not pain which moral virtue should try to restrain. Finally, while Bruni's concern for linguistic harmony had led him to insist that the opposite of virtue was always vice (*vitium*), the other translator had shown wisdom and foresight in sometimes rendering it as evil (*malitia*). The reason for this was that the term "vicious" should be reserved for actions which were intentional departures from virtue. Other kinds of nonvirtuous actions, committed out of ignorance or impotence, should be clearly labeled as evil, but they should not be confused with truly vicious actions. Alonzo was concerned with preserving these philosophic distinctions, which Bruni had obscured.[66]

Bruni replied to Alonzo's criticism in two letters to Francesco Pizolpasso, the archbishop of Milan (Alonzo's treatise had also been addressed to Pizolpasso, who was a prominent patron of learning).[67] He also wrote a short note to Alonzo himself, assuring the Spaniard that he harbored no ill will against him. Of course Bruni seized on Alonzo's ignorance of Greek for his first line of attack. The question, he observed, was one of translation, not of divination.

---

sed in hoc examinanda est, an simplicitatem rerum et restrictam proprietatem verborum observet. Saepe enim elegantia sermonum, si non stricto iudicio dirigitur, simplicitatem rerum confundit, quod maxime rectum scientiae intellectum perturbat."

[66] *Ibid.,* pp. 182-85. For Cicero's discussion of *vitium* and *malitia,* on which Bruni based his usage, see *Tusc. Disp.* IV, xv, 34.

[67] On Pizolpasso, see Angelo Paredi, *La biblioteca del Pizolpasso* (Milan, 1961), and Riccardo Fubini, "Tra Umanesimo e Concili," *Studi Medievali,* 3rd series, VII (1966), 323-70.

Alonzo seemed to want to engage in the second. Or else he wanted to argue about what Aristotle should have said rather than what he did say.[68] One who was ignorant of Greek could not question the actual meaning of Greek words or the appropriateness of Latin equivalents for them. In Bruni's view there were only two ways to talk about the meanings of words: through etymological analysis, or by reference to the usage of trustworthy authors. Alonzo could do neither with Greek words.[69]

Bruni did not stop with his comments on Alonzo's ignorance of Greek. He also insisted that no Latin words should be used unless they have been "tested and recommended by the best authors." The vocabulary of the older translator showed that he "snatches at random at whatever is offered."[70] In connection with this, Bruni included in his answer to Alonzo the reply he had made to the contention of Ugo Benzi of Siena that Leonardo's substitution of the Ciceronian phrase *summum bonum* for the scholastic *bonum per se* was incorrect. Alonzo had not raised this point, but the premise on which Bruni based his defense was the one that the Spaniard had attacked, namely that all usage should be based on "the best authors."[71] Bruni re-

---

[68] Birkenmajer, pp. 189-94. "[Alonzo] putat eum, qui libros Aristotelis de Graeco in Latinum transfert, non ad verba Aristotelis respicere debere nec quid dicat Aristoteles, sed quid dicere debeat in Latinum transferre" (p. 194). Bruni was referring here to Alonzo's assertion that one could always assume that Aristotle's language corresponded to "reason"; he was not, as some scholars have supposed, claiming that Alonzo in his treatise was concerned to link Aristotelianism and Christianity. Cf. G. Voigt, *Die Wiederbelebung* (1893), II, 170, and A. Buck in *Bibliothèque d'Humanisme et Renaissance*, XXI, 278. Recently the same view of Alonzo's purpose has been more subtly and interestingly stated by Riccardo Fubini, "Tra Umanesimo e Concili," pp. 337-40 (esp. 339). However, such an interpretation does not seem to be supported by Alonzo's treatise. It is true, as Fubini points out (p. 340), that in his reply Bruni did not explicitly take up the question of the relationship between rhetoric and philosophy, but other of his remarks show that this question was central to his own new view of Aristotle. See, for example, notes 36 and 37 above.

[69] Birkenmajer, p. 202.

[70] *Ibid.*, p. 191.

[71] *Ibid.*, pp. 189, 204-05. Among the modern writers who accept

fused to consider whether the kind of analysis of logical and linguistic distinctions practiced by Alonzo (and other philosophers) might constitute another valid way of thinking about the meanings of words. Nor did he discuss the question of whether the usage proper to oratory might differ from that of philosophy. Alonzo offered Bruni an excellent chance to deny that his purpose was to subordinate the search for wisdom to the pursuit of eloquence, but Bruni did not take it.

This debate between Alonzo of Cartagena and Leonardo Bruni on the proper way to translate Aristotle is a revealing episode in the history of humanism in the early fifteenth century. It shows how closely the dispute between humanism and scholasticism was linked to the question of the correct relationship between rhetoric and philosophy. The subject of the dispute between the bishop of Burgos and the chancellor of Florence was not merely the relative merit of two translations of Aristotle. On a deeper level, the questions at issue were the nature of moral philosophy and the proper standards for philosophic discourse. The answers given depended on what each man thought the proper relation of rhetoric to moral philosophy to be. Both men claimed to understand the linguistic standard which Aristotle—as an exemplar of the best kind of philosophy—employed. For Alonzo this standard derived from "reason." For Bruni it reflected Aristotle's supposed sympathy for literary and rhetorical culture and his involvement in the pursuit of eloquence. For the defender of the scholastics, the terms of philosophy had to meet certain standards of precision. For the humanist, they had to bear the pedigree of a literary tradition which had not been formed in the philosophic schools.

It should be noted that both men accepted some form of the ideal of a combination of rhetoric and philosophy; they disagreed about the point at which rhetoric should enter

Bruni's attribution of this argument to Alonzo is Giuseppe Saitta, *Il Pensiero Italiano nell' Umanesimo e nel Rinascimento* (Bologna, 1949), I, 172ff.

into the union. Alonzo stated that eloquent speech might be used to incite men to virtue, but only after the philosophic inquiry into the nature of virtue had been completed. To allow the orator his methods at the start opened the door to imprecision and error.[72] Bruni, on the other hand, thought that philosophy should be clothed in the language of rhetoric during the process of inquiry as well as at the moment of presentation. The proper style for any treatise in moral philosophy was the style of Cicero. To understand Bruni's attitude we must remember Cicero's declaration that practical philosophy, the part which pertains to *vitam et mores*, was the province of the orator. Bruni could not accept Alonzo's distinction between Cicero as orator and Cicero as philosopher in this context. The question between the two men was whether the orator, as orator and without departing from the standards of rhetoric, could be a philosopher too. Aristotle was the occasion for the dispute rather than its subject. He served as a symbol of philosophy, and each of the contestants tried to claim him for his own side. To Alonzo, Bruni's treatment of Aristotle represented the subjugation of philosophy to rhetoric. To Leonardo, the Bishop's view of Aristotle left philosophy stumbling in ignorance of the orator's literary art.

Unfortunately the present writer cannot claim to judge which of the two translations is the better one. To do so would require a good knowledge of Greek, in order to collate the two versions fully with the Greek text. No modern scholar has undertaken this task in full; it is to be hoped that someone will. The few partial attempts which have been made have not yielded results favorable to Bruni.[73]

[72] Cf. above, p. 127.

[73] The negative judgment of Susemihl is accepted by Beck, *Studien zu Leonardo Bruni*, p. 37, and by Martin Grabmann, *op.cit.* The most extensive comparison is that made by S. Troilo, "Due traduttori dell' Etica Nichomachea: Roberto di Lincoln e Leonardo Bruni," *Atti del R. Istituto Veneto di Scienze, Lettere, Arti*, XCI (1932). Troilo seems to share Alonzo of Cartagena's opinion in all respects, concluding that Grosseteste's version was far more faithful to the rigorous and scientific spirit of Aristotle than was Bruni's: "Barbara e ispida parve all' eleganza umanistica la traduzione medievale; ma è

Even so sympathetic a student of early Quattrocento humanism as Eugenio Garin has, as we mentioned earlier, referred to Bruni's "strange way of conceiving of translation."[74] Professor Kristeller emphasizes the improvement Bruni and other humanists made in syntax and in the rendering of idioms, but he describes their changes of terminology as "a serious matter in an author who served as a standard text in philosophy."[75] Such a judgment is moderate, and is probably as accurate a one as we are likely to have. An objective and definitive assessment of whether Bruni's translation is better or worse than the scholastic one may not even be possible, given the continuing relevance of the issues which divided him from his predecessor. It is well to remember, however, that even if Bruni's version was flawed, he inspired other fifteenth-century efforts which may have been better. The best use we can make of the controversy between Bruni and Alonzo of Cartagena in the present context is to offer it as an illustration of the different views of moral philosophy represented by these two men.

It is possible to say something about the respective views that these men held of Aristotle as a moral philosopher. Here there seems to have been a measure of reason on both

---

grande ventura se Aristotele, il tecnico e rigoroso e quasi matematico pensatore, fu ripensato e studiato prima e più dal Medio Evo che dall' Umanesimo: al quale molto celò e falsò del Filosofo antico il considerarlo sopra tutto sotto l'aspetto formale di maestro d'eloquenza" (p. 282).

[74] Garin, "Le traduzioni umanistiche di Aristotele . . . ," p. 65. Professor Garin offered a different judgment in *L'Educazione in Europa, 1400-1600* (Bari, 1957), p. 101n. There he argued that the technical fidelity of Bruni's translations was not the important question about them. "The point is not to make a mechanical calculation, but to understand what a term means in a context, in a certain time, in a certain moment of the mental development of an author. . . ." This is all very well, but it attributes much more sophistication to Bruni than he demonstrates, and ignores completely the propaganda for rhetoric and oratory which played so large a part in Bruni's Aristotelianism. I have found no basis for believing that Bruni thought in terms of Aristotle's "mental development," save in the sense indicated above.

[75] Kristeller, *Renaissance Thought* (New York, 1961) p. 39.

sides. Alonzo's picture of Aristotle may have been excessively abstract, and he was certainly less conscious than Bruni of the distance between the Stagirite's world and the Middle Ages. On the other hand, the Spaniard seems to have reflected the Aristotelian position on the relationship between rhetoric and philosophy more accurately than Bruni did. Like Aristotle, Alonzo attributed a definite value to eloquence, and saw that it had a certain connection with philosophy. Like him also, however, he insisted that both the value and the connection had clear limits. Alonzo's declaration that oratory and philosophy were separate enterprises and should be kept separate was faithful to Aristotle's *Rhetoric*, as were his strictures on rhetoricians who attempted to expand the scope of their techniques and activities outside their proper field.[76] Of the two contrasting interpretations of the combination of rhetoric and philosophy, the one offered by Alonzo of Cartagena was closer to Aristotle than Leonardo Bruni's was. This conclusion may perhaps help us to account for the strange circumstance that, though he often spoke about Aristotle's interest in oratory, Bruni preferred to translate the *Ethics* and the *Politics*, rather than to make the philosopher's *Rhetoric* available to the men of his time.

(5)

SCHOLASTIC writers might attack Bruni, but his new translations drew strong praise from other humanists. Moreover, his views about Aristotle were echoed and even amplified by his colleagues. Some of their comments should be noted before we conclude our discussion of Bruni's new image of Aristotle.

The first such comment was from the pen of Francesco Filelfo, the stormy opponent of the Medici who, before his exile in 1434, knew Bruni in Florence. In *De laudibus eloquentiae* (*In Praise of Eloquence*), an oration delivered in 1429 (probably the year in which Bruni wrote his *Life of Aristotle*), Filelfo elaborated on the theme of Aristotle's

---

[76] See Aristotle, *Rhetoric* I, 4, 1359[b].

"conversion" to eloquence. Like other humanists, Filelfo drew this idea from Cicero, who told how Aristotle had been led to join rhetoric to his teaching of philosophy because of the fame of the rhetorician Isocrates. But Filelfo developed the theme further than Cicero, Petrarch, or Bruni had. He greatly exaggerated Aristotle's plight in the period before he began to pay attention to his style. There was no evidence to support Filelfo's claim that Aristotle "was regarded as uncultured and boorish by everyone, and was even nearly deserted by his own followers" in the period when he taught only philosophy. Moreover, Filelfo asserted that when Aristotle learned that all his students had gone to Isocrates, "who was most elegant in writing and speaking," he then devoted himself "no less to the study of oratory for the rest of his life than he had to philosophy before, thus making himself not only useful to his hearers, but pleasing and entertaining to everyone." In Filelfo's view, therefore, Aristotle had turned from philosophy to rhetoric because he found that philosophy by itself made him unpopular as a teacher.[77] Petrarch and Bruni had taken this same passage in Cicero to mean that Aristotle had joined rhetoric to philosophy, while Filelfo seized on it as an indication that he had deserted the second for the first. This went well beyond Bruni's position, but Filelfo was not known for his moderation.

The same may be said of the second writer who made use of this theme, the Greek émigré George of Trebisond, also known as Trapezuntius. After having studied with Guarino and Vittorino da Feltre, Trapezuntius taught in Florence for a short time in 1442. He seems to have written his *Rhetoric* in 1436 or 1437, though he made a formal presentation

[77] In *Reden und Briefe Italienischer Humanisten*, ed. Muellner, pp. 153-54: "cum itaque ipse Aristoteles minus exculta in docendo, minus elimata minusque auditoribus grata dictione uteretur, non solum et ipse incultus est et ineptus existimatus ab omnibus, quin imo et a suis ipsis cunctis propemodum desertus. quoscum ad Isocratem rhetorem, qui et dicendo et scribendo esset ornatissimus, confluxisse intueretur, illico non minus studii oratione in omnem deinde vitam, quam antea philosophiae consuerat, accomodavit effecitque, ut non utilis solum auditoribus, sed et gratus omnibus ac iocundus esset."

of the work to the city of Venice in 1472.[78] In this work he cited Aristotle in support of his assertion that all the great philosophers of the past had been men of eloquence, and therefore very far removed from the scholastics who neglected rhetoric. Everyone knew that Socrates, Plato, the Stoics, and the Academics had all excelled in eloquence, Trapezuntius said. He gave his main attention, however, to Aristotle, since it was to him that contemporary philosophers looked as their guide and teacher. Did he despise eloquence? No one had spoken more elegantly, more clearly, more rhythmically; moreover, the Greek said (echoing Bruni), Aristotle had sought to teach rhetoric to others, and had left to posterity more of rhetorical ornament than had many men who were professed orators. "Therefore one should sooner take philosophy from him than not concede eloquence to him." In the mornings Aristotle had taught natural philosophy, but in the afternoon, "much the greater part of the day," he had given instruction in the art of oratory and the precepts of eloquence.[79]

Like Filelfo, Trapezuntius carried the transformation of the Philosopher into a rhetorician significantly further than Bruni had. Alonzo of Cartagena's accusation that the humanist purpose was to subordinate philosophy to oratory is much more easily brought against these two men than

---

[78] On Trapezuntius, see Giorgio Castellani, "Giorgio da Trebisonda, Maestro di Eloquenza a Vicenza e a Venezia," *Nuovo Archivio Veneto,* XI (1896), 123-42. Also R. Sabbadini, in *Giornale Storico della Letteratura Italiana,* XVIII (1891), 230ff., and XLIII (1904), 244ff. For the content of his *Rhetoric,* see Ciro Trabalza, *La Critica Letteraria* (Milan, 1915), pp. 11ff.

[79] *Rhetoricorum libri quinque* (Lugduni, 1547), pp. 373-74: "Quid ergo is philosophiae caput, et oculus, eloquentiae praecepta contemnit? At nemo, iudicio meo, ornatius, nemo distinctius, nemo numerosius simul et gravius locutus est: adeo ut si quis deum fingat humana oratione uti, non praestantiore, neque elegantiore dicendi forma eum uti, contendere ausim, qui non se solum, sed nos quoque docere cupiens, plura huius artis ornamenta reliquit, quam hi qui sese rhetores profitebantur. Itaque citius quis philosophiam ei ademerit, quam eloquentiam non concesserit. Fertur enim in Lycio ante prandium quidem ea deambulando secreta naturae explicasse, quae ipse *acroamatica* [in Greek in text] nuncupabat, post prandium maiore medius fidius diei parte, oratorias artes, elocutionisque praecepta tradidisse."

against Bruni. Bruni's declared goal had been the combination of rhetoric and philosophy, not the subjection of one to the other, and he often insisted on the independent place he reserved for philosophy in the union. Yet it is clear that Bruni sought to combine the two arts in a way which differed from that proposed by Petrarch and Salutati. As Bruni conceived of this union, philosophy did not play the same role within it; the search for wisdom did not make moral and intellectual claims which required that the pursuit of eloquence be regarded at times with suspicion and hostility. In other words, the ideal of the mixture of philosophy and oratory as Bruni worked it out was clearly the property of the orator. If Aristotle was the kind of thinker Bruni described him to be, then the philosophy which derived from him would not try to lord it over rhetoric in the way Salutati, in the last years of his life, had suggested it might. Bruni's reform of Aristotle was one way of shielding the rhetorical culture of humanism from possible attacks in the name of philosophy. It was not the only way, however. A different and more radical path was to be chosen by Lorenzo Valla.

When Bruni died in 1444 he received an elaborate funeral, and he was honored by a remarkable marble tomb in the Franciscan church of Santa Croce. According to the inscription, his passing from life caused history to grieve and eloquence to be silent, while none of the Latin or Greek muses could hold back their tears. This monument is testimony to the respect with which his contemporaries regarded Bruni, but it is noteworthy that philosophy was not listed among the mourners.

CHAPTER V

LORENZO VALLA
AND THE SUBORDINATION OF
PHILOSOPHY TO RHETORIC

colourful
individual
as well as
humanist

(1)

OF ALL the humanists who lived and wrote in the first half of the fifteenth century, Lorenzo Valla is probably the most celebrated. Talented, colorful, restless, a disdainful opponent of the temporal claims of the papacy and an acid critic of the pretensions of his own and past ages, Valla typifies the spirit of free inquiry and spiritual independence which many students find to be the essential quality of the Italian Renaissance. It was Valla who carried the humanist cultivation of *litterae* furthest, and who built, through his enthusiasm for linguistic study, the foundations of philology and historical criticism. His *Elegantiae linguae latinae* was the product of an intense and detailed study of the Latin language and its literature. Reprinted many times, this work provided a storehouse of material for later writers. The same intimate knowledge of Latin usage which filled the *Elegantiae* made possible the most important features of Valla's famous attack on the supposed Donation of Constantine. The authenticity of this best known of medieval forgeries had been denied before, but never on grounds like these, which—as modern scholars were later to recognize—established basic principles of textual criticism. Armed with an excellent knowledge of Greek, Valla also became the first of the humanists to bring the techniques of grammatical analysis to bear on the interpretation of scripture. In his *Notes on the New Testament* he criticized many of the Latin renderings of the Vulgate and suggested better ones, a procedure which was to be of great moment in the sixteenth century. Valla would become Erasmus' guide in both secular philology and textual criticism of scripture.[1]

Students of the Renaissance have differed in their accounts of what underlying purposes gave unity to Valla's

[1] On Valla's life, see L. Barozzi and R. Sabbadini, *Studi sul Panormita e sul Valla* (Florence, 1891); G. Mancini, *Vita di Lorenzo Valla* (Florence, 1891); M. von Wolff, *Lorenzo Valla, sein Leben und seine Werke* (Leipzig, 1893). On Valla's thought, see the perceptive discussion by Hanna H. Gray, "Valla's *Encomium of St. Thomas Aquinas* and the Humanist Conception of Christian Antiquity," in *Essays in History and Literature . . . Presented to Stanley Pargellis*, ed. Heinz Bluhm (Chicago, 1965), pp. 37-52, which anticipates some of the conclusions of the present chapter. Also, see Franco Gaeta, *Lorenzo Valla, Filologia e Storia nell' Umanesimo Italiano* (Naples, 1955); Giorgio Radetti, "Introduzione" to his edition, in Italian, of a number of Valla's works: Lorenzo Valla, *Scritti Filosofici e Religiosi* (Florence, 1953), pp. vii-xxxvii; Charles Trinkaus, Introduction to Valla's *Dialogue on Free Will*, in *The Renaissance Philosophy of Man*, ed. E. Cassirer, P. O. Kristeller, and J. H. Randall (Chicago, 1948), pp. 147-54; J. Freudenthal, "L. Valla als Philosoph," *Neue Jahrbücher für das Klass. Altertum*, XXIII (1909); also F. Adorno, "Di alcune orazioni e prefazioni di Lorenzo Valla," *Rinascimento*, V (1954); G. Radetti, "Nota bibliografica sulla filosofia del Valla," *Archivio di Filosofia* (1949), pp. 127-35. For Valla's influence on Erasmus, see E. H. Harbison, *The Christian Scholar in the Age of the Reformation* (New York, 1956), esp. pp. 43-49. For additional bibliography, see the notes to Hanna H. Gray's study, cited above. The only modern edition of several of Valla's major works is the Italian translation by Radetti noted above, cited hereafter as *Scritti*. The sixteenth-century edition of Valla's *Opera* (Basel, 1540), has been reissued by a photographic process, with a foreword by Eugenio Garin, in the series *Monumenta Politica et Philosophica Rariora* (Turin, 1962). The editors have collected the following works, not printed in the Basel *Opera*, as the second volume of this edition: *De rebus a Ferdinando Hispaniarum rege et maioribus eius gestis* (Paris, 1528); *Sermo de mysterio Eucharistiae* (Florence, 1479); *Opuscula quaedam* (Venice, 1503); *Opuscula tria*, ed. J. Vahlen, originally published in *Sitzungsberichte der Akademie der Wissenschaften, Hist.-phil. Classe*, LXI-LXII (1869); *Encomium Sancti Thomae Aquinatis*, originally ed. J. Vahlen in *Vierteljahrsschrift für Kultur und Literatur der Renaissance*, I (Leipzig, 1886); R. Sabbadini, *Cronologia documentata della Vita di Lorenzo Della Valle, detto il Valla*, in the above-cited L. Barozzi and R. Sabbadini, *Studi sul Panormita e sul Valla*; G. Mancini, "Alcune lettere di Lorenzo Valla," *Giornale Storico della Letteratura Italiana*, XXI (1893), with some omissions; and also one minor oration, three additional letters, and a poem. References below are to Vol. I of the Turin *Opera* (or to the one-volume Basel *Opera*) unless otherwise indicated.

many activities, but his own declarations were not at all ambiguous. The foundation of his career as a thinker and writer was rhetoric. "My resolve," he declared in a letter to Pope Eugene IV in 1434, "has always been to please God and help men through the study of oratory."[2] In Valla's view, the philological erudition of the *Elegantiae* provided support for rhetorical culture. "I proceed thus," he wrote at one point, "so as to exhibit the defense of eloquence against those who accuse her falsely, which is my larger purpose. Now I am not writing of that, but of the elegances of the Latin language, from which, however, an approach is made to eloquence itself."[3] It was rhetoric, more than grammar, which set Valla's standards of linguistic usage. When the grammarian Priscian erred at one point, Valla said he had faltered because he was "not practiced enough in the oratorical style."[4] Lorenzo was a historian as well as a grammarian, but he described oratory as the mother of history.[5] The revival of ancient learning was also

[2] Mancini, "Alcune lettere di Lorenzo Valla," p. 30 (omitted from the Turin *Opera*): "Ego quidem beatissime Pater, ab ineunte aetate cum ceteris liberalibus disciplinis, tum maxime oratoriae studui, quam ita me adamasse et ita complexum esse toto pectore confiteor, ut hac tempestate pauci vehementius; non ea caussa, qua multi solent, ut illam haberem aut jactantiae sociam, aut avaritiae ministram, aut peccatorum adjutricem. Longe enim ii homines absunt ab officio ac munere oratoris, si quidem orator est vir bonus dicendi peritus; sed is mihi semper animus fuit ut oratoriis studiis Deo placerem hominibusque prodessem."

[3] *Elegantiae linguae latinae*, IV, preface; *Opera*, p. 120: "Et ego sic ago, tanquam eloquentiae contra calumniantes patrocinium praestem, quod est maius proposito meo. Non enim de hac, sed de elegantia linguae Latinae scribimus, ex qua tamen gradus fit ad ipsam eloquentiam."

[4] *Elegantiae*, II, i; *Opera*, p. 43: "Et licet non pauca in hanc rem mihi dicenda sint, non prosequar tamen parvula et minuta quaedam, et tot verbis, quot ille fecit, sed quae eruditissimis evadere volentibus, sint gratissima: quae quum ignota fuerint Prisciano, declarant eum non satis stylo oratorio fuisse exercitatum."

[5] *De rebus a Ferdinando Aragoniae rege gestis libri tres* (Rome, 1520), preface, f. a^iii; *Opera*, II, 5: ". . . conditores oratoriae artis, quae historiae mater est." The central importance of rhetorical ideals and procedures in Valla's historical work emerges clearly from the discussion in Gaeta, *Lorenzo Valla*, pp. 169-92, despite the author's reluctance to admit it. It is true that Valla's account of the deeds of

Value of
eloquence

VALLA & THE SUBORDINATION

closely tied up with the pursuit of eloquence. In criticizing
the writings of members of the religious orders, Valla said
he would prefer "that they were composed more learnedly,
in the manner of orators rather than in that of philosophers, as the ancients used to do."[6] Not only had the
ancients written as orators; those who studied them were
orators too. Noting that St. Thomas Aquinas was said to have
never encountered a book which he could not understand
with ease, Valla commented, "I don't know if this has ever
happened in our day, whether to any jurist in the study of
civil law, or to any physician in medicine, or any philosopher in philosophy, or to any orator in the study of antiquity."[7] Thus all of Valla's own major interests were clearly
linked in his own mind to rhetoric. No bond could have
been more exalted, since eloquence was "the queen of truth
and perfect wisdom."[8]

Valla's various comments praising oratory, especially those
in which he compared it with philosophy, are much less moderate and restrained than the statements of the other humanists we have discussed here. Several considerations may help
to account for this. First, Valla was the most precocious of
the humanists, and his writings are full of youthful vigor,
not to say impertinence. Born in 1407, he was clearly of a
younger generation than Bruni and Poggio (who were
born in 1374 and 1380, respectively), even though he pub-

Ferdinand of Aragon included some realistic touches which displeased
other humanists—see Felix Gilbert, *Machiavelli and Guicciardini*
(Princeton, 1965), p. 217—but these did not clash with Valla's own
understanding of the intellectual standards of the orator. See the discussion of *On the True Good*, below.

[6] *Opuscula tria*, ed. Vahlen, in *Opera*, II, 321: "Fratres . . . ad
mores, ad virtutes, ad sanctitatem pertinentia multa componunt, mallem tamen eruditius magisque ad oratorum quam ad philosophorum
consuetudinem, quod prisci factitaverunt."

[7] *Ibid.*, pp. 349-50: "Eum omnino nullum legisse librum, quem non
plane intellexerit, quod haud scio an nulli nostri temporis contigerit,
vel iuris perito in iure civili, vel medico in medicina, vel philosopho
in philosophia, vel oratori in antiquarum rerum lectione. . . ." (Also
in *Scritti*, pp. 464-65.)

[8] *Elegantiae*, IV, preface; *Opera*, p. 120: "Vides quam mirabili
ornamento vestes Aaron distinguantur, quam arca foederis, quam
templum Salamonis, per hoc mihi significari eloquentia videtur, quae
(ut ait nobilis tragicus) regina rerum est, et perfecta sapientia."

lished his treatises in the same years their works appeared and was in fact outlived by Poggio. Bruni had been educated in the *studia humanitatis* under the moderating influence of Salutati, and he was probably restrained by the memory of the old Chancellor even while he rebelled against some of his procedures. Yet it is unlikely that Bruni, who was one of Valla's teachers, passed on to him any of the suspicion of rhetoric which Salutati had sometimes felt. Beyond this, something in Valla's character caused him to inject a note of polemic into practically everything he wrote.[9] He was the most argumentative and uncompromising of the humanists. Thus his comments on philosophy, while they remind us of certain remarks of Bruni, are much more consistent and determined in their hostility than Bruni's had been. In his *Dialogue on Free Will* Valla said that Boethius erred and departed from the Pauline position because "he was too ardent an admirer of philosophy." Valla declared that "no such ardent admirer of philosophy can please God."[10] In another work he denounced the pride of religious orders, whose members appropriated the name "religious" for themselves; this reminded him of the practice of philosophers "who restrict to themselves the name of friends of wisdom," without conceding it to legislators, statesmen, orators, and kings "whose wisdom governed states before philosophers rose up, and after their appearance as well."[11] The claim of Aristotle and others that the life of contemplation rendered man similar to God was, Valla several times asserted, only an attempt on the philosophers' part to glorify their own activity.[12] Thus Valla's opposition to philosophy and philosophers

[9] A number of writers have remarked on the polemical quality of Valla's writings. See G. Saitta, *Il pensiero italiano nel' umanesimo e nel rinascimento* (Bologna, 1949), I, 209; also E. Garin, *L'Umanesimo Italiano* (Bari, 1958), p. 59, where Valla is called "sempre crudelmente polemico"; Hanna H. Gray, "Valla's Encomium . . . ," p. 38.

[10] *Dialogue on Free Will*, trans. Trinkaus, in *The Renaissance Philosophy of Man*, p. 179.

[11] *Dialogo intorno alla professione dei religiosi, Scritti*, p. 387. Cf. Quintilian, *Institutiones Oratoriae*, I, preface, 14.

[12] *On the True Good, Scritti*, pp. 140-45. Also, *Dialectical Disputations*, I, viii, in *Opera*, p. 660.

went well beyond that of Bruni. Moreover, it is clear from several of these statements, as well as from others which will be discussed below, that Valla's defense of rhetoric required an opposition not only to the scholastic philosophy of his own day, but to the whole of the activity which claimed the name of philosophy, whether practiced by medieval men or by the ancients themselves.

The proper status of philosophy in Valla's view, was not one of equality with rhetoric, but of subordination to it. "Philosophy is like a soldier or a tribune under the command of oratory, the queen, as a great tragedian calls it," he wrote. Orators treated the questions of ethics "much more clearly, weightily, magnificently" than did "the obscure, squalid, and anemic philosophers." Orators had begun to discuss the most important matters "in the midst of civic life, before the philosophers began to chatter in their corners," and it was they, not the philosophers, who deserved to be regarded as leaders of other men.[13] Valla recognized—indeed, insisted—that his own devotion to rhetoric was greater than Cicero's had been. For the most part Valla admired Cicero, especially when the Roman "spoke not as a philosopher, but as an orator." But Cicero had sometimes claimed to speak as a philosopher too, a practice which Valla found blameworthy.

> I should prefer that he had said to treat these matters not as a philosopher, but as an orator, and that he had exercised the same license, or rather liberty [i.e., in not adhering to any philosophic sect] to reclaim from the philosophers all the oratorical equipment found among them (all that philosophy claims for itself is ours). And if someone had opposed him, I wish he would have attacked the thieving philosophers with the sword of eloquence—queen of all things—entrusted to him, and had punished the malefactors.[14]

[13] *On the True Good, Scritti*, pp. 30-31; *Opera*, pp. 906-07: "Siquidem philosophia velut miles est aut tribunus sub imperatrice oratione, et ut magnus quidem Tragicus appellat, regina."

[14] *Scritti*, p. 30; *Opera*, p. 907: "Sed tamen mallem, ut non tanquam

142

Much of Valla's own work would be to try to carry out oratory's revenge on philosophy, which Cicero had begun but not fully accomplished. Probably it is this determination which caused Valla, in a youthful work which has been lost, to prefer Quintilian to Cicero. Quintilian had declared that moral philosophy was properly the province of rhetoric, without ever reversing himself on this question, as Cicero had sometimes seemed to do.[15] Certainly Valla learned a great deal from Cicero, both about rhetoric and about philosophy, but he used this knowledge to further a much more radical commitment to oratory than Cicero had expressed.

From this altered perspective, Valla found Bruni's attempt to link Aristotle to the humanist program without real interest. Having deserted the earlier humanist idea of a union of rhetoric and philosophy in a nominally equal partnership, Valla gave up the attempt to "rediscover" Aristotle's "golden stream of eloquence." Aristotle belonged to philosophy, not to rhetoric; therefore he was not to be numbered among the most distinguished men. He did not devote himself to politics, military affairs, law, medicine, history, or poetry. Nor did he make any mark in those disciplines which were clearly the most difficult, namely literary and linguistic studies.[16] Such a description of Aristotle was not merely different from the one offered by Bruni; it was based on a denial of precisely those things about the

---

philosophum se illa tractare praedicasset, sed tanquam oratorem, et in hoc vel magis eandem licentiam aut potius libertatem exercuisset. Ut quicquid oratoriae supellectilis apud illos invenisset, omnia autem quae philosophia sibi vendicat, nostra sunt, id omne ab illis fortiter repoposcisset, et si qui repugnassent gladium illum quem a regina rerum tanquam Imperator acceperat, in latrunculos philosophos strinxisset, et male meritos male mulctasset." (Cf. also *Scritti*, p. 145; *Opera*, p. 954, where Valla praised Cicero for having spoken elsewhere as an orator, not a philosopher.)

[15] See, with regard to Valla's youthful comparison of Quintilian and Cicero, Sabbadini, "Cronologia documentata . . . ," p. 54, also in *Opera*, II, 360; and also *In Poggium Antidoti*, IV, *Opera*, p. 352. Cf. Quintilian, *Inst. Orat.*, I, preface, 10-11.

[16] *Disputationes dialecticae libri tres*, preface; *Opera*, pp. 644-45.

philosopher which Bruni had taken the most pains to affirm: his literary culture and his concern with everyday life. Valla was friendly to Bruni (at least for a time), and he expressed his gratitude for the older man's help in the Elegantiae.[17] But aside from an occasional approving reference to Bruni's translations, Valla paid no heed to his friend's new image of Aristotle. His own defense of rhetoric had no place for it.

There is still a sense in which Lorenzo Valla's cultural ideal should be described as the combination of rhetoric and philosophy. He treated many traditionally philosophic subjects (indeed, a larger number than either Petrarch or Bruni had) in a fashion appropriate to oratory. Furthermore, the traditional demand that the power of eloquence be kept out of the hands of those who would turn it to evil purposes sometimes reappeared in his writings. The true orator must be a good man, he said; moreover, no one can speak effectively about things he does not know well.[18] Yet to the extent that these are not mere commonplaces, they have a meaning in Valla's context different from any we have so far encountered. To understand the kind of union of wisdom and eloquence that Valla sought, we must now examine his attitude toward three questions: the significance of the various schools of moral philosophy; the relationship between philosophy, rhetoric, and the Christian religion; and the true nature of dialectic.

(2)

VALLA discussed the chief questions of moral philosophy in a treatise which he variously called *On Pleasure* and *On the True Good*.[19] The first version of this work was prob-

---

[17] *Elegantiae*, II, preface; *Opera*, pp. 41-42.

[18] *Scritti*, pp. 40, 167.

[19] On the composition of this work, see M. de Panizza, "Le tre redazioni del *De voluptate* del Valla," *Giornale Storico della Letteratura Italiana*, CXXI, 1-22; and Radetti, "Introduzione," *Scritti*, pp. xviii-xxv. A critical edition of this work has been expected for a number of years, but has not yet appeared. The Italian translation by Radetti in *Scritti* is based on a later version of the treatise than the

ably written and published (though not very widely) in 1431, during a brief period the humanist spent at Piacenza. He had stopped there on a journey from Rome to Pavia, where he was to take up a post as professor of rhetoric at the university. The original version of the treatise was afterwards elaborated, and the title changed from *On Pleasure* to *On the True Good*. The book was composed primarily of three set speeches: the first a short statement of what was called a "Stoic" position; the second, much longer, an attack on this position and a defense of "Epicureanism"; and the third a declaredly Christian exposition which refuted both the pagan schools, but found more to praise in the Epicurean position than in the Stoic. In the earlier versions of the treatise, Valla pretended that the discussion had taken place among the papal secretaries at Rome; he gave the Stoic part to Bruni (who had worked in Rome in the early 1420's), the Epicurean speech to Antonio Beccadelli (called Panormita), and the Christian judgment of the debate to Niccolò Niccoli, the Florentine. Other men appeared more briefly in the dialogue. Later, when Valla's relations with some members of this group became less friendly, the scene was transferred to Pavia, and Lombard figures replaced the Tuscan and Roman ones. The three speeches were then assigned to Catone Sacco, Maffeo Vegio, and Antonio da Rho, respectively. These men will appear as the speakers in the discussion below.

The support Valla gave in this work to the Epicurean doctrine of the pursuit of pleasure has received much attention, especially from writers who believe in the essentially "pagan" quality of the Renaissance. Yet Valla was almost certainly a loyal Christian, even though he may have been a somewhat eccentric one.[20] Here, however, we will

---

one published in the Basel *Opera*. Reference will be made to both texts below. The English translations given here have profited from Radetti's Italian version.

[20] For a somewhat over-enthusiastic affirmation of Valla's faith, see Giorgio Radetti, "La religione di Lorenzo Valla," *Medioevo e Rinascimento: Studi in onore di Bruno Nardi* (Florence, 1955), II, 595-620.

not try to determine Valla's religious loyalties, but to understand the way in which *On the True Good* and its Epicureanism fit into the general body of Valla's work. First we must note that no indication of any firm loyalty to the teaching of Epicurus appears in the humanist's other writings. There is no hint of Epicureanism in the *Dialogue on Free Will*, and no celebration of it in the *Dialectical Disputations*. Only when Valla defended his whole literary production and thus referred directly to *On the True Good* did he speak at any length about his Epicureanism, as in the *Apology to Eugene IV*.[21] Valla sometimes repeated the fifteenth-century commonplace that Plato was universally considered the prince of philosophers.[22] He also noted the kinship of his own procedures to those of the Academics (though as a Christian he rejected their denial that knowledge was possible), and he enthusiastically approved of Cicero's practice of speaking freely about philosophical questions without belonging to any one sect.[23] If Valla felt any loyalty to Epicurean doctrine, it was a very limited one.

This conclusion is also true in another sense, for the so-called Epicureanism of *On the True Good* was neither complete nor very accurate.[24] It lacked the whole of the

---

For a more balanced view, see P. O. Kristeller, *Eight Philosophers of the Italian Renaissance* (Stanford, 1964), pp. 31ff.

[21] Edited and translated by Radetti in *Scritti*, pp. 429-54; see esp. 436ff.

[22] *Disputationes dialecticae*, in *Opera*, p. 644; see also Sabbadini, "Cronologia documentata . . . ," p. 88, or in *Opera*, II, 394.

[23] In the letter just cited, Valla said that his criticism of philosophers of various schools was "quasi more Academicorum." In *On the True Good* he claimed support for his assertion of the superiority of utility to *honestas* from the Academics. His statement—in the *Dialogue on Free Will* (*The Renaissance Philosophy of Man*, pp. 158-59)—that the Academics "wrongly" denied that man can attain knowledge seems to have a Christian motivation. On Cicero, see *Scritti*, p. 30; *Opera*, p. 907.

[24] See B.J.H.M. Timmermans, "Valla et Erasme défenseurs d'Epicure," *Neophilologus*, XXIII (1938), 414-19, who notes that Valla's Epicureanism even lacked Epicurus' essential rule: that one should avoid pain.

physical theory (based on the atomic view of nature) which was the foundation of classical Epicurean doctrine. Lacking the "swerve" of the atoms, Valla's Epicureanism was also free of the denial of causality or Providence which had been a basic philosophical tenet for Epicurus. The defender of Epicureanism in the dialogue acknowledged these omissions. He could make them, he said, because, speaking as an orator rather than as a philosopher, he had the right to take his arguments from wherever he liked.[25] All these considerations allow us to suspect the genuineness of Valla's Epicureanism. As one of the speakers in *On the True Good* noted, "Sometimes one says not what he thinks, but what his own position requires."[26] Valla did not necessarily agree with the Epicurean opinions he put forth in his treatise.

Valla explained the position from which he spoke, and why it led him to defend Epicurus, in the preface to the dialogue. The work was, he said, a defense of Christianity against paganism, and an attack on those men of his own time who regarded the pagans more highly than was proper for Christians. He especially chastised those who lamented the banishment of the ancients to Hell, and who claimed that the virtue of the pagans was as great as that of some Christians. To entertain such opinions, Lorenzo asserted, was to deny that Christ's coming served any purpose; indeed, it was to deny that He had come at all. Thus it was necessary to show that the ancients had not lived according to virtue. "Paganism did nothing that was virtuous or morally right." The Athenians, the Romans, the very teachers of virtue in antiquity "were very far from the practice or the understanding of virtue."[27] Such state-

[25] *Scritti*, pp. 30-31; *Opera*, pp. 906-07.
[26] *Scritti*, p. 184; *Opera*, p. 971.
[27] *Scritti*, pp. 3-5; *Opera*, pp. 896-97: "Et quando illi quos dixi, tantum tribuunt antiquitati, Gentilium dico, ut eos omnibus virtutibus affectos esse contendant, ego contra planum faciam, non nostris sed ipsorum philosophorum rationibus, nihil cum virtute gentilitatem, nihil recte fecisse. Magnum opus profecto et arduum, et nescio an magis audax quam aliquod antiquorum. Non enim video scriptorum quem-

ments may sound strange indeed in the mouth of a humanist of the Renaissance who devoted so much of his own effort to the revival of antiquity. When we remember, however, that humanist culture as Valla understood it was the specific domain of the orator, then we are prepared to understand the sense in which Valla meant this attack on the Greeks and Romans. For it was not ancient culture in general, but ancient philosophical culture which was Valla's target. It was the ancient philosophers who had failed in the understanding of virtue while pretending to seek it. Valla said he would demonstrate his case "by arguments of the philosophers themselves." "Part of the philosophers' throats we shall cut with their own sword, the other part we shall incite to an internal war and a mutual destruction." Valla said he would do this by showing the worthlessness of the moral ideals which the philosophers had discovered. The highest of these ideals was *honestas*, moral worth. Valla would therefore show the emptiness of it, and of those who pursued it. "Because the Stoics support *honestas* most vigorously of all, it seems enough to me to refute these adversaries, taking the defense of the Epicureans." In other words, Valla's defense of Epicureanism had the specific purpose of discrediting the Stoics, and through them all ancient philosophers. The earlier humanists we have considered here—like their model, Cicero—had regarded Stoicism as the school which best embodied the ideals of philosophy. Valla was clearly aware of this exalted position often assigned to the Stoics, just as he was conscious of the disdain with which the upholders of *voluptas* were regarded by most philosophers. To show that the Epicureans were superior to the Stoics, therefore, was equivalent to demonstrating that the "best" of the ancient philosophers were inferior to the "worst." Valla explained this in quite specific terms: "Not only have I pre-

---

piam hoc pollicitum esse, ut ostenderet non modo Athenienses, Romanos, caeterosque qui summis laudibus feruntur, sed ipsos etiam virtutum praeceptores longe abfuisse ab illarum tum actione, tum intelligentia."

ferred the Epicureans, vulgar and despised men, to the guardians of honor, but I will show that these very seekers of wisdom followed not virtue, but the shadow of virtue, not *honestas*, but vanity, not duty, but vice, not wisdom, but madness, and that they would have done better to give themselves to pleasure, if in fact they did not give themselves to it."[28] This was what Valla meant by cutting the philosophers' throats with their own sword, and inciting them to a war of mutual destruction. It is not explicitly stated in the preface that the result of this strategy would be the exaltation of oratory; there Valla emphasized only that his aim was to support the Christian faith. But in the rest of the treatise it is clear that rhetoric will profit from the attack on philosophy as much as Christianity. Not only did Valla assert the superiority of oratory to philosophy in terms we have already noted, he also specifically described antiquity as excellent in rhetoric but not in philosophy. The third or Christian speaker declared in Book III of the treatise: "To antiquity I concede the merit of letters, of studies, of learning, and of that which always had greater value, rhetoric; however, I deny that it arrived at wisdom or the knowledge of true virtue."[29] Valla's purpose in *On the True Good* was to attack the philosophers and show that their wisdom could not stand up

[28] *Scritti*, pp. 5-7; *Opera*, p. 897: "Philosophos partim suo mucrone ingulemus, partim in domesticum bellum ac mutuam perniciem concitemus. . . . Cum Stoici acerrime omnium honestatem afferant, satis nobis videmur hosce adversarios contra nos statuere, assumpto patrocinio Epicureorum. . . . Non modo enim anteferimus Epicureos abiectos homines et contemptos honesti custodibus, sed etiam probamus hos ipsos sapientiae sectatores, non virtuteum sed umbram virtutis, non honestatem sed vanitatem, non officium sed vicium, non sapientiam sed dementiam fuisse sectatos, meliusque fuisse facturos, si voluptati operam, nisi dederunt, dedissent."
[29] *Scritti*, pp. 193-94; *Opera*, p. 975: "Cui antiquitati concedo literas, studia doctrinarum, et quod semper plurimum valuit, dicendi scientiam. Sed quod ad mores attinet, vereor Leonarde, ut tibi persuadeas illos veteres plane fuisse sapientes, et ad ipsorum virtutes nihil ex nostra religione posse accedere." (The English version above follows the clearer text given by Radetti. The second part reads: ". . . pero nego sia pervenuta alla saggezza e alla cognizione della vera virtù.")

against the truths of faith, while at the same time defending
rhetoric and showing its (harmony with Christian belief.)
This, then, was the reasoning behind his defense of the
Epicureans.

From a strictly Ciceronian point of view, a defense of
Epicureanism does not appear to be a very good vehicle for
the vindication of oratory. In *De oratore* Cicero had declared the Epicureans unsuitable teachers for the man of
eloquence, because they preferred the quiet of their garden
to the orator's active life.[30] This did not prevent Valla from
turning the doctrine of Epicurus into a sword for rhetoric's
defense, however. Valla's rhetorical culture was, as we have
seen, not strictly that of Cicero, nor was his Epicureanism
that of Epicurus. He invoked the orator's privilege as a
justification for taking from the Epicureans whatever argument suited him; and what suited him was what best fitted
the needs of oratory. The Epicureanism which Cicero rejected had turned its back on everyday life and its standards; the doctrine which Valla claimed to endorse accepted
these things. The advocate of the Epicurean position in the
dialogue insisted on his acceptance of the standards of his
community. By this means he tempered his most outra-
geously hedonistic flights of philosophical fancy. He followed an amusing and provoking attack on chastity with
this qualification:

> I am not ignorant of the secret thought that might now
> arise in the listener: that one cannot escape the eyes, the
> ears, the opinion of the people. To block every way to
> my opponents, I shall comport myself so as to avoid, with
> the greatest diligence, anything which is repugnant to
> commonly accepted opinion, or which might be sus-
> pected of damaging the benevolence of men toward me—
> not because those things I avoid are evil, but because it
> is more important to be loved by people.[31]

[30] *De oratore* III, 63.
[31] *Scritti*, p. 76; *Opera*, p. 926: "Nec ignaro quae tacita possit
audientem subire cogitatio, non fugies interim publicos oculos, non
aures, non opinionem. Ego ut omnem oppositioni viam intercludam,

He went on to list a number of things which he would not do because "it is prohibited to do the things which are not commonly accepted." An Epicureanism which sets such limits on its actions is not primarily committed to any philosophic doctrine at all, but simply to custom and common sense. Valla was aware that this was precisely the orator's commitment. The representative of Stoicism is also described as behaving in accordance with the common standards, despite his adherence to doctrines far removed from them; because he too was an orator, and "being an orator, you must also appear as one."[32] Valla had his Epicurean argue in favor of an almost complete licentiousness, but the humanist's purpose was not to undermine morality. It was only to deny that *philosophy* had any right to restrain men's actions. This right lay elsewhere: with custom (in Book II), and with the teachings of the true religion (in Book III).

The Epicureanism Valla supported in Book II, therefore, was primarily an orator's morality uncorrupted by philosophy. Sometimes the cleavage which appeared in *On the True Good* was not between Stoicism and Epicureanism, but frankly between Stoicism and oratory. At one point the Epicurean speaker chided the Stoics for their lack of persuasive power.[33] At another he asserted that the Stoics had shared with ancient orators the desire to achieve glory for themselves, but had failed because they had not followed the orators' lead: "As if anyone could ever attain glory without men, and with the sole testimony of mute solitude. Much better are the actions of orators, among whom whoever has greater favor with the crowd is considered to be

---

ita me geram, ut si quod receptae persuasioni repugnat, aut si quod offensum ire benevolentiam hominum suspicabor, id quam diligentissime declinem, non quia illa quae declino, mala sint, sed quia hoc ut ameris a populo, praeponderat."

[32] *Scritti*, p. 34; *Opera*, p. 908: "Nihil fere ab usu communi ac civili ac publica vita abhorres. Et scienter, sane, et graviter. Ut enim es orator, ita et videri debes."

[33] *Scritti*, pp. 88-89; *Opera*, p. 930.

the better orator."[34] Save for the reversal of the values given
to the two roles, this statement nearly reproduces the one
in which Petrarch, in his *On the Solitary Life*, had declared
the purposes of rhetoric and of philosophy to be at odds.[35]
What really concerned Valla was not the opposition between Stoics and Epicureans, but that between orators and
philosophers. Just as he sometimes set Stoicism against
rhetoric, so he sometimes used Stoicism as a synonym for
philosophy in general. Many of the opinions against which
the Epicurean argued in the treatise were not properly
Stoic, but Aristotelian: for example, the doctrine that each
virtue is a mean between two vices. As an instance of the
"Stoic" flight to contemplation Valla cited Aristotle, "your
Aristotle."[36] On one occasion he wrote, curiously, that
Boethius spoke on a certain matter "almost as a Stoic, following, as I maintain, the *Gorgias* of Plato."[37] Cicero had
once written that Stoic doctrines were "in the highest degree Socratic," meaning that they were the worthiest expression of the philosophic ideals which Socrates had first
proclaimed.[38] Valla stood this notion on its head, making
Stoicism represent all the most typical, and therefore to him
worst, aspects of philosophy. Moreover, he described the
origin of Stoicism in terms which denied it any serious
moral purpose, and which pictured it as the opposite of
oratory. The first Stoics, he asserted, had not been philosophers at all, but lazy men who preferred to live a "rude
and horrid life because of the trouble involved in procur-
ing the common necessities." Criticized for this preference,
they obstinately defended it. "And thus they introduced a
new dogma, as far removed from common sense as their

[34] *Scritti*, p. 110; *Opera*, pp. 939-40: "Quasi quis esse possit sine
hominibus, et ipsa muta solitudine teste gloriosus. Oratores praeclarius,
inter quos ut quisque plurimum multitudini probatur, ita optimus
numeratur orator."

[35] See above, Chap. II.

[36] *Scritti*, p. 137; *Opera*, p. 951.

[37] *Scritti*, p. 202; *Opera*, p. 978: "Quos prope imitatus Boetius ac
pene Stoicus, Gorgiam Platonis, ut reor, secutus. . . ."

[38] Cicero, *Paradoxa Stoicorum* 3-4.

life was from common practice."[39] Stoic doctrine was, then, the negation of the orator's basic moral imperative: that he must not disdain the standards of his community. The defeat of the Stoics was both a defeat for philosophy and a victory for the orator.

The defense of Epicureanism in *On the True Good* thus takes on a significance different from that usually attributed to it, if we interpret it in the context of Valla's other work and of the treatise itself. It constituted an attack on ancient philosophy (not only on medieval scholasticism) as well as, in Book II, a defense of rhetoric against the philosophers' claims to have discovered a morality superior to custom and common sense. The Christian exposition contained in Book III does not require any alteration of this interpretation, but, as we shall now see, confirms it.

(3)

MOST discussions of *On the True Good* have concentrated on classifying the treatise either as an expression of Renaissance paganism or as a Christian confession of faith. The truth is that while Valla's work is each of these things in a certain sense, it is able to partake of both because it is primarily neither one. Valla was serious about the "Epicureanism" he defended in Book II, in the sense we have just described; he was also serious about the Christianity he upheld in Book III, but he did not write the treatise in order to affirm his faith. He wrote it to show that while

[39] *Scritti,* pp. 150-51; *Opera,* p. 957: "Quod mihi, ut originem honestatis aperiam, non consilio videntur fecisse, sed inertia. Equidem sic statuo existimoque fuisse quosdam homines, ut hodie quoque sunt amatores negligentiae et ignaviae, qui taedio rerum comparandarum, quae sunt necessariae, in vivendo praelegerunt vitam hanc incultam et horridam, caeterum cum sibi ab hominibus id vitio verteretur, contumacissimum excogitaverunt suae turpitudinis patrocinium, ut sunt nonnulli crimen suum malentes defendere quam deponere, introduxeruntque novum dogma sic abhorrens a sensu communi, ut a communi usu ipsorum vita recesserat." Some aspects of the ethics of early Stoicism provided a good basis for Valla's remarks. See E. Zeller, *The Stoics, Epicureans and Sceptics,* trans. O. J. Reichel (London, 1880), pp. 307-08, on the connections between early Stoics and Cynics.

the Christian religion must necessarily regard philosophy with suspicion, oratory and Christianity were perfectly harmonious.

Before examining Valla's statement of these relationships in Book III of his treatise on moral philosophy, we may note that he also affirmed them in an important passage in the *Elegantiae*.[40] There he referred to the famous dream of St. Jerome, in which the Father found himself accused of being not a Christian, but a Ciceronian. Petrarch had defended himself against the same accusation while admitting his love for Cicero's language. Valla reacted differently. He admitted that the story should stand as a warning to Christians of the dangers of giving their loyalty to pagan pursuits, but he strenuously objected to the interpretation of the dream which made it an admonition against rhetoric. One finds not only elegant language in Cicero, he noted, but other achievements as well; nor is eloquence found only in Cicero, but in Plato and others too. "Why should we not think that it was Cicero's philosophy which harmed Jerome, rather than his art of speaking? I do not want to make a comparison here between philosophy and eloquence, or say which can do more harm; many have spoken of this, and they have shown that philosophy can scarcely be consistent with the Christian religion, since all heresies have derived from philosophical sources. Rhetoric, on the other hand, has been shown to have nothing which is not praiseworthy in it."[41] Rhetoric could harm only a man who neglected the other arts, and especially true wisdom, which St. Jerome did not do. Eloquence had always been an aid to the church; all the great fathers made use of it, Valla said. "Surely, only eloquent men like these are the pillars of the Church." St. Paul "seems to be distinguished

[40] *Elegantiae*, IV, preface; *Opera*, pp. 117-20.
[41] *Ibid.*, p. 119: "Cur non potius Ciceronis philosophia nocuisse putanda Hieronymo est, quam ars dicendi? Nolo hoc in loco comparationem facere inter philosophiam et eloquentiam, utra magis obesse possit, de quo multi dixerunt, ostendentes philosophiam cum religione Christiana vix coherere, omnesque haereses ex philosophiae fontibus profluxisse. Rhetoricam vero nihil habere nisi laudabile. . . ."

for no other thing than for eloquence."[42] Thus Christianity was foreign to philosophy, but perfectly at home with rhetoric.

The same conviction underlay the Christian exposition in Book III of *On the True Good*. Antonio da Rho (in the first version, Niccolò Niccoli) declared that both the schools had been in error, seeing only a shadow of the truth. Yet in deciding between them, the Christian must choose the Epicureans, because they had recognized that virtue was not an end in itself but served a higher purpose. Christianity taught, he pointed out, that no man can be truly virtuous unless he has faith in God, as several Pauline citations made clear. The virtuous man must also possess hope and charity. Of these two virtues, Valla emphasized hope: men do not perform virtuous acts for the sake of virtue; they are inspired by the hope of enjoying the fruits of their labors. It was hope which caused men to strive for virtue, because the struggle against vice did not produce happiness in the present. St. Paul himself often complained of the unhappiness which his work brought him; if Paul was miserable in his fight against evil, what man can expect virtue to bring him happiness in this life? The Stoics were wrong in making virtue itself the basis of happiness. Virtue and wisdom brought only trouble in this world, as scripture testified. This being so, man should enjoy the pleasures which were rightfully his, as Solomon himself declared. From this argument it followed that since the Stoics had thought *honestas* to be the highest good, bringing no reward beyond itself, whereas the Epicureans thought the highest good was pleasure, the latter were to be preferred. This was especially true because the Stoics had not lived as they taught, but had in reality sought glory. They were like the Pharisees, hoping to gain glory through a show of virtue. The Epicureans were hardly better; like the Sadducees, they denied immortality and the existence of angels. Yet

---

[42] *Ibid.*, pp. 119-20: "Et certe soli eloquentes, quales ii quos enumeravi columnae ecclesiae sunt, etiam ut ab apostolis usque repetas, inter quos mihi Paulus nulla alia re eminere, quam eloquentia videtur."

at least they recognized that virtue was not its own reward, but was sought for an end beyond itself.[43] Moreover, the proper name for this ultimate goal of man, even as Christianity understood it, was pleasure. In Latin it had to be called *voluptas*, not *delectatio*, because it was the most intense of pleasures. Only the pleasure of the next life was desirable in itself; the happiness of the present life lay in the hope of salvation in the next, the joy of the Lord. To be sure, the condition for obtaining this beatitude was *honestas*, but it was moral worth as the Christians—not the philosophers—understood it.[44]

Valla did not deny that the ancient philosophers had sown some good seed, but he insisted that it could not yield fruit until Christ came and purified the ground in which it lay. The philosophers had not shared in the good of Christianity. They had put their hope in the most abject things, and their reward matched their desires and their deserts. "I am not ashamed to despise and condemn philosophy, since Paul found fault with it, and Jerome and others called the philosophers fomenters of heresy. Away with philosophy, therefore, away with it!" Philosophy must be displaced by the true love of God. Thus the Christian speaker in *On the True Good* ended his confutation of the pagans.[45]

Urged on by his listeners, however, Antonio then turned to another theme. In a peroration, he described the state of true Christian happiness. He told how much greater were heavenly pleasures than earthly ones, how the life of the next world would cause men to forget about the things they had thought enjoyable in this, and finally, how the soul of the blessed man enters in triumph and glory into the heavenly city. This final discourse was necessary, Valla tells us, to erase from the minds of the audience any remaining

[43] *Scritti*, pp. 191-98; *Opera*, pp. 974-76. The text used by Radetti is somewhat more expanded than that in the *Opera*.

[44] *Scritti*, pp. 199-201; *Opera*, pp. 977-78.

[45] *Scritti*, pp. 201-02, 204-05; *Opera*, pp. 978-79: "Nec verebor philosophiam aut contemnere, aut damnare, cum Paulus eam arguat, et Hieronymus cum quibusdam aliis, philosophos haeresiarchas appellet." The text in the *Opera* varies slightly from that in Radetti.

effects of the powerful exposition of Epicureanism they had previously heard.[46] Thus eloquence secured the final triumph of Christianity over paganism.

It is clear that Valla thought the defeat of the philosophers at the hands of Christian truth left the dignity of rhetoric untouched. The best indication of this comes from Valla's references to Boethius. In concluding his refutation of the philosophers, the speaker of Book III found it appropriate to include Boethius among their number and to convict him of two related faults. First, Boethius had given his loyalty to philosophy, honoring it more than he did Christianity; and he had concluded that virtue was the highest good, that the virtuous were always happy and the wicked ever miserable, things which true religion showed to be false. Like other philosophers, Boethius had been confused by the use of the word "good" in connection with both virtue and happiness. He had argued thus: whoever is virtuous is good; whoever is good possesses the good; the good for man is happiness, therefore the virtuous man is happy. To argue in this way, Valla said, was to fail to see that "good" is used in two different senses: to describe *actions* according to virtue on the one hand, and the *state* of happiness on the other. The virtuous man indeed possesses the good of virtue, but not the good of happiness. While both virtue and happiness are called "goods," the only men who are "good" are those who are virtuous, not those who are happy.[47] This analysis led Valla to the second part of his accusation against Boethius. "In this way Boethius, more a lover of dialectic than of rhetoric, deceived himself. How much better it would have been for him to speak as an orator instead of as a dialectician! What is more foolish than the ways of philosophy? If one word is wrong, the whole argument is in danger." The orator did not rely on a single, supposedly rigorous line of reasoning, but used many and varied procedures, examining contrary arguments, examples, analogies, and so on. His conclusions were not subject

[46] *Scritti*, p. 210; *Opera*, pp. 980-81.
[47] *Scritti*, p. 202; *Opera*, p. 978.

to the same weaknesses as the deductions of the philosophers: if one argument failed, he had another at hand. Thus he found truths the philosopher could not find.[48] The total indictment of Boethius therefore charged that he had preferred philosophy to Christianity on the one hand, and to rhetoric on the other. His failure to understand the truth derived from both these errors.

Valla did not elaborate here upon the most important implication of all this, namely that the moral perspectives of oratory and of Christianity were harmonious. The basis of this harmony must be inferred, but it is not difficult to understand. From different starting points, the orator and the Christian reached the same conclusion. The Christian rejected the teachings of the philosophers because he accepted the contrary doctrine of faith; the orator rejected it because he accepted the contrary opinion of common sense. To be sure, this acceptance by itself did not allow the orator to understand the truth of faith, the promise of the next life. But as far as the question of happiness in this life was concerned, his attitude agreed with that of Christianity. The orator rejected the philosopher's attempt to define a happiness on earth different from the one which common sense and ordinary speech recognized; thus he resembled the Christian, who insisted that man can transcend his everyday life on earth only in the life to come. On earth, man could rightly put his trust in rhetoric, but not in philosophy.

Valla did not explicitly state these conclusions in *On the True Good*, but in concluding the dialogue he did describe the Christian exposition in Book III as a form of rhetoric, closely akin to the Epicurean oration of Book II. He put this final comment on the whole treatise in the mouth of the noted humanist teacher, Guarino of Verona. Guarino praised both the Epicurean and the Christian speaker for having sought not only to teach their hearers, but also to move and to please them, "like the best orators."[49] The dif-

---

[48] *Scritti*, p. 204; this passage does not seem to be included in the version of the treatise printed in the *Opera*; it was probably inserted after Valla completed the *Dialectical Disputations*.

[49] *Scritti*, pp. 246-47; *Opera*, p. 997.

ference between the two speeches he described by an analogy. The first speaker had used the voice of the swallow, the second that of the nightingale. The comparison with these two birds was appropriate, he said, because the poets thought them to be sisters and used them to represent the sister arts of oratory and poetry. The difference between them was that the swallow preferred to live on roofs and in cities, the nightingale in trees and forests. Thus the swallow "was similar to civic eloquence," while the nightingale resembled "the rustic eloquence of the poets," who sought solitude and the places frequented not by men but by the muses. Poets, Guarino noted, went on to argue from this distinction that their own eloquence was superior to that of orators, just as the nightingale sang more sweetly than the swallow. He did not wish to judge whether this was true, but he thought no one would deny his own application of the analogy to the two speeches.[50] In this way Valla explained the relationship between the Epicurean and Christian expositions. The first was an example of the kind of eloquence which was appropriate to the everyday life of men, the second of that eloquence which sought to transcend the everyday world in search of a superior kind of life. The second, Christian form of eloquence was the sister of the first, secular form.

In this way Valla brought his treatise *On the True Good* to the same conclusion we have already met in the *Elegantiae*: rhetoric harmonized with Christianity and supported it, but philosophy was true religion's enemy. With this assertion, Valla carried the defense of rhetoric well beyond the point at which the earlier humanists had left it. Petrarch and Salutati had felt that the Christian's commitment to true wisdom sometimes led him to seek the teachings of philosophy and to regard the pursuit of eloquence with suspicion. Valla tried to lay this suspicion to rest. Bruni had sought to quiet the philosophic suspicion of oratory by picturing the best philosophers—especially Aristotle—as friendly to rhetoric, but his new image of Aristotle only

[50] *Scritti*, pp. 247-48; *Opera*, pp. 997-98.

159

brought eloquence into harmony with the secular pursuit
of wisdom. He gave little attention to the relationship between eloquence and Christian doctrine. Thus Valla's demonstration of the harmony between oratory and Christianity built a stronger shield for the pursuit of eloquence
than any of the other three humanists had been able or
willing to construct. This was not the only way in which
Valla went beyond his predecessors. He also broke new
ground in his attempt to reform dialectic.

(4)

VALLA's opposition to philosophy was, as we have noted
above, much more thoroughgoing and determined than
that expressed by any of the other humanists. In *On the
True Good* it is perfectly clear that his strictures are not
directed primarily against the scholastics, but against
ancient philosophers. Yet even Valla could not disdain the
pursuit of wisdom with complete consistency. The attrac-
tiveness of the ideal of philosophy was too great for him to
resist entirely. He, too, was forced to substitute for the philosophy of the philosophers a different, true philosophy. He
addressed himself to this task primarily in a work called the
Dialectical Disputations, finished some years after *On the
True Good*.[51] The two treatises are related: he mentions the
Dialectical Disputations in the earlier work, and a number
of arguments appear in both.[52] At least once he spoke of
publishing the two together, referring to the later treatise
as "On True Philosophy."[53] He also described the work on
dialectic at times as the "rediscovery" or "digging up"
(*repastinatio*) of philosophy, and some of the manuscripts

[51] The *Disputationes dialecticae* was finished in 1439. It will be
cited below (by book and page) as *D. D.*; references are to the *Opera*.
On this work, see the discussions of Gaeta and of Freudenthal cited
in note 1, above. Also, see Cesare Vasoli, "Le 'Dialecticae disputationes' del Valla e la critica umanistica della logica aristotelica,"
Rivista Critica di Storia della Filosofia, XII and XIII; though recent
writers have criticized the discussion by Carl Prantl, *Geschichte der
Logik im Abendlande*, IV (Leipzig, 1870), 161-67, it is still valuable.
[52] See *Scritti*, p. 204; also, above, note 12.
[53] See Mancini, "Alcune lettere di Lorenzo Valla," p. 35.

are entitled *On the Restoration [Reconcinnatio] of Philosophy.*[54]

Most commentators on humanism take these titles to mean that Valla intended to lead philosophy back from the detour on which the scholastics had taken it, and to return it to the main highway of ancient thought. This account will not quite do, however. Valla's purpose was to redefine philosophy in a way acceptable to him as a humanist, but this does not mean that he wished to define the term as ancient philosophers had. Rather, Valla sought to rediscover a philosophy which accepted its proper place under the domination of oratory. As he wrote in the *Apology to Eugene IV*, his aim had been to show that, among other things, "the major part of Latin logic is false, while my logic is true; that the orator is the true wise man, insofar as it is given to man to be such, and that he is more than a philosopher, namely a *sophos*."[55] The title *sophos*, which Valla wished to give to the orator, was the very name that Socrates and other Greek thinkers had thought inappropriate and presumptuous for the man of wisdom, preferring to style themselves "lovers of wisdom" rather than "wise men." The kind of learning which Valla sought to foster in the *Dialectical Disputations* resembled that of Greek philosophers much less than it did that of the rhetorical sophists.

The ancient writer on whom Valla most relied in this treatise was the rhetorician Quintilian, whom he had once said he preferred to Cicero. Quintilian had never written a treatise on dialectic, but Valla claimed to know his *Oratorical Instruction* almost by heart. This was a proper source for his own *Disputations*, in Valla's view, because dialectic was only a part of rhetoric.

Dialectic is quite a simple and brief thing to learn, as can be determined by a comparison with rhetoric. For what else is dialectic but one kind of confutation, the

---

[54] See Radetti's note in *Scritti*, pp. 445-46.
[55] *Scritti*, p. 446.

various sorts of which are part of *inventio* [discovery]? *Inventio* is one of the five parts of rhetoric. It falls to the dialectician to use the syllogism. Doesn't the orator do the same? . . . But look at the difference: the dialectician uses so to speak a nude syllogism, the orator uses one which is clothed and armed, and decorated with gold and purple and precious gems.[56]

Valla went on to praise the orator and true eloquence, concluding that rhetoric was far more excellent than dialectic, and more difficult. He did not mean to disparage his subject, he added, but only to speak in the modest terms that were appropriate to it, and to encourage students to learn dialectic quickly and easily. It could be mastered in as many months as grammar took years.

The method Valla followed, to assure that dialectic kept its proper place in relation to rhetoric, was to tie the dialectician firmly to the linguistic standard of the orator. This standard, as has been pointed out in connection with each of the thinkers we have considered here, was the common language of everyday life. Even though the humanists could not reasonably expect the Latin they wrote and studied to be understood in the marketplace as Cicero's spoken Latin had been, they all nonetheless regarded the commitment to common sense and ordinary, nonphilosophical language to be characteristic of rhetorical culture. In the debate between Leonardo Bruni and Alonzo of Cartagena on Aristotle's linguistic practice, Bruni rejected the attempt to construct a terminology especially fitted to philosophical inquiry, preferring the usage of "the best authors." This may appear to differ from the usual rhetorical

[56] *D. D.*, II, preface; *Opera*, p. 693: "Erat enim dialectica, res brevis prorsus et facilis, id quod ex comparatione rhetoricae dijudicari potest. Nam quid aliud est dialectica, quam species confutationis, hae ipsae sunt partes inventionis. Inventio una est ex quinque rhetoricae partibus. Dialectici est syllogismo uti: quid non orator eodem utitur? . . . Sed vide quid interest, dialecticus utitur nudo (ut sic loquar) syllogismo, orator autem vestito armatoque, auro et purpura, ac gemmis ornato. . . ."

standard. But in Valla's prescription for dialectic and philosophy, the usage of "the best authors" and the speech of ordinary men alternate as correctives for the corrupt terminology of philosophers, and sometimes merge into one. Most often Valla appealed to everyday speech. "Philosophy and dialectic neither usually do nor ought to depart from the most common usages of speech, or, so to say, from the paths and pavements frequented by the crowd."[57] "Let us see," he proposed at one point, "whether the people or the philosopher speaks better." The answer appeared in another place: "How much more satisfying it would have been [for Aristotle] to follow the common custom of speech!"[58] At other times, Valla's measure was more clearly the speech of learned men. "After this," he demanded, "let not dialecticians and philosophizers [*philosophantes*] persist in their ignorance of certain of their terms, but let them turn to a speech which is natural and commonly used by learned men."[59] The two standards were combined, however, in Valla's conclusion that "The people speak better than the philosopher, and the best authors agree with them."[60] The reason for this agreement was that "the best authors," in Valla's view, were those who belonged to a tradition which respected common usage, namely the tradition of oratory. In the *Dialectical Disputations* Valla regarded custom with a reverence even greater than that shown in *On the True Good*. "If anyone departs from this [custom] he should not only be driven out of the company of the learned, but expelled from the city as one contemptuous of laws and *mores.* And as *mores* and laws differ among nations and peoples, and the differing nature of language among them is each holy and inviolate, therefore,

[57] *D. D.*, I, iii; *Opera*, p. 651 (misnumbered p. 653 in Basel edition, but corrected in Turin edition): "At philosophia ac dialectica non solent, ac ne debent quidem recedere ab usitatissima loquendi consuetudine, et quasi a via vulgo trita et silicibus strata."
[58] *Ibid.*, pp. 684, 678.
[59] *D. D.*, III, preface; *Opera*, p. 731.
[60] *D. D.*, I, xvii; *Opera*, p. 685.

usage [*consuetudine*] ought to be fixed as a kind of civil law."[61] This was the law Valla wished to lay down for philosophy. Tied in this way to the common practice of everyday life, it would never depart from the moral and intellectual world of ordinary men, as Valla criticized (and as Cicero and Petrarch had sometimes praised) the Stoics for doing.

This reform of dialectic was far-reaching. Some aspects of it primarily affected the practices of medieval philosophers: as for example the denial of the meaningfulness of the medieval "transcendentals," *ens, aliquid, res, unum, verum, bonum,* all of which Valla described as simple variations on the fundamental notion *res;*[62] and similarly, Valla's famous assertion that the medieval Latin words ending in *itas—entitas, quidditas, haecceitas,* and so forth—were inadmissible in any serious discussion because they were ungrammatical.[63] Other of Valla's arguments were directed primarily against Aristotle, whom he especially attacked, and whose great prestige among the scholastics he lamented in this treatise. Of this sort were the attempt to reduce the ten Aristotelian categories to three (had Valla been more careful he might have pointed out that Aristotle himself sometimes limited the number to five, four, or three);[64] the attack on the Aristotelian treatment of the syllogism (a form of argument which, Valla said, should be dealt with in very simple terms, since it was used without any training even by children);[65] and the denial that one could reach general conclusions by means of induction (though it was legitimate to use induction in what Cicero had described as the rhetorical fashion—to compel agree-

[61] *D. D.,* II, xi; *Opera,* p. 709: "A qua si quis desciverit non secus a choro literatorum explodendus quam legum morumque contemptor e civitate expellendus est. Et ut sunt varii mores variaque leges nationum ac populorum, ita variae naturae linguarum apud suos unaquaque intemerata et sancta, itaque consuetudine tanquam quodam iure civili standum est."
[62] *D. D.,* I, ii and iii.
[63] *D. D.,* I, iv; cf. also I, xiv.
[64] See Freudenthal, "L. Valla als Philosoph," p. 730.
[65] *D. D.,* III, i-xiv.

ment in a particular case by pointing out acceptance of a series of similar propositions).[66]

A number of Valla's arguments in the *Dialectical Disputations* dealt with questions which were not strictly in the domain of logic. In a chapter entitled "De anima" he attacked Aristotle's view of the soul, and in another, "De virtutibus," he repeated some of the points made in *On the True Good*.[67] Certain of Valla's ideas seem quite interesting today, especially in connection with the anti-metaphysical stance of many contemporary philosophers. For instance, he ridiculed the Aristotelian terminology of "act" and "potency," saying that it was silly to describe some timber as "potentially" the bow of a boat, when all that was meant was that a carpenter could make a bow from the wood.[68] In a similar way he attacked Aristotle's statement that an "empty" vessel was not really empty as long as it remained full of air. Valla insisted that emptiness be considered in a practical, everyday sense: a thing is empty when it is void of what it usually holds. A jug is empty when it has no water; the marketplace is empty when there are no men in it. Air should be considered only when it is of real importance to the matter at hand: a sail may be described as empty when it is not filled with air, so may a ball; but not a water jug, or the marketplace.[69]

In such passages Valla showed real philosophical talent, ✕ but the effect of his argument was to hold all philosophical discussion within extremely narrow limits. His criticisms of traditional logic and metaphysics seem to foreshadow those of sixteenth- and seventeenth-century philosophers, and perhaps even some opinions that have become popular in the twentieth century. Yet it is incorrect to confuse Valla's philosophical position with that of Descartes or Galileo, or of Wittgenstein. Some connections may be discerned between the humanist attempt to reform philosophy and the scientific revolution of the seventeenth century;

[66] *D. D.*, III, xvi.   [67] *D. D.*, I, ix-xi.
[68] *D. D.*, I, xvi; *Opera*, p. 678.
[69] *D. D.*, I, xvii; *Opera*, pp. 684-85.

certainly both shared a healthy suspicion of scholasticism. But the reasons for this suspicion were very different in the two cases. The scientists of the seventeenth century sought to free the investigation of the physical universe from the restraints imposed by scholastic modes of thought; the humanist's purpose was not to separate physics from traditional metaphysics, but to restrict the independent pursuit of either. The discussion of "emptiness" mentioned above is evidence of this: any scientific discussion had to respect the rules of common speech.[70] The same uncompromising insistence on the everyday sense of words divides Valla from the "linguistic philosophy" of the twentieth century. A number of contemporary philosophers, influenced especially by Ludwig Wittgenstein, have asserted that many of the traditional problems of metaphysics are meaningless: they are not genuine questions about existing things but pseudo-questions, which "result from the fact that we do not understand the logic of our language."[71] These twentieth-century thinkers believe that earlier philosophers have been confused by language; they therefore try to understand clearly what ordinary language actually means, in order to avoid being misled by it. Their procedures may seem to resemble Valla's, but the similarity is only superficial. Wittgenstein and his followers have not sought to model philosophical discourse on the language of business or politics, nor have they tried to align their conclusions with all the usual notions of common sense. These were Valla's purposes; they were the consequences of subjecting philosophy to rhetoric. To any philosopher who attempted to refine common language or criticize common ideas of morality, Valla's answer was ready: "Let the people respond that

[70] For a very different view of this question, see Eugenio Garin, "Gli umanisti e la scienza," *Rivista di filosofia*, LII (1961), 259-78; also Gaeta, *Lorenzo Valla*, Chap. III.

[71] Ludwig Wittgenstein, *Tractatus Logico-Philosophicus*, 4.003, quoted by Suzanne K. Langer, *Philosophy in a New Key* (New York, 1951), p. 79. In connection with the comments here, see Mrs. Langer's discussion, especially of Carnap, on pp. 77-81. Also, Albert William Levi, *Philosophy in the Modern World* (Bloomington, 1959), Chaps. IX, XI.

the rules of speech and all decisions about it lie with them."[72]

Valla's conception of the function of logical discourse is especially clear in his discussion of negation and of contrary statements. The traditional law of contrary statements holds that of two contraries (for example, "all horses are black" and "no horses are black"), both cannot be true, but both may be false. Simple as it is, this principle is basic to the construction of any consistent body of discourse. Valla denied, however, that it could ever aid in the pursuit of knowledge. One could not decide about the truth or falsehood of simple statements by any logical test, but only by means of some independently acquired knowledge. Our knowledge that both statements about the color of horses cannot be true has nothing to do with the fact that they contradict each other. Both are false because they each contradict our experience, and for no other reason.[73] Valla did not specifically discuss in the *Dialectical Disputations* the question of where man's knowledge comes from; but he made it quite clear that he did not believe reason, by itself, could add to this knowledge. Valla's treatment of dialectic, despite his disclaimer, was essentially a negative one. He did not think that there was any place in education or in intellectual life for a dialectic independent of oratory. He was aware of the tradition which distinguished dialectic from rhetoric as an instrument for conducting investigations in private rather than in public, but he did not think that dialectic was therefore any more rigorous a procedure than rhetoric. It was only cruder and less polished.

Valla's redefinition of philosophy had the primary effect of making philosophy a part of rhetoric, and thus of helping to accomplish that revenge on behalf of oratory which Valla criticized Cicero for not having carried far enough. Valla would not have objected to having his own overall purpose as a thinker described in just this way. He be-

---

[72] *D. D.*, I, xvii; *Opera*, p. 685: "Respondeat populus penes se esse arbitrium et normam loquendi."
[73] *D. D.*, II, xiv; *Opera*, pp. 711-12.

longed to the same Ciceronian tradition as the other humanists we have discussed, and in several ways his concerns were an extension of theirs. Many of his writings centered on the question of the relationship between rhetoric and philosophy, and he understood the aims and characteristics of the two disciplines in the same general terms as Cicero and Petrarch did. But the combination he made of the two, while formed out of the same basic elements, was shaped in a different way. He sought to join rhetoric to philosophy in a manner which guaranteed that the freedom and prestige of the orator would never be threatened by the claims of the philosopher. In Valla's intellectual world, the ideal of wisdom was defined in a way which gave free play to the pursuit of eloquence. Thus Valla avoided the problems which arose for the orator in the more moderate union of philosophy and rhetoric envisioned by Petrarch and Salutati, and which came to the surface most visibly in the Petrarch Controversy of 1405-06.

In his attempt to shield the orator from the attacks of philosophers, Valla departed from many of the positions held by his onetime friend Leonardo Bruni, but the basic aims and viewpoints of the two men did not differ. Both attempted to add to the prestige of rhetorical culture by establishing a new relationship between oratory and ancient philosophy, even though their views of this relationship were not the same. Confronted with the scholastic image of ancient philosophy, Bruni sought to replace it with one which stressed the harmony between Greek thinkers and the art of rhetoric. Valla admitted the separation and hostility between ancient philosophers and the art of oratory, thereby declaring all traditional philosophy to be outside the pale of true learning.[74] Only Bruni's posi-

[74] A remarkably similar range of alternatives was covered by Petrus Ramus, a later thinker with interests resembling those of the humanists. One of Ramus' critics (Pierre Galland) described his development as follows: "First you denied that the works of Aristotle which have come down to us were by Aristotle, on the grounds that you could not find in them the golden river of eloquence which Cicero so often says he found in Aristotle. . . . When your friends had with great trouble

168

tion recognized a sharp distinction between ancient and medieval philosophical culture. Valla was as vehemently hostile to ancient philosophers as to their medieval successors. His position was far more radical than were the stands taken by most of his humanist colleagues, but his subordination of philosophy to rhetoric was a response to problems which inevitably were present in more moderate attempts to join eloquence to wisdom. Although many of his conclusions would have been rejected by Salutati or Bruni, it was Valla who went furthest along the intellectual path opened up by Petrarch.

---

won you away from this position, you began to say that the books were not Aristotle's in the sense that they were corrupted from their original grace and beauty and contaminated. . . . Then suddenly, changing sail as sailors do in a storm, you took another tack. You no longer denied that these books were Aristotle's, but when you were passed over and another lecturer on Aristotle was appointed to our college, you opened your attack, and, openly declaring yourself his enemy and the enemy of all Aristotelians, you struck out at these distinguished persons . . ."; in Walter J. Ong, S.J., *Ramus, Method, and the Decay of Dialogue* (Cambridge, Mass., 1958), pp. 39-40.

Part Two

Some Contexts of Petrarchian Humanism

CHAPTER VI

RHETORIC AND PHILOSOPHY
IN MEDIEVAL CULTURE

O UR STUDY of humanist thought in Part One has shown that Petrarch and his followers had a pervasive interest in the relationship between rhetoric and philosophy. Their concern to combine these two arts in a manner suitable to the man of eloquence shaped their thinking in significant ways. This conclusion accords with those of several other recent studies, which have also found rhetoric to be at the center of the humanist cultural program.[1] The altered view of the humanist movement which thus begins to emerge modifies our understanding not only of the internal history of humanism, but of its external history as well. This view offers a new perspective from which to examine the relationship of the humanist movement both to earlier intellectual tendencies and to its contemporary environment. To explore this perspective is the purpose of the present chapter and of the two which follow it. These chapters differ from those of Part One in that they take a wider focus and are more speculative and less fully documented than the earlier treatments of individual humanists. The conclusions stated below are tentative, but the questions posed are important enough to justify such a discussion of them here. In this chapter we shall compare humanist views of the relationship between oratory and philosophy to medieval ones; in Chapter VII our subject will be the development of humanism from its medieval roots;

[1] Paul O. Kristeller, "Humanism and Scholasticism in the Italian Renaissance," in *Studies in Renaissance Thought and Letters*, p. 560; Hanna H. Gray, "Renaissance Humanism: The Pursuit of Eloquence," *Journal of the History of Ideas*, XXIV (1963), 497-514; Charles Trinkaus, "A Humanist's Image of Humanism: The Inaugural Orations of Bartolommeo della Fonte," *Studies in the Renaissance*, VII (1960), 90-147; Peter Herde, "Politik und Rhetorik in Florenz am Vorabend der Renaissance," *Archiv für Kulturgeschichte*, XLVII (1965), 141-220.

the final chapter discusses the place of the humanists in the intellectual and social life of their time.

MUCH OF the present uncertainty about the historical significance of the Italian Renaissance has arisen from a growing awareness of the richness and diversity of the culture of the Middle Ages. We can no longer speak of medieval civilization in terms which derive from humanist polemics against the schoolmen. Yet to question the humanists' assertions that their learning was superior to that of the scholastic philosophers is not necessarily to deny that the concerns of the two groups were qualitatively different. It is wrong to set the Renaissance against the Middle Ages as light against darkness, but it may still be correct to paint the two eras in quite different colors. In seeking to define the unique achievement of the fifteenth-century Renaissance while still recognizing the existence of other, medieval moments of rebirth, one of the foremost cultural historians of our time has formulated what he calls the "principle of disjunction." In Erwin Panofsky's words: "Wherever in the high and later Middle Ages a work of art borrows its form from a classical model, this form is almost invariably invested with a non-classical, normally Christian, significance; wherever in the high and later Middle Ages a work of art borrows its theme from classical poetry, legend, history or mythology, this theme is quite invariably presented in a non-classical, normally contemporary form."[2] Thus did Nicolo Pisano introduce the figures of Dionysius, Hercules, and Phaedra into his Pisa pulpit, but transformed respectively into St. Simeon, Christian Fortitude, and the Virgin Mary. A number of medieval artists preceded Botticelli in depicting the birth of Venus, but their versions of the scene, while sometimes charming, were hopelessly confused. Misreading their literary sources, they showed the goddess holding her shell, or in the company of an animal of uncertain lineage called a "sea-goose." The Quattrocento sought to end this divorce of form and content. Renaissance

[2] Erwin Panofsky, *Renaissance and Renascences in Western Art* (Stockholm, 1960; 2nd edn., 1965), p. 84.

artists reunited classical images and classical ideas, and the reunion was permanent. Without denying either the value of medieval achievements or the medieval knowledge of and involvement in ancient culture, therefore, Panofsky has subtly and persuasively distinguished the medieval "renascences" from the major Renaissance.

Panofsky's work has centered on (though it has not been limited to) the history of art, and his terminology is that of art history. Yet his insight is relevant here because it can further illuminate the issues of intellectual history we have considered. The principle of disjunction prepares us for the clear differences we will find between medieval and humanist discussions of the relationship between rhetoric and philosophy. The terms "form" and "content" cannot be applied to the history of ideas in precisely the sense in which Panofsky has used them for art history. Nevertheless, medieval discussions of the relations between philosophy and oratory reveal a species of "disjunction" strikingly similar to the medieval divorce of theme and image in the figurative arts. Before attempting to define the exact nature of this disjunction, we must take note of some distinguishing characteristics of rhetoric in the Middle Ages. In doing so, we do not mean to offer even a summary history of medieval rhetoric. What follows is merely an attempt to examine the ways in which some representative medieval thinkers approached the theme we have examined in the writings of the humanists: the relationship between rhetoric and philosophy. The pages which follow have been placed here— rather than earlier in our study, where a chronological history of medieval rhetoric would belong—because they are intended only to provide a context within which to consider the historical importance of humanist thought.

Rhetoric had many uses in medieval society.[3] Even

[3] Charles Sears Baldwin, *Medieval Rhetoric and Poetic to 1400* (New York, 1928); Ernst Robert Curtius, *European Literature and the Latin Middle Ages*, trans. W. R. Trask (New York, 1953); Richard McKeon, "Rhetoric in the Middle Ages," *Speculum*, XVII (1942), 1-32; P. Abelson, *The Seven Liberal Arts: A Study in Medieval Culture* (New York, 1906); L. J. Paetow, *The Arts Course at Medieval*

though it lost the preeminence it had enjoyed among the liberal disciplines in classical Rome, it served many needs and affected many facets of life. Perhaps its most pervasive application, in a society so largely organized around religious institutions and so much driven by Christian aspirations, was in preaching. A large branch of medieval rhetorical literature was made up of sermons and manuals for preachers. But rhetoric did not entirely abandon its secular role. Law and politics retained some of their classical association with rhetoric. Rulers and ruling bodies relied on rhetoricians to draw up charters and other state documents, and in the tenth century Gerbert of Aurillac, later Pope Sylvester II, regarded training in rhetoric as necessary for those who participated in public life.[4] Medieval rhetoric also retained (sometimes in a restricted form) its ancient function in literature. Literary theory usually derived from classical rhetorical manuals, and the classical bond between rhetoric and poetry lasted throughout the Middle Ages. Given these recognitions of the importance of rhetoric, it is not difficult to understand why it should have remained one of the principal subjects of primary instruction in medieval schools. Together with grammar and logic (or dialectic), it was one of the arts of the trivium.

The prominence of rhetoric in medieval culture helped to keep alive the old problem of its relation to philosophy. The educational curriculum included classical rhetorical manuals—at the very least Cicero's *De inventione* and the pseudo-Ciceronian *Rhetorica ad Herennium*, sometimes together with other works of Cicero or with Quintilian's *Institutiones*.[5] Thus classical discussions of the relationship between eloquence and wisdom could be one source of

Universities with Special Reference to Grammar and Rhetoric, Un. of Illinois Studies, III (Champaign, 1910); D. L. Clark, "Rhetoric and the Literature of the English Middle Ages," *Quarterly Journal of Speech*, XLV (1959); Eduard Norden, *Die Antike Kunstprosa vom VI. Jahrhundert v. Chr. bis in die Zeit der Renaissance* (Leipzig and Berlin, 1915).

[4] See R. W. Southern, *The Making of the Middle Ages* (New Haven, 1953), p. 176.

[5] Paetow, *The Arts Course*, Chap. III.

medieval concern about it. In addition, such concern may have been aroused when medieval men turned to the study of philosophy and began to ask themselves how other disciplines were related to it. The contrast between various tendencies in medieval intellectual life has sometimes been described in terms of the distinction between rhetorical and philosophical procedures.[6]

While the question of the relationship between wisdom and the pursuit of eloquence remained alive, however, it underwent significant transformations. Christianity itself was responsible for some of these. The Christian commitment of medieval men demanded that they devote themselves to wisdom, and it might also lead them to desire to propagate the truth by eloquence. Both the wisdom they cherished and the eloquence they sought had to be distinguished from those of the pagan past, however, and the relationship between the two had to take a different form.[7] Other fundamental features of medieval society also helped to give a new shape to the rhetorical tradition and its bearing on philosophy. The disruption of society in the early medieval period broke the continuity of all educational activities; in the centuries that followed, the texts available for study at different times varied considerably. Equally important were the changed social and political conditions under which the study of rhetoric was carried on. Though the uses of rhetoric were many, they were not the same as those that existed in Greece and Rome. The medieval preacher or chancellor might be an accomplished speaker or writer, but he was a different figure from Cicero's Crassus or Antonius. His environment, his purposes, and his needs differed from those of the classical men whose art he shared.[8]

[6] See H. I. Marrou, *St. Augustin et la fin de la culture antique* (Paris, 1938), p. 173. Marrou also writes of St. Augustine in terms of his "conversion from rhetoric to philosophy."

[7] In this connection, see the discussion of St. Augustine by McKeon, "Rhetoric in the Middle Ages," pp. 5ff.

[8] For a similar view, see R. R. Bolgar, *The Classical Heritage and its Beneficiaries* (Cambridge, Eng., 1954), Chap. I.

These changes are summarized in the disappearance of the classical orator, the figure idealized in *De oratore*. Rhetoric survived as a learned tradition, a body of literature, a technique, a subject of study; the rhetorician remained as the representative of the tradition, the interpreter of the literature, the expert in the technique, or the teacher of the subject. But he was not an orator in the classical sense: he could not claim to fill the many-sided role of the classical orator. The varied tasks performed by the classical orator either fell into disuse or were distributed among separate occupational and social groups, none of which was primarily identified with the art of rhetoric. Whereas Cicero's orator had derived his identity from his practice of rhetoric and thus had tended to regard many other aspects of life and thought from the viewpoint of oratory, most medieval practitioners of rhetoric had some other primary identity and hence regarded rhetoric as an adjunct to some other task. Thus the salient features of the history of rhetoric in the Middle Ages are the loss of the art's identity as a single coherent tradition, the diffusion of its various elements among other disciplines, and the failure of professional rhetoricians to retain Cicero's conception of rhetoric as the doorway to general education and political life.

The prominent position of rhetoric as one of the three arts of the trivium must not be allowed to hide the fundamental transformation of its place in social and intellectual life. In the first place, the trivium was usually dominated by grammar or dialectic.[9] More important, the boundaries between the three arts often fluctuated mightily; by a kind of intellectual imperialism, both the techniques and the purposes of one might be taken over by another. Medieval considerations of the relations between the arts sometimes had the purpose of distinguishing one from another, but often such discussions sought to identify one art with another, to have one exchange tasks with another, or to sub-

[9] Baldwin, *Medieval Rhetoric and Poetic to 1400*, p. 151.

178

ordinate one to another.[10] Thus the techniques of rhetoric and the content of classical rhetorical treatises turn up in unexpected places during the Middle Ages: in discussions of grammar or logic (both of which were sometimes said to seek "eloquence") and in various parts of philosophy, as well as in law and literature. So pervasive was this diffusion of rhetoric in medieval intellectual life that one perceptive student of its history insists that "if rhetoric is defined in terms of a single subject matter—such as style, or literature, or discourse—it has no history during the Middle Ages."[11] As rhetoric gave up many of its earlier functions to the other disciplines, its own purpose was reduced to the mere providing of ornament.

The precise frontier in the history of rhetoric between the classical period and the appearance of these medieval features is difficult to draw. Some of the characteristics just cited (especially the fluctuations in the boundaries between the arts) can be found in ancient writers as well as medieval ones, and they do not disappear in the Renaissance. Yet, as the following discussion will indicate, medieval treatments of the relation between rhetoric and philosophy are easily distinguished from both classical and Renaissance ones. The "disjunction" described earlier appears clearly in representative writers from the Carolingian period through the thirteenth century.

The nature of this disjunction was that medieval writers disassociated the question of the relationship between wisdom and eloquence from the range of issues with which it had been connected in classical thought. The ideal of a union of philosophical knowledge and verbal skill by no means disappeared in the Middle Ages; on the contrary, it was often invoked. When medieval writers called upon it, however, they did so in a manner similar to that of medieval artists illustrating classical themes: they gave the ideal a nonclassical, contemporary form. Whereas in antiquity

[10] McKeon, "Rhetoric in the Middle Ages," p. 3 and *passim*. See also McKeon's article, "Poetry and Philosophy in the Twelfth Century," *Modern Philology*, XLIII (1946), p. 217.
[11] McKeon, "Rhetoric in the Middle Ages," p. 32.

discussions of the relationship between eloquence and wisdom commonly took the form of a confrontation between the two rival disciplines of oratory and philosophy, in the Middle Ages this was no longer the case. The question of how wisdom could be joined to eloquence was not formulated in terms of the relations between the orator and the philosopher. Conversely, while some of the issues which had arisen in classical debates about the proper relationship between orators and philosophers reappeared in medieval writings, they were characteristically employed to treat some separate and usually unrelated problem. Thus the classical theme was clothed in a nonclassical form, or elements of the classical form were employed in the service of nonclassical themes. Only with Petrarch would an integral revival of this important ancient debate —form and content together—occur. The contrast between his understanding of the elements of the debate and medieval writers' use of them is clear.

The first figure we shall consider is Alcuin, Charlemagne's friend and tutor.[12] Called by Charlemagne from York in 782, Alcuin was one of the intellectual leaders of the Carolingian renaissance. His activities included instruction in all three arts of the trivium. His treatise on rhetoric took the form of a dialogue between himself and Charlemagne.[13] In many ways it followed classical precedent. Alcuin's immediate authority for many of his opinions on rhetoric was the fourth-century writer Julius Victor, but since Julius had borrowed freely from *De oratore*, there is reason to describe Alcuin's doctrine as "thoroughly Ciceronian."[14] Alcuin included a discussion of the virtues in his *Rhetoric*, thus maintaining the classical tie between rhetoric and moral philosophy.

[12] See Bolgar, *The Classical Heritage*, Chap. III; Eleanor S. Duckett, *Alcuin, Friend of Charlemagne* (New York, 1952); David Knowles, *The Evolution of Medieval Thought* (Baltimore, 1962), Chap. VI.

[13] Alcuin, *The Rhetoric of Alcuin and Charlemagne*, ed. and trans., with intro., Latin text, and notes, by Wilbur Samuel Howell (Princeton, 1941).

[14] See W. S. Howell's comments in his introduction to *The Rhetoric of Alcuin and Charlemagne*, pp. 28-30.

While Alcuin was certainly aware of the need to join eloquence to wisdom, however, his ideas on how to accomplish this show none of the sophistication of Ciceronian theory. In approaching the question in the dialogue, he is either perfunctory or else treats the problem in a markedly unclassical manner. The first instance, which raised the question of this union only by implication, arose in connection with Alcuin's demonstration of the technique of induction. The type of induction he illustrated was that employed by the orator rather than the philosopher: i.e., it did not attempt to establish a general conclusion from a set of particular examples, but sought to force agreement in a particular instance by pointing out agreement to a series of analogous instances. As an example, Alcuin cited an ancient philosopher who convinced Xenophon that he would prefer his neighbor's spouse (on the analogy of his house, his land, etc.) if she appeared more perfect than his own. To Charlemagne this seemed a dangerous conclusion, and he primly observed that "This philosopher was not a Christian." Thus Charlemagne showed his distrust of rhetoric's power to encourage beliefs not in accord with Christian teaching. After raising this problem, however, Alcuin gave it very little attention. "Not a Christian," he replied, "but nevertheless a good rhetorician." "Why do we consider him an authority?" Charlemagne desired to know. "He followed the principles of his art," Alcuin answered, and changed the subject.[15]

Later in the treatise Alcuin stated much more explicitly the need to combine eloquence with wisdom. The passage dealt with the question of style. "How is style made eloquent?" Charlemagne inquired. In *De oratore* Cicero had answered that true eloquence required wisdom, and that the ideal orator would give splendor to his speech through his understanding of the philosophical basis of the case he urged. Petrarch echoed this idea in *De remediis*. Alcuin's initial reply to Charlemagne was only that style "will be made eloquent if it observes the rules of grammar, and is

---

[15] *The Rhetoric of Alcuin and Charlemagne*, pp. 118-19.

supported by the authority of the ancients."[16] A few pages later he gave a more extended answer:

> Coming now to the most important observation, we say that, just as wisdom is the foundation of everything else, so is it the true foundation of eloquence. As in life, so in speech, nothing is more praiseworthy than to do everything wisely. Therefore, the speaker should train himself to have above all an understanding of what befits himself and his subject, a sense of decorum in his choice of ideas and of words. He should not express himself in identical thoughts and phrases when he speaks to the different degrees of fortune, rank, prestige, age; his style should not be insensitive to the adaptations suggested by the place and time of his speech, and by the audience he faces; in every part of his speech, as in every minute of his life, he should let his sense of decorum be his guide.[17]

While Alcuin appealed here to the traditional ideal of a combination of eloquence and wisdom, he deprived this ancient theme of its common classical form and thus of most of its import. Both Plato and Cicero, despite their disagreements, had conceived of the problem in the same terms, and the humanists would follow them: to join eloquence to wisdom meant to place the orator in some definite relationship to philosophical truth. The demands made on the orator by the practical nature of his tasks had somehow to be reconciled with the philosopher's commitment to abstract truth. In Alcuin's *Rhetoric* this whole range of issues has disappeared. There, to combine eloquence with wisdom was not to join rhetoric to philosophy; it was only to vary speech according to the demands of decorum. Alcuin's student was not made aware of the problems which had arisen from the classical confrontation of rhetoric and philosophy, but only told to adjust his speech according to time, place, and circumstance. Such considerations had of course been part of classical discussions of

[16] *Ibid.*, p. 133.   [17] *Ibid.*, p. 137.

oratory, but they had not displaced the more basic issue of the relationship between persuasive speech and philosophical content. Thus Alcuin's combination of wisdom and eloquence did not take the form of the classical union of philosophy and oratory. For this reason, it failed to retain the full significance of the ancient ideal.

The reasons for this failure may be sought in the general observations about medieval rhetoric made above. Alcuin's knowledge of the ancient rhetorical tradition was limited by the paucity of his sources. More important, perhaps, is the difference which existed between his environment and that of the classical writers. For them the figure of the orator was a familiar and important aspect of the cultural and political scenes. For Alcuin the orator and his tasks had little reality. The problem faced by the Carolingian educator was neither one of making the orator as useful and beneficent a figure as possible, nor of justifying his techniques and concerns. It was simply the problem of making the techniques of rhetoric available to men whose education would not center on it as classical education had, and whose fundamental commitment to wisdom—Christian truth—was not to be called into question. In these circumstances the ideal of a combination of wisdom and eloquence survived, but the classical understanding of it did not.

Three centuries later Europe experienced another important intellectual advance, often referred to as the renaissance of the twelfth century.[18] Corresponding to the upsurge of activity in all fields around the time of the First Crusade, the movement was marked by the expansion of schools, the accessibility of new texts, and the dissemination of new techniques. One of the representative figures of the age was John of Salisbury, and one of its representa-

[18] Charles Homer Haskins, *The Renaissance of the Twelfth Century* (Cambridge, Mass., 1927; reprinted New York, 1957); G. Paré, A. Brunet, and P. Tremblay, *La Renaissance du XIIe siècle* (Paris, 1933); W. A. Nitze, "The So-called Twelfth Century Renaissance," *Speculum*, XXIII (1948); E. M. Sanford, "The Twelfth-Century: Renaissance or Proto-Renaissance?" *Speculum*, XXVI (1951).

tive books, his *Metalogicon*. John's work shows the great importance that ancient literature and the rhetorical tradition had for twelfth-century writers and thinkers. It demonstrates with equal clarity, however, that its author looked upon ancient learning with the eyes of his own day, and that his evocation of the union of eloquence and wisdom carried the accents of the Middle Ages, not those of the ancient world.

John has often been compared to the humanists of the Renaissance.[19] Certainly his knowledge of ancient Latin literature was impressive, and among his most important sources were Cicero and Quintilian. In a general sense, it is correct to label his basic orientation as humanistic. He regarded ethics as the highest part of philosophy, and he insisted, in words that would later be echoed by Petrarch, that its first commandment was "know thyself."[20] Moreover, this praise of moral philosophy was accompanied, in the *Metalogicon*, by an insistence on the value of eloquence. Save for virtue and wisdom, John affirmed, eloquence was to be desired above all things. The man of eloquence gained distinction because he surpassed his fellows "in those sole respects wherein man surpasses other beings."[21] John of Salisbury made the ideal of the combination of eloquence with philosophy the starting point of his defense of liberal studies in the *Metalogicon*. To attack the union of the two was to "undermine and uproot all liberal studies, assail the whole structure of philosophy," and to reduce man to

[19] See H. Liebeschütz, *Mediaeval Humanism in the Life and Writings of John of Salisbury*, Studies of the Warburg Institute, XVII (London, 1950); *The Letters of John of Salisbury*, ed. W. J. Millor, H. E. Butler, and C.L.N. Brooke (London, Edinburgh, and New York, 1955), of which only one volume has so far appeared; Ioannis Saresberiensis Episcopi Carnotensis, *Metalogicon*, ed. C.C.J. Webb (Oxford, 1929); *The Metalogicon of John of Salisbury*, trans. and ed. by D. D. McGarry (Berkeley and Los Angeles, 1955). Douglas Bush, *The Renaissance and English Humanism* (Toronto, 1939), p. 60, compares John explicitly to the humanists on the basis of his view of language and culture, and his emphasis on eloquence.

[20] *Metalogicon*, trans. and ed. D. D. McGarry, pp. 269-71. Cited below by book and chapter, with page references to this edition.

[21] *Ibid.*, I, 7; p. 27.

the state of the beasts.[22] John embraced the ancient conception with an enthusiasm closely akin to that of the humanists of the Renaissance.

John wrote his treatise in opposition to a group of his contemporaries whom he disguised under the name "Cornificians."[23] While it is difficult to connect John's description of these men with any precise movement in twelfth-century education, it is clear that he regarded them as enemies of the three arts of the trivium. If, as he asserted, Cornificius and his sect were opposed by such diverse figures as Gilbert de la Porrée, Thierry of Chartres, William of Conches, Bernard of Chartres, and Abelard, then it is hard to dispute John's claim that the "Cornificians" were the enemies of all learning. Combating their position, John praised "logic," by which he meant all the arts of the *logos*, all means of training human reason and speech. These means included grammar, rhetoric, and dialectic, plus logic in the more restricted sense of the term. John also included sophistical reasoning as a genuine form of logic, despite its dangers.[24] The various parts of "logic" in its broader sense all contributed to eloquence, which John defined as fitting and efficacious speech. This eloquence was to be joined to wisdom. John several times insisted that the logical arts (especially dialectic) had to be joined to knowledge gained from other disciplines in order to bear their promised fruit.[25] Thus he referred often to the need to combine skill in speech with a knowledge of things. His statements to this effect often remind one of classical and Renaissance demands for the union of eloquence and wisdom.

Yet John of Salisbury's vision of this union was not a revival of the classical understanding of the ideal, as Petrarch's would be. In John's hands, the classical theme was molded into a contemporary form, and in the process it lost its most distinctive features. The first suggestion of this alteration comes from John's terminology, which was often

[22] *Ibid.*, I, 1; pp. 11-12.   [23] See *Metalogicon*, I, 3-5.
[24] *Ibid.*, I, 9-10 and II, 3.
[25] See *ibid.*, I, i; II, 9; and elsewhere.

that of the fourth-century writer Martianus Capella. Martianus had written an allegorical description of *The Marriage of Mercury and Philology,* which served as the basis for many medieval discussions of the seven liberal arts. As John interpreted the allegory, Mercury stood for eloquence and Philology for the love of reason and knowledge, i.e., for philosophy.[26] Their union was indeed a kind of combination of rhetoric and philosophy, but as such it clothed the classical ideal in a strikingly nonclassical form. It is a literal example of Panofsky's principle of disjunction. For medieval writers, including John of Salisbury, *The Marriage of Mercury and Philology* served both to preserve the old ideal and to remove it from its classical context.

One indication of the changed context in which John defended eloquence is that in his mind eloquence had no special connection with rhetoric or oratory. He described it as the product of each of the three arts in turn, or of the three together ("logic" in the broad sense).[27] In fact, he gave very little space to rhetoric. He described dialectic as the most useful of the three arts; since it sought only probable conclusions, its goal was not as elusive as the certainty aimed at by demonstrative logic. "Nor does it become the plaything of political currents," as rhetoric was liable to do.[28] Thus John of Salisbury's praise of eloquence had very little to do with oratory in the classical sense. Dialectic sought to achieve persuasive force in the same way rhetoric did; the difference between the two was not that rhetoric was more concerned with persuasion, but only that it "aims to sway the judgment of persons other than the contestants."[29] John seems to have made no distinction between the relationship of eloquence to rhetoric and its relationship to dialectic.

[26] *Ibid.,* I, 1; II, 3; IV, 29.

[27] For the role of grammar in producing eloquence, see the last few chapters of Bk. I; for dialectic as the "ever-ready servant of eloquence," to which knowledge must be joined, see II, 9 (p. 93), and II, 15; for rhetoric as the source of eloquence "where persuasion is in order," I, 24 (p. 67); for all the three arts as parts of "logic" in the broadest sense, and productive of eloquence, see I, 9-10.

[28] *Ibid.,* II, 3; p. 79.   [29] *Ibid.,* p. 102.

John of Salisbury's discussion in the *Metalogicon* did not promote a revival of the ancient problem of the relationship between rhetoric and philosophy, but rather covered over those very contrasts between the two disciplines which had created the problem in the first place. In Plato and Aristotle, as in Cicero, the proper relation of oratory to philosophy presented a challenge first of all because the linguistic standards appropriate to the composition of a moving speech contrasted with those which seemed requisite for strict logical inquiry. The language of the orator sacrificed precision for general intelligibility; the philosopher's speech subordinated communication with the untrained to the search for rigor and consistency. Therefore, while classical writers recommended that the orator be trained in dialectic, they remained aware of the differences between the orator's art and the dialectician's. These differences were present to the author of the *Metalogicon* only in the vaguest terms. He drew no clear distinction between logical inquiry in the manner of dialectic and the effective expression of ideas in the manner of oratory.

Thus, the essential observation with regard to John's place in the history of the ideal we are considering here is that for him the relations between eloquence and wisdom were not a problem at all, in the ancient sense. He accused the Cornificians of breaking the sacred union of the two, and made a defense of this relationship the starting point of his attack on them. But Cornificius, whoever he may have been, was neither an orator who neglected philosophical learning nor a philosopher who turned his back on oratory. He regarded the elaboration of certain dialectical techniques and their use for the detailed study of dialectic itself as the most admirable, and perhaps the only genuine or necessary, intellectual pursuit. John's prescription for this illness was a good dose of learning in substantive, nonverbal disciplines such as ethics and theology.[30] In John's terms, the result of such treatment would be the joining of eloquence to philosophy (since John regarded the Cor-

[30] *Ibid.*, I, 3ff.

nificians' sophistry as a corrupt form of eloquence).[31] But neither this problem nor its solution had very much to do with the relative standing of oratory and philosophy in the classical or Renaissance sense.

The distance between John's version of the union of wisdom and eloquence and the classical or humanist one is further revealed by his references to the various classical philosophical schools. While taken for the most part from Cicero, John's comments on the Stoics, Peripatetics, and Academics preserve only a small part of the Roman orator's interest in these philosophers. Doubtless John meant to associate himself with Cicero when he declared himself a follower of Academic skepticism "in matters that are doubtful to a wise man."[32] Perhaps he was also influenced by Cicero in his general preference for the Peripatetics. His statement that this school had "made careful investigations into the nature of all things, so as to determine which should be avoided as evil, discounted as useless, sought after as good, or preferred as better, and finally which are called 'good' or 'bad' according to circumstances," has a Ciceronian ring.[33] So has his comparison of Aristotle's followers with those of Plato: "The Peripatetics, who philosophize in a more human manner, refrain from being mentally transported for themselves and for God, as do the Platonists. On the contrary, they remain sober for [the sake of their fellow] men. . . ."[34] Yet John did not grasp the implication of Cicero's juxtaposition of Stoic and Peripatetic ethics. He never connected the moral doctrines of the Peripatetics with their "humanity" as Cicero did; in the passage just quoted, he cited Peripatetic logic, not ethics. Nor did he specifically contrast the Peripatetics with the Stoics, though he noted that the latter school "held that all sins are equally grave."[35] John possessed the materials to understand the distinction between the Stoics and the Peripatetics as Cicero had outlined it, but he failed to reconstruct

[31] *Ibid.*, pp. 91, 93.
[33] *Ibid.*, p. 76. Cf. above, Chap. I.
[35] *Ibid.*, p. 76. See also p. 180.

[32] *Ibid.*, p. 6.
[34] *Metalogicon*, pp. 261-62.

188

this contrast. The differences between the two schools did not suggest to him two fundamentally separate moral and intellectual perspectives. This was true because, unlike Cicero and Petrarch, John of Salisbury never considered the opposition between the two schools in connection with the rival perspectives of the "orator" and the "philosopher." He did not regard the contrast between Stoics and Peripatetics as relevant to the combination of rhetoric and philosophy which he himself championed.

Like other medieval writers, John of Salisbury reveals his historical position through his lack of interest in the orator as a distinctive kind of thinker or speaker. John's man of learning was neither a philosopher who had clothed his wisdom in eloquence, nor an orator who had steeped himself in the search for truth. The closest the author of the *Metalogicon* came to either was in his picture of the ideal teacher of grammar, who "will more fully perceive and more lucidly explain the charming elegance of the authors in proportion to the breadth and thoroughness of his knowledge of various disciplines." The authors had incorporated knowledge of all the various disciplines into their works, and the grammarian who was able to reveal the learning they contained could teach them best.[36] John's grammarian (he cited Bernard of Chartres as a contemporary model) would combine linguistic skill with philosophical knowledge, and would thus recall the old ideal of the combination of rhetoric and philosophy. In such a form, however, the combination differed markedly from the classical understanding of it. Like John's other evocations of the union of wisdom and eloquence, this one was carried out in contemporary terms. The classical theme appeared only in a nonclassical guise.

One of John of Salisbury's most famous contemporaries was Abelard.[37] As a chief figure in the early development of scholastic philosophy, Abelard is seldom claimed as a precursor of the humanists. Like other twelfth-century in-

[36] *Ibid.*, I, 24.
[37] On Abelard, see Etienne Gilson, *History of Christian Philosophy in the Middle Ages* (New York, 1954), pp. 153ff.

tellectual figures, however, Abelard was well read in many classical authors, and he often quoted Cicero. To be sure, he did not approach ancient literature in the same spirit as John of Salisbury tells us that Bernard of Chartres did, but neither could he be considered to resemble John's "Cornificius." He is relevant in this context because he seems to represent a disjunction of a different sort from that seen in John of Salisbury. He did not employ the ideal of the union of wisdom and eloquence to serve a contemporary need; but he did adapt some elements of the classical confrontation of oratory and philosophy for use in his discussion of a theme which had little to do with the relationship of wisdom to eloquence.

Abelard was never primarily concerned with rhetoric as such. The art that most attracted him was dialectic. He declared dialectic to be the chief science, and he used it as an approach to other parts of philosophy.[38] Yet he certainly believed that rhetoric had legitimate uses, for he once wrote that "the intention of all divine Scripture is to teach or to move in the manner of a rhetorical speech," an idea which was shared by other medieval writers.[39] Moreover, Abelard made use of a series of techniques derived from rhetoric in his famous *Sic et Non*. Here, it will be remembered, he collected a large number of seemingly contradictory texts, prefaced by a set of rules for interpreting and reconciling them. These rules, as several writers have pointed out, stemmed from rhetoric. Richard McKeon describes them as involving "such directions as careful consideration of context, comparison of texts, specification of time, place, and person, determination of original cause of statement, differentiation of general measures from particular." He goes on to observe, "Although this method led to a further step in the dialectical resolution of the contradictions, the method at this stage is rhetorical rather than

[38] Abelard, *Intro. ad Theologiam*, in Migne, *Patrologia Latina*, clxxviii, 979. On this work, see Maurice de Wulf, *History of Medieval Philosophy*, trans. from the 6th French edn. by E. C. Messenger (London, 1953), I, 196.
[39] McKeon, "Rhetoric in the Middle Ages," pp. 20-21.

190

dialectical."[40] That is, Abelard proposed that the apparent contradictions between the various texts could be understood by keeping in mind the fact that their authors followed rhetorical precepts of composition, and by tracing the effects of these precepts on their statements.

The prologue to *Sic et Non* was thus based on a clearly articulated understanding of the rhetorical basis of ancient and patristic literature. What is especially striking about Abelard's discussion is his recognition that differences of circumstance would impose not only different styles of speaking or writing, but modifications of substance as well. Abelard quoted Cicero's statement that "the style of speech which is polished with truth itself, through disputation, differs from that which is accommodated to the understanding of all. For this reason, we speak like the crowd, and say that some men are strong, others good, others prudent, when we are employing common language and popular speech." (The contrast was with the Stoic insistence that the man who possessed any one virtue must possess all virtues.)[41] Thus an author who spoke to two different audiences, each in terms accommodated to its particular level of understanding, would change the content of his speech when he modified its form. Abelard did not actually say that some of the authorities collected in *Sic et Non* had spoken as philosophers while others had spoken as orators, but he nonetheless made use of one aspect of the classical division between the two roles.

It is important to recognize that Abelard's thought included this reminiscence of the classical confrontation of oratory and philosophy. Yet this circumstance does not blur the line we have drawn between the medieval adaptations of the classical rhetorical tradition and the humanist revival of it. Abelard drew upon some traditional rhetorical techniques and perceptions which John of Salisbury had ignored, but he did so in a context radically different from

[40] *Ibid.*, p. 21.
[41] Abelard, *Sic et Non*, "Prologus," in Migne, *P. L.*, clxxviii, 1344. Note also *ibid.*, 1339-40.

classical discussions of oratory. He used rhetorical methods to serve an enterprise which had nothing to do with the pursuit of eloquence. It was philosophical consistency that Abelard sought; rhetorical principles were helpful only because they might explain why some men failed to achieve it. The philosopher was to make use of certain elements of rhetoric, but his goal was not the union of wisdom with eloquence. John of Salisbury had invoked the classical theme without preserving its classical form; Abelard employed elements of the form to serve a different —even an opposed—theme. The separation of classical form and classical content marked both applications.

Both John and Abelard belonged to the first half of the twelfth century. In the century and a half that followed, intellectual activity (at least north of the Alps) moved further away from the classicism of the twelfth-century renaissance, and rhetorical ideals played an increasingly smaller part.[42] No late-twelfth- or thirteenth-century writer matched John of Salisbury's concern for the union of wisdom and eloquence; the grammatical culture represented by Bernard of Chartres came more and more to be subordinated to dialectical and theological interests. Echoes of the old controversies could still be heard; indeed, they were amplified by rivalries between various disciplines which accompanied the changes in intellectual life. But these echoes were also distorted by the peculiar features of the intellectual landscape which reflected them. The participants in the disputes did not see the issues dividing them in terms of the classical distinction between the pursuit of eloquence and the search for wisdom. Rather, they spoke of rivalries between the "authors" and the "arts" (that is to say, between the study of classical literature and the new program of education which was dominated by dialectic), or of "battles of the arts." The latter notion was given a bizarre allegorical form in a thirteenth-century

---

[42] See Gilson, *History of Christian Philosophy*, Part Six, Chap. II; De Wulf, *History of Medieval Philosophy*, I, 54; Paetow, *The Arts Course, passim.*

poem which envisioned the arts and their champions engaged in a pitched battle with one another.[43] A third common variety of learned conflict was the dispute about the nature of a particular art of the trivium, usually grammar. As the study of language, grammar became the focus of a quarrel between those who wished to teach language in connection with literature and those who sought to remake language as an instrument of philosophical inquiry.[44] Each of these disagreements reflected some aspect of the ancient problem of the relationship between eloquence and wisdom. At the same time, they all show that men of the twelfth and thirteenth centuries could perceive this problem only in terms and categories directly related to their own experience, and not in those of the classical world.

The general outcome of these debates was a reduction of the importance given grammatical and rhetorical studies, in favor of more strictly philosophical pursuits. By the time scholastic philosophy reached a mature stage of development in the thirteenth century, rhetoric was a subject of only secondary interest in the main scholastic centers, and the problem of the relationship between wisdom and eloquence had ceased to be a very lively issue. The main topics of learned discussion derived either from theology or from the rediscovered treatises of Aristotle; wisdom in some form was stated to be the goal of most intellectual

[43] Paetow, pp. 13-15; on the "battle of the arts," see *Two Medieval Satires on the University of Paris: La Bataille des vii arts of Henri d'Andeli and the Morale Scolarium of John of Garland*, ed. L. J. Paetow (Berkeley, 1927). Also, Bolgar, *The Classical Heritage*, pp. 207ff.

[44] On these matters, see Paetow, *The Arts Course*, Chap. II; Gilson, *History of Christian Philosophy*, pp. 312-14; R. H. Robins, *Ancient and Medieval Grammatical Theory in Europe* (London, 1951), pp. 77ff.; R. W. Hunt, "Studies on Priscian in the Eleventh and Twelfth Centuries," *Mediaeval and Renaissance Studies*, I (1943) and II (1950); R. W. Hunt, "The Introductions to the 'Artes' in the Twelfth Century," *Studia Mediaevalia in honorem . . . R. J. Martin* (Bruges, 1948?), pp. 85ff.; Heinrich Roos, S.J., "Die Stellung der Grammatik im Lehrbetrieb des 13. Jahrhunderts," *Artes Liberales*, ed. Josef Koch (Leiden and Cologne, 1959).

activity, and the bearing of eloquence upon it did not become a pressing question.

Even a thinker like St. Bonaventure, who attributed a certain dignity to rhetoric among the liberal arts, was concerned about the relation of wisdom to eloquence only in a perfunctory way. Bonaventure knew what functions classical authors had attributed to rhetoric, and he adapted these classical conceptions to preaching: the mind is moved to assent by rational arguments, he observed, but real conviction (*affectus*) requires rhetorical persuasion.[45] Sometimes he stated that the mind was taught by logic and moved by rhetoric, but at other times he placed both *docere* and *movere* in the orator's domain.[46] He wrote an *Art of Preaching*, and seems to have applied the rules of Latin prosody to some of his writings.[47] Certainly he warned against the dangers of rhetoric, advising preachers to take care lest they become more interested in eloquence than in Christian wisdom. But he also cautioned against an inordinate attachment to secular philosophy, a failing which he probably found more widespread among his contemporaries than a love of oratory.[48]

Bonaventure was concerned to establish the proper place of both eloquence and philosophy in the Christian life. This concern defined his interest in the proper relationship between the two disciplines themselves. For Bon-

[45] See J. G. Bougerol, O.F.M., *Introduction à l'Etude de Saint Bonaventure* (Paris, 1961); McKeon, "Rhetoric in the Middle Ages," pp. 24-25; S. Bonaventurae, *Collationes in Hexameron*, ed. R. P. Delorme (Quaracchi, 1934), Visio I, Collatio i, p. 68. Also, Baldwin, *Medieval Rhetoric and Poetic to 1400*, pp. 176-78.

[46] Compare Bonaventure's *De reductione artium ad sacram theologiam*, 4, in *Opera Omnia* (Quaracchi, 1891), V, 321 (quoted by McKeon, p. 24n.), with his *Collationes in Hexameron*, ed. Delorme, p. 71.

[47] Bougerol, *Introduction à l'Etude de Saint Bonaventure*, p. 97.

[48] Bonaventure, *Ars concionandi*, 31, in *Opera Omnia* (Florence, 1901), IX, 16: "cavenda sunt in sermone nimis ornata eloquia vel eloquentia." Sermon for the fourth Sunday in Advent, quoted by Bougerol, p. 207: "cogitationes humanae philosophiae subiiciendae sunt secundum dictamen veritatis aeternae, non secundum dictamen rationis philosophicae." See Bougerol's discussion of Bonaventure's cautions against philosophy, pp. 207ff.

194

aventure it was essential and sufficient that both eloquence and wisdom recognize their origin in Christian truth and their dependence on divine illumination. Rhetoric was one of the several branches of philosophical knowledge, all of which were founded on the wisdom of God. The recognition of this principle Bonaventure called the *reductio artium ad sacram theologiam,* "the return of all the arts to their origin in divine wisdom."[49] Eloquence was thus to be tied firmly to the wisdom which was its source, but the problem of establishing this connection was submerged in the larger question of the relationship between all forms of rational activity and the superrational Christian revelation. While the question of the relation of wisdom to eloquence sometimes occurred in Bonaventure's writing, therefore, it never took any of its classical forms. Bonaventure asked not that the orator satisfy the claims philosophy made on his art, but that both orator and philosopher accept the challenge of Christian wisdom.

Somewhat more complicated are the features assumed by our problem in the writings of St. Bonaventure's great rival, St. Thomas Aquinas. St. Thomas gave rhetoric a lower place among the arts, but his greater sympathy for secular intellectual pursuits in general led him to make broader use of ideas drawn from ancient writers on rhetoric than St. Bonaventure did. In its main features, Thomas' view of oratory was Aristotelian. Rhetoric was one of the acts of reason, but a fairly lowly one, ranking below both "judicative logic" and dialectic. "Judicative logic" was the logic of certitude and therefore the highest form. Dialectic came next, leading not to certain knowledge but only to conviction or opinion. Rhetoric was similar to dialectic in that it dealt with probable matters in a legitimate, rational way, but inferior to dialectic because its product was not conviction or opinion but only "a kind of suspicion" that one of two contrary possibilities was the correct

---

[49] St. Bonaventure, *De reductione artium ad theologiam,* a commentary with intro. and trans. by Sister Emma Thérèse Healy (St. Bonaventure, N. Y., 1939).

one. (Rhetoric, however, was superior to both poetry and sophistical reasoning.)[50] This, at least, was the schema Thomas drew up when he dealt with the matter systematically. At other times he referred to both dialectic and rhetoric as forms of reasoning about matters of contingency, in which opposite possibilities must be faced.[51] The second manner of relating the two arts was somewhat closer to Aristotle's description of rhetoric as the "counterpart" of dialectic, but both conceptions have Aristotelian sources.

Not all of St. Thomas' references to rhetoric derived from Aristotle, however. The Dominican theologian was also well read in a number of Cicero's works, and his attitude toward the Roman orator seems to have been generally friendly.[52] He had of course read St. Augustine's *De doctrina christiana*, in which much of classical rhetorical theory was adapted to the needs of the Christian preacher, and from it he quoted the classical description of the purposes of rhetoric: to teach, to please, and to move.[53] He was also aware of the common classical notion that rhetoric was concerned with civic life and the subjects connected with it, and he attributed the orator's failure to achieve certainty to the nature of his material as well as to the place of rhetoric among the logical disciplines.[54] At least once he spoke of the orator simply as a man whose excellence lay in speech.[55]

[50] McKeon, "Rhetoric in the Middle Ages," pp. 23-24. Aquinas, *In libros Posteriorum Analyticorum Expositio*, I, Lectio 1.

[51] Aquinas, *Summa Theologica*, I, 83, 1, c: "Ratio enim circa contingentia habet viam ad opposita, ut patet in dialecticis syllogismis, et rhetoricis persuasionibus."

[52] E. K. Rand, *Cicero in the Courtroom of St. Thomas Aquinas* (Milwaukee, 1946).

[53] *Summa Theologica*, II-II, 177, 1, 1.

[54] *In X. libros Ethicorum*, I, Lectio iii (where the point is made that less certainty is possible in rhetoric than in mathematics): "Rhetorica autem negotiatur circa materiam civilem, in qua multiplex variatio accidit." Cf. *Summa Theologica*, I-II, 105, 2, ad 8: "in negotiis humanis non potest haberi demonstrativa probatio et infallibilis, sed sufficit aliqua coniecturalis probabilitas, secundum quam rhetor persuadet." Cf. Bonaventure, *Collationes in Hexameron*, Visio I, Collatio, i, pp. 69-70.

[55] *Summa Theologica*, I-II, 47, 3, c.

196

Yet Thomas was very little concerned with eloquence as an ideal or a goal. He saw a close connection between reason and speech, but this meant that speech, if it were to have good effects, had to depend strictly on reason. He thought that reason was an essential characteristic of speech. He seems to have felt the need to justify calling the works of orators "speeches" (and orators "speakers"), on the grounds that speeches included rational arguments.[56] He does not seem to have ever discussed the problem of the relation between wisdom and eloquence in explicit terms. In describing the task of the preacher he once coupled *sapientia* and *eloquentia*, stating that Christian preaching should not rely on "worldly wisdom and eloquence," but he said no more on the subject.[57] In other contexts he sometimes discussed related issues. Thus he once wrote that "the knowledge of things is more noble than the knowledge of words," and added that the mind is edified only by knowledge, not by speaking.[58] He regarded speech as a means for the transmission of grace, but as such it was only "a kind of tool"; the internal persuasion was accomplished not by the language but by the Holy Spirit itself.[59]

Thus there are a number of echoes of the ancient questions about wisdom and eloquence in the writings of St. Thomas Aquinas. The instances mentioned here may not be the only ones that an extensive search would reveal, but they are probably representative. They show Thomas as a philosophical thinker with a basically Aristotelian view of rhetoric, but with a fundamentally nonclassical perspective on it. Thomas Aquinas followed Aristotle in defining rhetoric, but he gave much less attention to oratory than Aristotle had. More revealing than the narrow dimensions of the Dominican's interest in rhetoric are the contexts in which he chose to

---

[56] *4 Sent.* 15, 4, 1, 1, c: "oratio dicitur quasi oris ratio. . . . Et quia sermones rhetorici, qui conciones dicuntur, continent argumentationes ad persuadendum accomodatas; inde est quod etiam orationes dicuntur et rhetores oratores."

[57] *Summa Theologica*, I-II, 185, 6, ad 2.

[58] *Ibid.*, II-II, 176, 2, c.

[59] *Ibid.*, II-II, 177, 1, c.

speak about it. All the references to rhetoric and oratory just noted occur in contexts which have little or nothing to do with rhetoric itself. The reference to the orator as a man excellent in speech appears in a discussion of whether any kind of excellence may be a cause of anger; the connection between rhetoric and everyday life is pointed out in a defense of the Old Testament legal principle that the testimony of two or three witnesses shall be accepted as the truth; the terms *sapientia* and *eloquentia* are coupled in an attempt to allegorize the apostolic ideal of poverty and therefore to make it legitimate for bishops to own property. Similarly, the observations that the knowledge of things is superior to the knowledge of words, and that only understanding, not speech, edifies the mind, are part of a discussion of prophecy. Although as such they at least appear in connection with a problem analogous to that of the orator and philosophy, prophets being speakers, this does not alter the general conclusion. St. Thomas Aquinas employed ancient ideas about rhetoric only in relation to contemporary questions, not in connection with the kind of problems discussed in his classical sources.

In this he resembles the other medieval writers we have considered here, all of whom contrast in the same way with the humanists. Alcuin, John of Salisbury, Abelard, Bonaventure, and Thomas Aquinas all drew on the ancient rhetorical tradition in ways required by their quite different contemporary situations. They used ideas from classical literature to treat themes and subjects which bore little or no relation to the interests displayed in the ancient sources. Petrarch, Salutati, Bruni, and Valla, on the other hand, approached ancient rhetorical literature with a set of concerns much closer to those of classical writers; they employed classical material in connection with questions which ancient thinkers had sought to answer for themselves. Thus they brought to an end the disassociation between classical form and classical content which had prevailed during the Middle Ages. In this sense Panofsky's

198

principle of disjunction is indeed applicable to the history of ideas.

To be sure, such an application of Panofsky's principle is limited. It touches only the set of ideas we have examined in this study, leaving out much that was of interest both to medieval writers and to the humanists. An examination of other ideas or issues might yield quite different results.[60] Yet it must be remembered that rhetoric was one of the dominant intellectual interests of antiquity, the central educational discipline during most of the classical period of Greece and Rome. The ability of the humanists to discuss in a classical fashion the range of moral and intellectual issues raised by the philosophical criticism of rhetoric suggests a genuine rapprochement with their counterparts in the ancient world. In reviving the ideals of classical oratory, the humanists opened the way to the recovery of much more in ancient culture. Between medieval adaptations of classical literature and the humanists' return to the world of the classical orator, the dividing line should not be erased.

[60] For a similar conclusion in another context, however, see Rice, *The Renaissance Idea of Wisdom*, p. 28.

CHAPTER VII

FROM THE DICTATORES
TO THE HUMANISTS

CLEAR as the line between medieval writers and the humanists may be, however, one must be careful not to assume that it marks an absolute boundary between the Middle Ages and the Renaissance. Not only did many medieval elements (including some of those described above) persist into the fifteenth century; humanism itself also had medieval beginnings which we have not yet attempted to bring to light. Humanism evolved principally out of a medieval intellectual movement which was peripheral to such major developments as the Carolingian renaissance, the renaissance of the twelfth century, and the rise of scholastic philosophy. The main features of this movement were two: it was a species of professional rhetoric, and it was primarily an Italian phenomenon. While still conforming to the principle of disjunction described earlier, it carried the seeds of humanist classicism. Before looking at this medieval Italian rhetoric specifically, we must say something about its historical setting; that is, about the place of Italy in the civilization of the Middle Ages.

As most historians use the term, "Middle Ages" refers to Europe as a whole, while the traditional concept of the Renaissance relates (at least first of all) to Italy. This common usage has often obscured a very important point: Italy differed from the countries north of the Alps not only in the period of the Renaissance, but in the Middle Ages as well. As early as the twelfth century, the contrast between the largely agrarian and feudal society to the north and the predominantly urban life of the Italian peninsula was clear. Otto of Freising, the nephew of Frederick Barbarossa, was struck by it.[1] He found feudal values challenged by the

[1] Otto of Freising, *The Deeds of Frederick Barbarossa*, trans. and annotated by C. C. Mierow (New York, 1953), pp. 127-28.

urban character of Italian life and by the survival of Roman lore. By Otto's time, the economic expansion which accompanied the First Crusade had given vigor to the life of the Italian towns—as his Uncle Frederick was to learn to his sorrow. The communal revolutions of the late eleventh and twelfth centuries had proclaimed the independence of many towns from outside political control, and the dominance of the towns over the countryside was beginning to be established. Even before 1200, one finds evidence that town life in Italy could at times become the focus for patriotic sentiment, expressed through an identification with the achievements of the Romans.[2] In short, Italy did not wait until the fifteenth century to show its separateness from the dominant forms of medieval life; the unique character of Italian society was clear much earlier.

The most important aspect of this uniqueness was the strongly urban character of life in Italy. Yet Italy was not the only region of medieval Europe in which towns played a major role, and it is not sufficient simply to describe Italian society as urban or bourgeois. It must be emphasized that the town life of medieval Italy differed in quite fundamental ways from that of other parts of Europe. Italy maintained many ties to classical Rome which did not exist in other regions. This meant that certain vestiges of Roman urban life had survived more easily there, and that cities played a part in Italian society unlike their role in the North. Put in its simplest terms, the difference was this: in the North, the towns functioned as foreign elements within a society which was basically agrarian and feudal; in Italy, towns were the center of social life for the whole society,

[2] A Pisan poet celebrated his city's triumph over the Saracens in the eleventh century with these lines: "Inclytorum Pisanorum scripturus historiam,/ Antiquorum Romanorum renovo memoriam,/ Nam ostendit modo Pisa laudem admirabilem,/ Quam olim recepit Roma Vincendo Carthaginem." Quoted by H. O. Taylor, *The Medieval Mind* (London, 1927), I, 253, and by Garrett Mattingly, "Changing Attitudes Towards the State During the Renaissance," in *Facets of the Renaissance*, essays by Wallace K. Ferguson, Garrett Mattingly, *et al.* (New York, Evanston, and London, 1963), p. 39.

"feudal" elements as well as "bourgeois" ones.[3] Feudal nobles of middle rank were among the first members of Italian urban communes, and their descendants continued to be influential in town life.[4] From the earliest moment of their history, the towns in Italy were the scenes of cooperation and interaction between landed and commercial interests, between feudal aristocrats and middle-class merchants. Attempts by the towns to control the neighboring countryside sometimes expressed the hostility of city-dwellers toward rural nobles, but often they resulted when rights to rural areas, earlier claimed by aristocratic members of the communes, were taken over by the towns.[5] Within the towns, political struggles often involved elements of the rivalry between "bourgeois" and "aristocratic" interests, but each of the rival parties actually contained representatives of various economic and social groups. What characterized the magnates or aristocrats was not feudal origin, but long residence and powerful connections within the town itself; moreover, these periods of struggle were often followed by interludes of mingling and partial fusion of the two groups. Even in the fifteenth century, Italian urban society was marked by strong family loyalties and by widespread networks of aristocratic patronage.[6]

Italian towns, then, unlike those of any northern region, were the focus of activity—social, political, cultural—for all important social groups. Urban life and the values it stim-

[3] Nicola Ottokar, *Studi comunali e fiorentini* (Florence, 1948), pp. 4ff.

[4] Gino Luzzato, *An Economic History of Italy, from the Fall of the Roman Empire to the Beginning of the Sixteenth Century,* trans. Philip Jones (London, 1961), pp. 66-71; Enrico Fiumi, "Sui rapporti economici tra città e contado nell' età comunale," *Archivio Storico Italiano,* CXIV (1956), 18-68; P. J. Jones, "Florentine Families and Florentine Diaries in the Fourteenth Century," *Papers of the British School at Rome,* XXIV (1956), 183-205.

[5] Ottokar, *Studi comunali e fiorentini,* pp. 18ff.

[6] N. Ottokar, *Il Comune di Firenze alla fine del dugento* (Florence, 1926; reissued with an intro. by E. Sestan, 1962); David Herlihy, *Pisa in the Early Renaissance* (New Haven, 1958), p. xii; Gene A. Brucker, "The Structure of Patrician Society in Renaissance Florence," *Colloquium,* No. I (1964), pp. 2-11.

ulated were not the exclusive preserve of nonaristocrats, but conditioned the life of society as a whole. The pattern which historians have most commonly seen in the social history of the European countries—namely a class of townsmen "rising" within a society founded on nonurban forms of life—does not fit Italy in the Middle Ages and Renaissance. What existed in many parts of the Italian peninsula was rather a society centered around town life. The basic content of historical change here was not a shift in the balance of feudal and nonfeudal elements. It consisted rather of developments within a society where all major groups participated in the evolution of urban life. One cannot properly represent the coming of the Renaissance in Italy as the change from a primarily feudal to a predominantly urban way of life.[7]

What the traditional account describes is less the change from medieval to Renaissance society as it happened all over Europe, than the contrast between medieval society north of the Alps and the social order which emerged in Italy with the rise of the communes. Indeed, it is relevant to observe at this point that although the notion that a revival of certain kinds of activity had taken place was abroad in fourteenth- and fifteenth-century Italy, the modern concept of the Renaissance as a unified period was elaborated in the nineteenth century by northern Europeans, notably Jules Michelet and Jacob Burckhardt.[8] Both of them contrasted Renaissance Italian civilization with an image of the Middle Ages drawn in large part from the history of

[7] A recent attempt to describe the period of the Renaissance in these terms is Wallace K. Ferguson, *Europe in Transition, 1300-1520* (Boston, 1962). For an imaginative criticism of this "conventional wisdom" as it applies to English history, see J. H. Hexter, "A New Framework for Social History," *Reappraisals in History* (New York and Evanston, 1961), pp. 14-25. The weaknesses of the "rising middle class" approach as applied to Italian history are different from those pointed out by Hexter with regard to England, but a similar rethinking of traditional categories seems to be required.

[8] See Johan Huizinga, "The Problem of the Renaissance," *Men and Ideas* (New York, 1959), pp. 243-87; Wallace K. Ferguson, *The Renaissance in Historical Thought* (Cambridge, Mass., 1948).

203

the countries north of the Alps. Debate on the problem of the Renaissance has for the most part continued to set a medieval culture largely centered in France against a Renaissance which first emerged in Italy. It is precisely this contrast which we have affirmed in Chapter VI: all of the medieval figures discussed there (including the Italians among them) did their work in the North and belonged to intellectual currents which were primarily Northern in character.

The contrast between Renaissance Italy and the *Italian* Middle Ages (taking the death of Dante as the customary dividing line) is much less sharp. Indeed, one prominent Italian historian, Armando Sapori, has recently denied that the traditional boundary between the Middle Ages and the Renaissance can be drawn in Italian history.[9] If we take the term Renaissance in its literal sense, Sapori suggests, then we must apply it in a manner quite different from the usual one. The important moment of revival in most realms of Italian life was not the fourteenth or fifteenth century, but the onset of the Crusades. Arguing from the perspective of economic history, but considering politics and culture also, Sapori finds in Italy, from the twelfth century on, a society characterized by urban life, prosperity, individualism, and a high degree of education and sophistication. The necessary basis for this development was the economic advance of which the Crusades were both the sign and the implement. In this advance the Italian towns played a unique role; this period, initiated by the Crusades, may be said to end with the new economic and political conditions of the sixteenth century, which altered many features of European life as a whole and transformed the position of Italy within it.

[9] Armando Sapori, "Medioevo e Rinascimento, spunti per una diversa periodizzazione," *Archivio Storico Italiano*, CXV (1957); *idem*, "Moyen Age et Renaissance Vus d'Italie," *Annales, Economies-Sociétés-Civilisations*, XI (1956), 433-57; *idem*, *L'Età della Rinascita* (Milan, 1958). A similar periodization has been suggested on primarily political grounds by Frederic C. Lane, "At the Roots of Republicanism," *American Historical Review*, LXXI (1966), 403-20, esp. 417.

This view of Italian economic and social history may help to place the emergence of humanism in the fourteenth and early fifteenth centuries in its proper context. In order to account for the coming of humanism, it does not seem necessary to posit a fundamental change in the social order of medieval Italy. The following discussion of the growth of humanism from its medieval roots is based on the hypothesis that there was a large degree of continuity in the framework of Italian society from the thirteenth to the fifteenth centuries, and thus seeks to describe what we may call nonstructural changes. Petrarchian humanism was in some significant ways a new phenomenon in Italian life, but in other ways it reflected the continuity between Renaissance civilization and the Italian Middle Ages.

Just as the social and political organization of medieval Italian society differed from that of the North, so did the chief intellectual interests of the two regions diverge.[10] In the North, culture was dominated from the late twelfth century by the philosophical movement later called scholasticism. In Italy, however, the study of philosophy in the strict sense did not achieve a comparable place in intellectual life. There the universities fostered more practical activities, notably law and medicine. Closely related to legal studies was a discipline with closer ties to everyday life in Italy than either medicine or law, namely rhetoric.

Medieval Italian rhetoric was quite a different thing from the Ciceronian humanism of the Renaissance. For the most

[10] On the special character of medieval intellectual life in Italy, see first of all, Kristeller, "Humanism and Scholasticism in the Italian Renaissance," in *Studies in Renaissance Thought and Letters*, pp. 554ff. Kristeller points out that knowledge of classical literature was less widespread in medieval Italy than in France in the same period, and thus concludes that "there can be no doubt that there was an Italian Renaissance; that is, a cultural Renaissance of Italy, not so much in contrast with the Middle Ages in general or with the French Middle Ages, but very definitely in contrast with the Italian Middle Ages" (p. 556). On the same question, see also Hastings Rashdall, *The Universities of Europe in the Middle Ages*, new edn. by F. M. Powicke and A. B. Emden (Oxford, 1936), I, esp. 102, 234; Karl Vossler, *Medieval Culture*, trans. W. C. Lawton (New York, 1929), II, esp. 25ff.

part it was a quite mundane and practical activity, called *ars dictaminis* or *ars notaria*.[11] *Ars dictaminis* had to do primarily with letter-writing; its practitioners, called *dictatores*, wrote about the principles of epistolary composition, applied them in specified situations, and made formularies of letters for use on various occasions both by individuals and by town governments or princes. *Ars notaria* was the craft of the *notaio* or notary, whose chief tasks revolved around drawing up legal documents and contracts; his clients also might be either private individuals or public officials. While the two arts were distinct, they were very closely related. Often the *notaio* and the *dictator* were the same person; writers on *notaria* included precepts of composition in their works, and manuals of *dictamen* sometimes contained notarial forms. Both arts had the same general aim: to provide the written necessities of urban life.

[11] On this medieval rhetoric, see, in addition to the works cited above in Chap. VI, note 3, the following: L. Rockinger, *Briefsteller und Formelbuecher des elften bis vierzehnten Jahrhunderts* (Munich, 1863-64); A. Gaudenzi, "Sulla Cronologia delle opere dei dettatori bolognesi da Boncompagno a Bene di Lucca," *Bull. d. Ist. St. It.*, XIV (1895), 85-174; G. Manacorda, *Storia della Scuola in Italia* (Milan, 1913), II, 255-79; Charles Homer Haskins, *Studies in Medieval Culture* (Oxford, 1929), pp. 170-92; H. M. Willard, "The Use of the Classics in the *Flores Rhetorici* of Alberic of Monte Cassino," *Haskins Anniversary Essays* (Boston, 1929), pp. 351ff.; Francesco Novati, "Pier della Vigna," and "Il Notaio nella vita e nella letteratura Italiana dalle origini," both in *Freschi e Minii del Dugento* (Milan, 1908); idem, *La Giovinezza di Coluccio Salutati* (Turin, 1888); Ernst Kantorowicz, "An 'Autobiography' of Guido Faba," *Mediaeval and Renaissance Studies*, I (1943), 253-80; idem, "Anonymi 'Aurea Gemma,'" *Medievalia et Humanistica*, I (1943), 41-57; Helene Wieruszowski, "*Ars dictaminis* in the Time of Dante," *Medievalia et Humanistica*, I (1943), 95-108; idem, "Arezzo as a Center of Learning and Letters in the Thirteenth Century," *Traditio*, IX (1953), 321-91; Giuseppe Saitta, "Fra i Dettatori Bolognesi: Boncompagno da Signa," *Prospettive Storiche e Problemi Attuali dell' Educazione: Studi in Onore di E. Codignola* (Florence, 1960), pp. 16-27. For an excellent description of the diversity and importance of the notaries in a particular town, see J. K. Hyde, *Padua in the Age of Dante* (Manchester and New York, 1966), pp. 154-74.

One noteworthy aspect of this medieval rhetoric was its close association with the study of law.[12] The famous school of law at the University of Bologna had originally been a school of rhetoric, and even after the legal faculty became independent it retained many connections with rhetorical instruction. Notaries and public secretaries required some knowledge of legal forms and at least a smattering of legal principles. Even as late as the fourteenth century, students of rhetoric were required to devote some time to the study of law, and teachers of *notaria* sometimes lectured on legal texts. Lawyers and notaries formed a single guild in most towns, usually called the *arte di giudici e notai*. Many men followed both professions. One consideration which distinguished the two, however, was that a career as a rhetorician required fewer years of study than did a degree in law. As a result, there were many more notaries than lawyers, and a career as a notary seems often to have served as a vehicle for social advancement.[13]

Not all the activities of the rhetoricians had to do with letters and documents. Public speaking was cultivated too, both in sermons and in secular speech. Otto of Freising was struck by the strong interest Italians displayed in public oratory, and his successor Rahewin remarked that eloquence was a pursuit in which Italians were "accustomed to glory."[14] The usual name for public oratory in medieval

[12] See Novati, *La Giovinezza di Coluccio Salutati*, pp. 68-71; on lawyers who wrote on *dictamen*, see *ibid.*, pp. 45-46n. Also, Wieruszowski, "Arezzo as a Center of Learning and Letters."

[13] On the career of notary as a means of social advancement, see Kantorowicz, "An 'Autobiography' of Guido Faba," p. 266 and note. Also see Novati, "Il Notaio nella vita e nella letteratura . . ."; and Hyde's *Padua in the Age of Dante*, pp. 165ff., which emphasizes the importance of patronage in the career of Mussato. Note also the statement of Giovanni del Virgilio: "Cum tanta sit rhetorice dignitas, ut . . . solum eius particula que vocatur epistola rusticanos ad regum consilia provocet, divitiis locupletet egenos et indecores honoribus condecoret" (P. O. Kristeller, "Un 'Ars Dictaminis' di Giovanni del Virgilio," *Italia Medioevale e Umanistica*, IV [1961], 193).

[14] Otto of Freising, *The Deeds of Frederick Barbarossa*, pp. 146, 235.

Italy was *ars arengandi*; it was linked to *dictamen*. The thirteenth-century *dictator* Brunetto Latini was concerned with both sorts of eloquence.[15]

Like ancient oratory, the medieval *ars dictaminis* appeared sometimes as a form of legal training, sometimes as a form of literature. In the thirteenth century, especially under the influence of the Bolognese professor Boncompagno of Signa, the practical and legal side of rhetoric was heavily stressed.[16] Boncompagno wrote a *rhetorica novissima*, or "up-to-date rhetoric," which emphasized the practical tasks of the rhetorician and their connections with law, and which played down the usefulness of classical rhetorical precepts. Despite this mundane and pedestrian strain in thirteenth-century rhetoric, however, the *ars dictaminis* never became completely separate from literary study. In fact, the development of Italian poetry both in Dante's generation and the preceding one owed much to professional rhetoric. Most of the early *rimatori* were themselves judges and notaries, and the prose of Dante and his contemporaries was modeled on that of the *dictatores*. Classical studies were cultivated in the same circles. A recent study of the Paduan circle of "prehumanists" which included Albertino Mussato and Lovato Lovati has identified the members of this group as lawyers, but it is important to see that they were *dictatores* as well.[17]

Given their many activities, it is not surprising that the rhetoricians were respected members of medieval Italian society. As one of them remarked, the *dictamen* was in wide demand, and was "recognized as of great utility. It increases eloquence, promotes favor, enlarges honors, and

[15] On secular eloquence in medieval Italy, see Kristeller, "Humanism and Scholasticism in the Italian Renaissance," pp. 555-56; A. Galetti, *L'Eloquenza* (Milan, 1904-38), pp. 430ff. For Latini, see below.

[16] For the information in this paragraph, see Wieruszowski, "Arezzo as a Center of Learning and Letters."

[17] For the Paduan circle, see Roberto Weiss, *The Dawn of Humanism in Italy* (Inaugural Lecture, University College, London, 1947); *idem, Il Primo Secolo dell' Umanesimo* (Rome, 1949), and Hyde, *Padua in the Age of Dante*, Chap. X.

often enriches the needy."[18] In several towns the notaries were influential in politics.[19] Theirs was much the largest of the learned professions. Writing of Florence in 1330, Giovanni Villani noted that whereas there were eighty lawyers and sixty physicians in the town at that time, there were six hundred notaries.[20] Individual *dictatores* were sometimes men of great reputation. Pier della Vigna, who studied *dictamen* at Bologna, became a favorite of Frederick II, serving both as his chancellor and as a judge of his Magna Curia. Rolandinus Passagerius, who was the author of a standard textbook on *ars notaria* and who wrote against Frederick II on behalf of the city of Bologna, achieved both fame and wealth. He was given a marble tomb with the symbols of his craft on it, and an inscription on the Bolognese Palazzo de' Notai described him as *Ciceronis floridus ore*.[21] In Florence, at roughly the same time, Brunetto Latini gained a similar position. Giovanni Villani praised him as the first man to instruct Florentines in the art of politics, and Dante, who certainly learned much from him regardless of whether Latini was ever his teacher in a formal sense, treated him with reverence even when he encountered him in the Seventh Circle of the *Inferno*.[22]

[18] Bene of Florence (?), quoted by C. S. Baldwin, *Medieval Rhetoric and Poetic to 1400* (New York, 1928), p. 220. Cf. note 13, above.

[19] Bologna is the most notable example. See P. Valsecchi, *Comune e Corporazione nel Medio Evo Italiano* (Milan, 1949), pp. 82-94. For some indication of the notaries' importance in Siena, see David L. Hicks, "Sienese Society in the Renaissance," *Comparative Studies in Society and History*, II (1960), 412-20. On the political importance of *notai* in Orvieto, Elisabeth Carpentier, *Une ville devant la peste: Orvieto et la peste noire de 1348* (Paris, 1962), pp. 69-72, shows the notaries to have been more influential than either lawyers or physicians; on Padua, see Hyde, *Padua in the Age of Dante*, pp. 164-65.

[20] Villani, *Cronica*, Bk. XI, Chap. xciv; Eng. trans. in R. S. Lopez and I. W. Raymond, *Medieval Trade in the Mediterranean World* (New York, 1955), p. 72. On the even larger numbers of notaries in other towns, see Hyde, p. 162.

[21] See Novati's studies in *Freschi e minii del Dugento*, cited above in note 11.

[22] On Latini, see Demetrio Marzi, *La Cancelleria della Repubblica Fiorentina* (Rocca San Casciano, 1910), Chap. II. Dante's comment

The masters of *dictamen* made exalted claims for their art. Their descriptions of its place among the other learned disciplines sometimes recalled classical rhetorical ideals, and in particular the ideal of the combination of rhetoric and philosophy. They made these claims, however, in a manner much closer to that of the medieval writers discussed earlier than to the humanists. The *ars dictaminis* was described as "the empress of the liberal arts"; or grammar, rhetoric, and dialectic were listed as its handmaidens. Even theology might appear as an *ancilla artis dictandi*. A connection with moral philosophy seems implied in the assertion that *dictamen* was the *gradaria ad virtutes*, "the stairway to the virtues."[23] Sometimes the ideal of the union of wisdom and eloquence was explicitly stated, as it was by Brunetto Latini in his *Tresor*.[24] Moreover, the claim of Latini to combine oratory and philosophy was recognized by Giovanni Villani, who described Brunetto as "a great philosopher, and a perfect master in rhetoric, both spoken and written. He expounded the rhetoric of Tully, and wrote the good and useful book called the *Tresor* . . . and besides that other books of philosophy, and one about the vices and virtues."[25]

Despite these claims, however, the *dictatores* were far removed from a real understanding of the classical combination of rhetoric and philosophy. Few of them possessed any genuine knowledge of philosophy, though a number

---

to Latini in *The Divine Comedy* (*Inferno*, XV, 85)—"m'insegnavate come l'uom s' eterna"—indicates the esteem in which Latini was held, and suggests a connection between the culture of the earlier rhetoricians and the later humanist ideal of glory.

[23] For these comments, see Ernst Kantorowicz, "Anonymi 'Aurea Gemma,'" pp. 47-48n. Note also the comments of Mino da Colle cited by Helene Wieruszowski, "*Ars dictaminis* in the Time of Dante," pp. 104-05.

[24] Latini, *Li Livres Dou Tresor*, critical edn. by T. J. Carmody, Un. of Cal. Pub. in Modern Philology, Vol. 22 (Berkeley and Los Angeles, 1948), III, i, 2 and III, i, 6. See Aristide Marigo, "Cultura letteraria e preumanistica nelle maggiori Enciclopedie del Dugento: lo *Speculum* ed il *Tresors*," *Giornale Storico della Letteratura Italiana*, LXVIII (1916), 1-42, 289-326 (esp. 315-16).

[25] Villani, *Cronica*, Bk. VIII, Chap. x.

used philosophical maxims in their writings, and one might occasionally attempt to write about moral subjects. Brunetto Latini probably devoted more effort to the study of philosophy than most of the others; exiled from Florence for a time, he used his enforced leisure to gain a knowledge of philosophy as it was taught in thirteenth-century France. His encyclopedic *Tresor* was the result of this study. The *Tresor* is clearly the treatise of a rhetorician discussing philosophy, and in that sense it represents a combination of the two pursuits. It contains much information about rhetoric taken from Cicero (especially the *De inventione*). In it, Latini praised rhetoric as the foundation of political life: "The science of speaking well and of ruling men is the noblest art in the world."[26] The *Tresor* also included a general discussion of the divisions of philosophy and a fairly extended treatment of ethics, together with a vernacular translation of a medieval summary of Aristotle's *Ethics*. Latini described those who combined good sense with skill in speech as "the flower of the world," and inquired, "Where wisdom is joined to speaking well, who will say that other than good things can come of it?" But aside from this, he went no further in the attempt to combine rhetoric and philosophy.[27] He did not consider whether the attempt to join the two arts presented any special problems, or whether some philosophical positions or rhetorical procedures were better suited than others to such a union. The *Tresor* was not constructed on the basis of any characteristically rhetorical attitude toward philosophy. Aristotle's *Ethics* appeared prominently because it was widely known and admired, not because Peripateticism seemed to have any special relevance to the orator.

Other echoes of the ancient ideal among the *dictatores* seem even further removed from classical statements of it. Some of the claims for *dictamen* seem to have been made in response to the challenge posed by theology. Like the jurists, the *dictatores* sought "to raise their arts to a sphere

[26] Latini, *Li Livres Dou Tresor*, I, i, 4; cf. I, iv, 5 and I, iv, 9.
[27] *Ibid.*, III, i, 2; III, i, 6.

211

of quasi-holiness in order to compete with theology."[28]
Guido Faba spoke of a kind of union of celestial piety and
Latin eloquence, or of the coming together of "Tullian
experience," Ciceronian eloquence, and the wisdom of Solomon.[29] This was an adaptation of the ancient theme, but
it lacked the classical form.

In spite of this distance from the more genuinely classical culture of Petrarch, however, there can be no doubt
that these medieval rhetoricians, the Italian *dictatores* and
notaries, were the direct ancestors of the humanists. The
links between the two groups have been noticed by several
scholars, notably by Paul Oskar Kristeller. "The humanists,"
Professor Kristeller points out, "were not classical scholars
who for personal reasons had a craving for eloquence, but
vice versa, they were professional rhetoricians, heirs and
successors of the medieval rhetoricians, who developed the
belief, then new and modern, that the best way to achieve
eloquence was to imitate classical models, and who thus
were driven to study the classics and to found classical philology."[30] The clearest evidence for this conclusion is the
fact that the humanists occupied positions in society almost exactly like those held earlier by the *dictatores*. Both
groups made their careers as either secretaries of princes or
communes, or teachers of rhetoric and allied subjects. The
place of Salutati or Bruni in their day was analogous to
that of Rolandinus Passagerius or Brunetto Latini in theirs.
To most students of history the humanists are certainly better known than their medieval predecessors; but the more
one inquires into the place earned by the earlier rhetoricians, the clearer it becomes that the success of the humanists was foreshadowed. Members of both groups were able
to attain places in society to which their birth did not en-
title them, and in both cases this success derived from the
practice of an art which appeared to be at once learned

[28] Kantorowicz, "An 'Autobiography' of Guido Faba," pp. 261-62.
[29] *Ibid.*, pp. 263, 265.
[30] Kristeller, "Humanism and Scholasticism in the Italian Renaissance," pp. 560, 563-64.

and involved in the problems of civic life. These similarities between the medieval rhetoricians and the Renaissance humanists, each group representative of the character and needs of the society it inhabited, suggest the continuity of Italian civic life from the thirteenth century to the fifteenth. The link between the humanists and the medieval rhetoricians appears also from another point of view: many of the literary forms favored by Petrarch and his followers had also been cultivated by the *dictatores*.[31] These included theoretical treatises on rhetoric and grammar, particular forms of letter-writing, and spoken oratory. In the latter category, the most common occasions for humanist speeches were weddings, funerals, academic ceremonies such as occurred at the beginning of a course or a new term, and official or decorative speeches by ambassadors and other public officials. All had clear antecedents among the activities of the medieval rhetoricians. The ties between humanist letter-writing and that practiced by the *dictatores* are also well attested to, for instance by collections of letters which bring together the eminent humanist Salutati, his well-known rival Pellegrino Zambeccari, and the thirteenth-century *dictator* Pier della Vigna.[32]

It may seem at first glance that this description of the humanists as successors of the medieval rhetoricians does not apply to Petrarch. The career of the first and most influential of the humanists did not follow the pattern established by the *dictatores*. Petrarch did not exercise any profession, but supported himself with the income from certain benefices and by the favors of powerful friends like the Colonna, the Visconti, and the Carrara. Nonetheless, as Professor Kristeller has pointed out, "several facts of his bi-

---

[31] *Ibid.*, pp. 564ff.

[32] For the collection of letters entitled "Magistri Petri De Vineis, Colucii Florentini et Peregrini de Zambecariis epistolae," see *Epistolario di Pellegrino Zambeccari*, ed. Carlo Frati (Rome, 1929), preface, p. xvii. Frati finds that both Salutati and Zambeccari, who was chancellor of Bologna from 1389 to 1399, modeled their style on that of Pier della Vigna, adding to it classical citations and allusions (preface, p. xxi).

ography show that he too was regarded by his contemporaries from the point of view of the rhetorical and grammatical culture of the time." He was several times offered the post of secretary in the papal curia; he composed letters and discourses on behalf of the Visconti and perhaps for other rulers; and he was once offered a chair, with the task of expounding the Latin poets, at the University of Florence. All these activities were common to the medieval rhetoricians.[33] For instance, Petrarch's friend Pietro da Muglio, the Bolognese and Paduan teacher of rhetoric who was probably responsible for introducing Coluccio Salutati to the works of Petrarch and Boccaccio, engaged in most of them.[34] Moreover, the opportunity which Petrarch seized, that of pursuing a literary career largely independent of the practical activities which were the livelihood of his father and many of his friends, was one often longed for by the notaries themselves. The career of secretary to a commune or prince was an uncertain one, involved as it was in the confused and often violent political life of the day. Some of the prominent *dictatores* complained of the "servile yoke" of their profession and longed to give themselves to letters.[35] Petrarch's solitude at Vaucluse and elsewhere represented what many of them would have liked for themselves.

Yet Petrarch's originality is undeniable. Clearly it is not sufficient to regard him and his followers simply as successors of the medieval rhetoricians. Professor Kristeller has emphasized the novelty of the humanist enthusiasm for classical literature, and of the knowledge of the ancient world which it produced. The earlier rhetoricians betray little of the spirit of humanist classicism. The humanists

[33] On Petrarch's career, see Ernest Hatch Wilkins, *Life of Petrarch* (Chicago and London, 1961); for the matters mentioned in the text, see especially P. O. Kristeller, "Il Petrarca, l'umanesimo e la scolastica," *Lettere Italiane*, VII (1955), 373-74.

[34] See Novati, *La Giovinezza di Coluccio Salutati*, pp. 35ff., and more recently, G. Billanovich, "Giovanni del Virgilio, Pietro da Muglio, Francesco da Fiano," *Italia Medioevale e Umanistica*, VI (1963), 203-34, and VII (1964), 279-324.

[35] Novati, *La Giovinezza di Coluccio Salutati*, pp. 88ff.

themselves proclaimed their own originality, and often emphasized Petrarch's contribution to it. As Boccaccio, Bruni, and Poggio Bracciolini all declared, Petrarch "opened the way for us to show in what manner we could acquire learning."[36] Our study of humanist rhetorical culture, and a comparison of this culture with the attitudes of medieval writers—including the *dictatores*—toward rhetoric, leads us to agree. Petrarch carried the medieval rhetorical tradition to a new understanding of and sympathy with the classical study of oratory. He and his successors discussed the problems of rhetorical culture and its relation to philosophy in a manner which revived the classical concern for these questions. They brought about a reintegration of classical form and content, reviving the ancient debate about the orator's relation to philosophy and to culture in general, with its full range of issues and implications.

Given the many connections between the humanists and the medieval rhetoricians, what accounts for the differences between the two? What circumstances stimulated Petrarch to "open the way"? The considerations which follow are at best a sketch of the answers these questions deserve, but they may at least claim to focus our attentions on the areas where the explanation should be sought: in changes which took place in Italian intellectual life beginning around 1300, and in changes in the social and professional life of the rhetoricians brought on by developments within society at large. In the former category, the first new element to be noted is the growing importance of scholastic philosophy in Italy. Several kinds of evidence combine to persuade us that scholastic philosophy was gaining in influence and prestige in Italy in the years around 1300. Far from being a long-entrenched feature of medieval Italian intellectual life, Aristotelian philosophy became a regular aspect of

[36] On the humanist view of Petrarch, see Herbert Weisinger, "Who Began the Revival of Learning? The Renaissance Point of View," *Papers of the Michigan Academy*, XXIX (1944), 625-38; for the quote, see Baron, *Crisis*, I, 232ff.

Italian culture only in the second half of the thirteenth century. Before about the year 1250, the chief centers of scholastic activity had been located entirely in the North. Some of the most prominent schoolmen of this time were Italians, but they did most of their studying and teaching north of the Alps. Even though Aristotelianism found a ready acceptance in Italy among teachers of medicine and logic, there seems to be good reason to describe at least certain aspects of this new philosophical interest as imported from the North. Its bases in Italy included, in addition to university faculties of medicine and arts, the popular and influential schools of the mendicant orders. In all these places, both teachers who had studied at Paris and other northern scholastic centers and questions which had originated there played an important role.[37]

If Aristotelian scholasticism was in part an import from the North, it was complemented by another northern influence in a second area of learning, namely in the study of poetry. In the twelfth and early thirteenth centuries, verse-making and the study of Latin poetry had been cultivated more extensively in France than in Italy. The same seems to be true of commentaries on classical Latin literature, of which a significant number began to appear in Italy only after 1300. In the fourteenth century the flow of interest in literature from France to Italy seems to have been increased by the presence of many Italians at the papal court in Avignon.[38]

These changes had several effects on the culture of the

[37] On scholastic philosophy in Italy, see Rashdall, *The Universities of Europe in the Middle Ages*, I, 234; Kristeller, "Humanism and Scholasticism . . . ," pp. 575ff.; *idem, Die Italienischen Universitäten der Renaissance* (Krefeld, n.d.), esp. pp. 21ff.; Bruno Nardi, "L'averroismo bolognese nel secolo XIII e Taddeo Alderotto," *Rivista di Storia della Filosofia*, IV (1949), 11-22; Martin Grabmann, "L'Aristotelismo Italiano al tempo di Dante, con particolare riguardo all' Università di Bologna," *Rivista di Filosofia Neo-Scolastica*, XXXVIII (1946); and the other literature cited by Kristeller, *Studies in Renaissance Thought and Letters*, pp. 576-77n.

[38] Kristeller, "Humanism and Scholasticism . . . ," pp. 569-71; B. L. Ullman, "Some Aspects of the Origin of Italian Humanism," *Philological Quarterly*, XX (1941), 20-31.

rhetoricians. In the first place, it was they who were responsible for much of the growing interest in poetry and classical literature. Literary circles in Padua, Florence, and Naples all included notaries and *dictatores*; one thing which tied the three circles together was the exchange of chancery employees and functionaries between the three towns.[39] Perhaps the most advanced of the three groups was the one at Padua, where fairly well-known figures like Albertino Mussato and Lovato Lovati were active in both the writing of poetry and the study of classical literature.[40] Secondly, certain rhetoricians had absorbed some of the new ideas of scholastic philosophy as well. Brunetto Latini actually studied philosophy in France, and sought to convey some knowledge of it to men who knew no Latin. In the late thirteenth century one finds all these intellectual currents side by side, and sometimes even intermingled as in the group of poets who cultivated the *dolce stil nuovo*. The main formative influences on Dante and his friends were the rhetorical culture represented by Latini, the scholastic philosophy and theology beginning to be taught in the universities and the schools of the mendicant orders, and forms of poetry recently introduced from France. In Dante, as in some of his contemporaries, these various strains coexisted and merged.[41]

At the same time, however, these new features of Italian intellectual life made their appearance through conflict as well as through harmony. Some representatives of the rhetorical tradition found themselves engaged in polemics with

[39] Roberto Weiss, "Lineamenti per una Storia del Primo Umanesimo Fiorentino," *Rivista Storica Italiana*, LX (1948), 349-66.

[40] See the studies cited above in note 17, and Hyde, *Padua in the Age of Dante*, p. 163.

[41] The literature on Dante is too vast to cite here. For the influence of rhetoric and the *dictatores* on Italian literature, see especially A. Schiaffini, *Tradizione e poesia nella prosa d'arte italiana* (Rome, 1943); also E. R. Curtius, *European Literature and the Latin Middle Ages* (New York, 1953), Chap. 17; Wieruszowski, "Arezzo as a Center of Learning and Letters in the Thirteenth Century," pp. 375ff.; on Dante and scholastic philosophy, see Etienne Gilson, *Dante and Philosophy*, trans. David Moore (New York, Evanston, and London, 1963).

the increasingly prominent scholastics. The best known
of these debates was the one between the Paduan prehumanist Albertino Mussato and Giovannino of Mantua,
a teacher at the Dominican convent in Padua. The issue
over which the two disagreed was the value of poetry and
its relation to theology. The Dominican sought to place
poetry among the liberal disciplines in a firmly Thomistic
fashion: that is, according a lowly position to it. Mussato,
on the other hand, made poetry the most noble art and
equated it with both philosophy and theology. The debate
had a number of ramifications, including disputes over the
nature and purpose of metaphor, and the value of pre-
Christian intimations of divinity. But in more general terms
the conflict was between the Aristotelian philosophy which
had recently become prominent in Italy, and which sought
to organize all intellectual life according to its principles,
and the more traditional Italian culture of the rhetoricians,
which—especially at Padua in the early fourteenth century
—was coming to be increasingly associated with the study
of poetry and classical literature.[42] Even in the twelfth century the *dictatores* had responded to claims of primacy
made by other disciplines with assertions of the dignity of
their own activity. Mussato's defense of poetry was a similar response, but couched in different terms. For a member
of the Paduan literary circle of the early fourteenth century, it was natural to make this response in terms of the
dignity of the poet. Petrarch and Salutati would continue
to defend poetry against attack. For them, however, as we
have seen, the defense of poetry was integrated with the
wider defense of the *studia humanitatis et eloquentiae,*
which had rhetoric rather than poetry at its center. Mussato's defense of poetry was not equivalent to the human-

---

[42] On this dispute, see Alfredo Galletti, "La 'ragione poetica' di
Albertino Mussato ed i poeti teologi," *Scritti vari . . . in onore di R.
Renier* (Turin, 1912), pp. 331-59, and Curtius, *European Literature
and the Latin Middle Ages,* pp. 215ff. Curtius rightly points out that
Mussato represented "tradition" in this controversy, although he
perhaps does not see the contrast between Italy and the North
clearly enough (p. 220).

ist campaign for eloquence, but it was clearly related to it, and was provoked by some of the same challenges.[43]

One reason why humanist culture centered around the figure of the orator rather than around the poet was that the most influential enthusiasts for ancient culture continued to come from the circles of professional rhetoricians. During the same years that poetry and scholastic philosophy were finding an increasingly warm reception in Italy, certain developments in the Italian towns altered the position of the rhetoricians in ways which help to explain the emergence of Petrarchian humanism. The main area of activity for the rhetoricians as a group seems to have shifted away from private business and toward public questions. In the twelfth and thirteenth centuries much of the employment of the notaries was connected with business transactions, since all business contracts had to be drawn up by a notary in order to be legally valid. A number of the *notai* found most of their employment in public chanceries, but a larger percentage appears to have been involved with the affairs of private individuals. Beginning at the end of the thirteenth century, two factors operated to change this situation. First of all, notaries became less necessary to businessmen. Education among laymen was spreading (Giovanni Villani's figures on the number of Florentines in various schools in the early fourteenth century suggest quite widespread literacy),[44] and more and more businessmen were able to draw up the necessary contracts for themselves. In the fourteenth century, contracts drawn up privately became acceptable for the first time as evidence in legal actions. Notaries still performed many services for businessmen, but in comparison with the earlier situation, "busi-

[43] For a discussion of various humanist and prehumanist defenses of poetry, and an account of the growing importance of specifically rhetorical ideals in them, see Francesco Tateo, *"Retorica" e "Poetica" fra Medioevo e Rinascimento* (Bari, 1960).

[44] Enrico Fiumi, "Economia e vita privata dei fiorentini nelle rilevazioni statistiche di Giovanni Villani," *Archivio Storico Italiano,* CXI (1953), reprinted in *Storia del' economia Italiana,* ed. Carlo M. Cipolla (Turin, 1959), pp. 325-60, esp. 357ff.

ness . . . was dispensing . . . with . . . the services of the notary."[45]

At the same time that this process reduced the demand for notarial services in one sphere, another development offered notaries increased employment elsewhere. Evidence indicates that the administrative bureaucracies of most town governments in northern Italy expanded significantly after 1300. The communes took a larger burden of government upon themselves, and the need for functionaries grew accordingly. Most of these positions were filled by people trained in *dictamen* and *notaria*.[46] Taken together, these two developments suggest a significant shift in the kind of activity which primarily occupied the professional rhetoricians in Italy. Fewer rhetoricians must have earned their livelihood mainly from private commercial transactions; a larger group must have been supported by some kind of public employment. One sign of this trend is the appearance, toward the end of the thirteenth century, of the first collection of letters and formularies aimed solely at the municipal *dictator*. This manual was the work of Mino da Colle, who taught *dictamen* in several towns. Earlier collections had given attention to both private and public affairs.[47]

These developments are related to a less tangible but no

[45] Herlihy, *Pisa in the Early Renaissance*, p. 10 (also, for Florence, p. 20n.); Jacques Heers, *L'Occident aux XIVᵉ et XVᵉ Siècles, Aspects Économiques et Sociaux* (Paris, 1963), pp. 180, 184.

[46] For a recent description of the process through which "private interests" diminished in the face of a mounting concern with state affairs" during the fourteenth century, see Marvin B. Becker, "Economic Change and the Emerging Florentine Territorial State," *Studies in the Renaissance*, XIII (1966), 7-39; for a similar development in Pisa slightly earlier, Herlihy, p. 20; see also Hyde, *Padua in the Age of Dante*, p. 246. On the virtual monopoly of administrative offices by the guild of notaries, see Santi Calleri, *L'arte dei Giudici e dei Notai in Firenze nell' età comunale e nel suo Statuto del 1344* (Milan, 1966), reviewed by Niccolò Rodolico in *Archivio Storico Italiano*, CXXIV (1966), 126-27. Also Gene A. Brucker, *Florentine Politics and Society, 1343-1378* (Princeton, 1962), p. 60.

[47] On Mino da Colle's collection of formularies for the municipal *dictator*, see Wieruszowski, "Arezzo as a Center of Learning and Letters," pp. 370f.

less real set of circumstances which characterized Italian life in the late thirteenth and early fourteenth centuries. This was a moment of unusual importance for the maturing of Italian communal civilization. Economically, the years just after 1300 probably witnessed the height of the growth in wealth which had begun around the time of the First Crusade, and which was interrupted by the famines and troubles of the fourteenth century. Demographically, it marked the peak of medieval population growth for most towns as well. It was a time when many material indications of social growth stood at a high point, but also one in which many residents of the Italian towns seem to have sought to increase their range of nonmaterial satisfactions as well. Merchants no longer moved about with their goods, but became more settled and probably found more leisure for activities outside their business. Certainly the culture of the time was remarkably rich. This was the age of Dante, Giotto, Marsiglio of Padua. The prestige both of poetry and of scholastic philosophy appear to have risen at the same moment. At such a time, it seems likely that the rhetoricians would have felt especially called upon to present themselves as men of high culture as well as of practical utility.

These various elements of change in Italian life in the years after 1300 all help to explain how, in the fourteenth century, Renaissance humanism was able to develop out of medieval Italian rhetoric. The new directions which Petrarch gave to rhetorical culture in Italy may be seen in large part as responses to the several factors which we have just outlined. The rhetoricians were challenged by the increasing prestige of scholastic philosophy; their sphere of activity was shifting from the field of private transactions to that of the city-state; they probably also felt a need to present themselves as the representatives of a kind of culture which was not exhausted in their day-to-day occupation. Petrarch met all the needs brought on by these changes. To the challenge of scholastic philosophy he responded with the Ciceronian ideal of the combination of rhetoric and philosophy; to provide for the increasingly public nature of the rhetoricians' tasks he led the way back to the classical rhetorical culture, which had been tightly linked to the life of the city-state; in order that the culture of the rhetoricians might be of value even to men who did not employ it professionally, Petrarch made the exaltation of eloquence the vehicle for a return to the cultural standards of the ancient world. Petrarch transformed medieval Italian rhetoric by rediscovering its classical roots and scope, thus enabling practicing rhetoricians to remake themselves in something like the Ciceronian image. In his writings the culture of the orator emerged in its full classical stature, as it had not done for centuries. Thus rhetoric could claim a dignity it had not known before; the rhetoricians learned to understand and describe in classical terms the special relationship between their form of education and activity and the life of the city-state; and rhetoric became once more the doorway to general education, as it had been in classical Rome.

After Petrarch's death, humanist culture changed and evolved in response both to the intellectual exigencies described in Part One of this study, and to the changes in fourteenth- and fifteenth-century Italian society. We cannot speak of the latter at length here, but two important aspects of life in the early Renaissance must be mentioned briefly. The first is the series of disruptions caused by plague and war, beginning in the 1340's; the second is the previously unequaled degree of social peace which reigned in most Italian towns in the fifteenth century. The latter fourteenth century was the age of Salutati. It was a period in which innovation in art seems to have slowed down markedly, and in which both social disruption and psychological strain may have worked against innovation in other fields.[48] These features of life after 1350 may help to explain some of Salutati's caution toward classical ideals, and may suggest some of the reasons for the differences be-

[48] See Millard Meiss, *Painting in Florence and Siena after the Black Death* (Princeton, 1951).

tween his understanding of the combination of rhetoric and philosophy and that arrived at by Bruni and Valla. Bruni came to maturity as the social wounds of the fourteenth century were being healed; Valla grew up in an atmosphere still less tinged with crisis. Perhaps this changed environment was one thing which allowed the fifteenth-century humanists to work out intellectual positions in which the enthusiasm for rhetoric was less restrained by the fear of departure from traditional notions of Christian wisdom than it had been in Salutati's thought.

However this may be, Bruni and Valla must be understood in terms of both their reliance on Petrarch and their independence from him. The balance of change and continuity, here as in many questions involving historical development, is not easy to determine. In many respects, Bruni and Valla came into much closer contact with the classical world than Petrarch had; their consciousness had thrown off many elements which had characterized the Middle Ages. At the same time, their celebration of rhetoric and their position as professional rhetoricians placed them in a line of descent which reached back both to Petrarch and to the earlier Italian *dictatores*.

In attempting to make clear Petrarch's role in the development of humanism, we can be aided by an insight developed in a recent and highly suggestive essay in the history of science. Petrarch provided, to use Thomas S. Kuhn's term, a new "paradigm" of intellectual activity. That is to say, his work became both a model for others and a framework within which they could expand and develop his achievement. Such paradigms in the history of science "provide models from which spring particular coherent traditions of scientific research. . . . The study of paradigms . . . is what mainly prepares the student for membership in the particular scientific community with which he will later practice."[49] It is the relationship between model and community which Professor Kuhn emphasizes: what is

[49] Thomas S. Kuhn, *The Structure of Scientific Revolutions* (Chicago and London, 1962), pp. 10-11.

common to all the members of a particular scientific community at a given time is the acceptance of a single paradigm. This does not mean that, for example, all astronomers who accepted the Ptolemaic or the Newtonian paradigms agreed about all the details of planetary arrangements. But their disagreements arose from further investigation or reflection along lines laid down by the basic scheme.

This description of the way scientific communities cohere around an original model also sheds much light on the history of nonscientific ideas. It allows us to see why Petrarch was so important in the history of humanism. The usual observation that Petrarch "influenced" those who came after him does not satisfactorily describe his effect on his followers. The humanists of the early fifteenth century constituted a well-defined cultural community, hyperconscious of the distinctive nature of their learning, and closely tied to each other intellectually despite their many personal feuds and individual differences. What gave them this coherence was the Ciceronian thought-model which Petrarch had provided. This is what the humanists meant when they said that Petrarch "opened the way for us to show in what manner we could acquire learning."

Certainly the conclusions of the present study affirm the originality and importance of Petrarch's work. He and his successors were able to approach classical texts much more in the spirit of their ancient authors than were medieval writers, either in Italy or in the North. At the same time, however, Petrarch's place in the development of humanism should not be described only in terms of his originality. The tendency—met in much historical writing—to take sides with apparently "modern" elements in Renaissance culture against the Middle Ages may be satisfying in certain ways, but it is more an expression of personal preference than of historical understanding. The textbook image of Petrarch as a rebel against the scholastic culture which dominated the Middle Ages needs some correction, in the light of his many links with the distinct world of medieval

224

Italian rhetoric. Petrarch's thought evolved out of the culture of the medieval rhetoricians, and in part represented a response to challenges they felt. It contained elements of continuity, as well as of innovation. The humanist movement grew up in and grew out of a busy, complex, town-centered society, but the humanists were not the first group of intellectuals that this society produced, nor the first to meet its needs. This conclusion can be clarified by a consideration of the humanists' place in the overall intellectual and social life of the fifteenth century.

CHAPTER VIII

THE INTELLECTUAL
AND SOCIAL SETTING OF THE
HUMANIST MOVEMENT

THE HUMANIST movement was a success. Through their talent and effort, Petrarch and his followers achieved a high position for themselves and for the *studia humanitatis*. The extent to which their prestige exceeded that of the earlier *dictatores* is difficult to judge, since no one has attempted to make a careful comparison of Petrarch's predecessors with his successors in this regard. We do know that, at least in Florence, many of the men associated with the humanists were wealthy, respected, and well-connected citizens. By the standards which determined social place in the early fifteenth century, they ranked high in society.[1] All this is well established. Yet it would be hasty to conclude from these facts that humanism alone occupied the center of the cultural stage in the fifteenth century, or that humanism, simply because of its success, should be regarded as more in tune with Renaissance society than were other intellectual movements of the time. The question of humanism's place in the life of Renaissance Italy is considerably more complex than these simple conclusions suggest.

The first point which must be stressed is the persistence of strong currents of interest in scholastic philosophy throughout the fifteenth century in Italy. Renaissance humanism was not a replacement for medieval scholasticism.[2] The defenders of the *studia humanitatis et eloquentiae* were successful in assuring their own place in the intellectual

---

[1] For this conclusion, see Lauro Martines, *The Social World of the Florentine Humanists, 1390-1460*.

[2] Once again, our starting point is the work of Paul O. Kristeller; see "Humanism and Scholasticism in the Italian Renaissance," pp. 575ff., and the works cited above in Chap. VII, note 37.

life of their time, but they neither intended nor were able to deprive scholastic philosophers of theirs. In the fields of natural philosophy, metaphysics, and theology, the humanists did not challenge the scholastics' position in the universities. In ethics and logic, however, the two groups were rivals, as the careers of Leonardo Bruni and Lorenzo Valla show. While the humanists often succeeded in gaining the available university chairs in moral philosophy for themselves, in logic the predominance of the scholastics continued, at least in the Quattrocento.

Thus humanism and scholasticism coexisted in the universities, uneasily at times, but more harmoniously than humanist polemics suggest. This situation has been described by other writers. How did it affect society at large? How did each of these groups figure in the intellectual interests of educated laymen who were neither professional rhetoricians nor professional philosophers? Many accounts of Renaissance culture still seem to assume that educated members of the ruling families in the major Italian towns were wholly given over to the new interests of the humanists. Yet even a brief account of the intellectual concerns of educated laymen in the early fifteenth century is enough to cast doubt on this view. Humanism and scholasticism shared men's attention outside the universities, just as they did within them. At least this seems to have been the case in two important cultural centers, Venice and Florence.

In Venice, as Bruno Nardi has recently pointed out, the two cultural forces represented on the one hand by Petrarch, and on the other by the scholastic opponents he answered in *On His Own Ignorance*, coexisted throughout the fifteenth century.[3] It was in fact one of Petrarch's four critics, Tomà Talenti, who provided in his will for the establishment of a lectureship in logic and philosophy in Venice. The income he gave was later supplemented by the

[3] Bruno Nardi, "Letteratura e Cultura Veneziana del '400," in *La Civiltà Veneziana del Quattrocento* (Florence, 1957), pp. 99-145; *idem*, "La Scuola di Rialto e l'Umanesimo Veneziano," in *Umanesimo Europeo e Umanesimo Veneziano*, ed. V. Branca (Florence, 1963), pp. 93-139.

republic. Talenti's purpose was to create a place where those citizens who could not afford to go to Paris or Oxford could study philosophy, and the government of the city shared his desire. There was thus "introduced into Venice the study of Aristotelian philosophy and of Averroism."[4] The most famous incumbent of this chair was Paolo della Pergola, who had studied logic with Paolo Veneto at Padua, and who taught in Venice from 1421 to 1454. To his many students he conveyed an intellectual outlook clearly formed in the scholastic curriculum. In one of his writings on logic he attacked the "ignorant rhetoricians," whose lack of dialectical knowledge led them to deride logical subtlety, and who desired to appear learned only to the ignorant.[5] Of course he meant the humanists. The success of Paolo della Pergola suggests that scholastic philosophy was an important component of fifteenth-century Venetian intellectual life.

A public chair in the *studia humanitatis* can be found in Venice only toward the end of Paolo della Pergola's activity there, in the year 1446. This chair, which was later held by a number of distinguished men, was closely associated with the Venetian chancery. In this it resembled the chair of rhetoric in the *studio* at Florence. On the death of one of its incumbents in 1457, the senate declared that his instruction had been pleasant and useful both to "iuvenes cancellarie nostre" and to other youths of the city.[6] After

---

[4] Nardi, "Letteratura e Cultura Veneziana del '400," p. 109.

[5] *Ibid.*, p. 115: "rudes rhetorici, qui parentem ac progenitricem suam dialecticam ignorant, solent non nunquam argutiam logicorum deridere, obiicientes quod proprium nomen non audent nunciare, sed deliniti fuco sapientie sunt qui nec merentur rhetores appellari, cum per ianuam recto tramite non introiverint, et apparere rudibus solum laborent, nescientes longe esse prestantius unius sapientis iudicio commendari, quam totius vulgi clamore sapientissimus videri." It is interesting to compare this statement with Valla's criticism of philosophers for failing to seek glory among the masses (see above Chap. V, note 33). Valla's view of the respective purposes of humanists and philosophers agrees with that of Paolo della Pergola; but each writer upholds the value of his own group's activity. Paolo's statement also recalls some comments of Petrarch: see above, pp. 43-51.

[6] *Ibid.*, p. 120 (Latin text, p. 142).

228

1460 the commune supported two lecturers in the humanities.

The relations between these two centers of instruction reveal much about the intellectual life of Renaissance Italy. There was competition and hostility between the two, but each had a recognized place in Venetian education. Moreover, the rivalries between the professional teachers of these subjects were much muted in their students. Several Venetian patricians combined an interest in both kinds of studies. Lauro Quirini, who corresponded with Leonardo Bruni about Aristotle, was both a student of *humanitas* and held a doctorate in arts from the University of Padua. As a result of this double perspective he could refer to Averroës both as "a barbarous and uncultivated man" and as "a distinguished philosopher and an extraordinary judge of truth."[7] The physician Pier de Tommasi was a friend of the humanists Poggio and Filelfo; Ludovico Donato studied in both the scholastic and the humanistic school. In general, patrician Venetians did not confine themselves to one branch of learning; they sought instruction and cultivation from teachers of both sorts.

The evidence for a state of affairs in Florence similar to the one Bruno Nardi describes in Venice seems to have never been presented. Yet scholastic philosophy interested Florentine citizens too. Here we shall look at the literary activities of five prominent Florentines: Roberto de' Rossi, Cino Rinuccini, Gianozzo Manetti, Benedetto Accolti, and Alamanno Rinuccini. The information we possess is not equally complete for all five, but in each case it reveals a similar combination of scholastic and humanist interests.

Roberto de' Rossi was prominent in humanist circles.[8] The second book of Bruni's *Dialogues* inscribed to Pier Paolo Vergerio takes place in his garden. Like his friend Bruni he studied Greek with Manuel Chrysoloras, and like Bruni, too, he used his knowledge to make a new translation of

[7] *Ibid.*, p. 122.
[8] For what is known of Rossi, see Aldo Manetti, "Roberto de' Rossi," *Rinascimento*, II (1951), 33-55.

Aristotle. But Rossi's concern with Aristotle was different. He chose to translate not one of the moral works of Aristotle, but the *Posterior Analytics*. Aristotle interested him as a logician, and Rossi showed himself to be attracted by the powers of the syllogism in a way many humanists would have scoffed at.[9] Moreover, he wrote some vernacular poetry which has survived, and which exhibits certain arresting features. It resembles the poetry of the *dolce stil nuovo* in a number of ways; it uses similar kinds of allegories and is similarly burdened with philosophical content. Its vocabulary includes the word *quiditate*, which is of course the scholastic *quidditas* later derided by Valla and other humanists.[10] Finally, one of his extant writings is an oration against rhetoric, a complete catalogue of all the dangerous uses to which oratory can be put.[11] This speech is often viewed as an exercise, and in large part it was one. Even so, however, the arguments it contained cannot have been regarded with indifference by the humanists of the early fifteenth century. Salutati's expressions of doubt about the virtues of oratory led him to a rehabilitation of scholastic philosophy; perhaps for this reason, the next generation of humanists refused to question the pursuit of eloquence as Petrarch and Salutati had. It seems clear that Rossi's intellectual appetites were not fed by the humanists alone. Rossi was associated with the humanist movement, but only as an amateur, and his intellectual interests differed from those of professionals like Bruni and Poggio. A member of a family which had been declared magnates in 1293, but which still played a role in Florentine politics in the fifteenth century, Rossi belonged to the highest stratum of Florentine society.[12] As an educated and culti-

---

[9] See the preface to Rossi's translation of the *Posterior Analytics*, in Manetti, esp. p. 55.

[10] Manetti, p. 40: "La vera nostra regia è il sommo Idio: / in lui eterno siamo et increate;/ quivi si legge nostra quiditate,/ né altrove indi fora. . . ."

[11] In Manetti, pp. 48-52.

[12] On Rossi's social position, see Martines, *The Social World of the Florentine Humanists*, pp. 108-10.

vated patrician he participated in the activities of Forentine humanist circles, but he seems to have shared some of the interests of scholastics too.

A similar example of an educated layman with an interest in scholastic philosophy is presented by Cino Rinuccini.[13] While his name is often mentioned in connection with the humanist movement, the existing evidence about him indicates that he had an equal interest in the culture of scholasticism. Rinuccini is best known for his extravagant *Invective Against Certain Calumniators of Dante, Petrarch, and Boccaccio*.[14] This work is usually seen as a reply to the kind of criticism of these three poets which Bruni put in Niccoli's mouth in the first book of his *Dialogues*; that is, to the most militantly classical tendencies in early humanism.[15] It seems, however, that Rinuccini's purpose was not only to censure the most uncompromising form of humanist classicism, but also to defend traditional scholastic pursuits. His high praise for Dante centered on the poet's learning in the scholastic curriculum, and his indictment against the poet's detractors emphasized their neglect of this kind of culture.[16] One of the most interesting aspects of this work is Rinuccini's description of the traditional medieval disciplines as useful for the life of the city; the literary concerns of the humanists, he noted, lacked this utility.[17] Thus he rejected one of the humanists' favorite arguments for the superiority of their own kind of learning. Rinuccini was no cloistered monk, but an important figure in the life of Florence. He came from an old and wealthy family, pursued an active career as a mer-

---

[13] No comprehensive discussion of Cino exists. See Baron, *Crisis, passim*, and also Cesare Vasoli, "Polemiche Occamiste," *Rinascimento*, III (1952).

[14] "Invettiva contro a cierti calumnitori di Dante e di messer Francesco Petrarca e di messer Giovanni Boccaccio," summarized in Cesare Vasoli, "Polemiche Occamiste," pp. 133-36. Only a *volgare* version of this text survives; it is included in A. Wesselofsky's edition of *Il Paradiso degli Alberti* (Bologna, 1867).

[15] Baron, *Crisis*, I, 264.

[16] Vasoli, "Polemiche Occamiste," p. 135.

[17] *Ibid.*, p. 134.

chant, and belonged to several of the major guilds.[18] Yet he defended scholastic culture, and regarded it as relevant to the problems of practical life.

One of the most talented and best-known fifteenth-century Florentine citizens was Gianozzo Manetti.[19] Manetti had many humanist connections. He wrote a treatise *On the Dignity of Man.* He knew Greek and Hebrew, and delivered a funeral oration for Leonardo Bruni. He was admired as a speaker, and Vespasiano recounts a number of occasions when he excelled as a public orator.[20] While Manetti had clear ties with humanist culture, however, he was by no means alienated from scholastic philosophy. In the 1420's he frequented the study group which met in the Augustinian convent of Santo Spirito. Little is known about this group, but its character probably reflected the intellectual inclinations of its leaders. They were two Augustinian monks, Evangelista of Pisa and Girolamo of Naples, whose interests seem to have been not far removed from those of typical medieval philosophers and theologians. In 1431 both men were appointed to lecture publicly in the Florentine *studio*, Evangelista on logic, and Girolamo on natural and moral philosophy.[21] Whether from these men or others, Gianozzo Manetti learned to respect the tradition of scholastic philosophy. This is revealed in his attitude toward Dante. In recounting the story that Dante went to Paris to study, he took the opportunity to praise the University of Paris as a center of learning in philosophy and theology. Moreover, Manetti referred to some of the subjects Dante supposedly studied at Paris as *studia humani-*

---

[18] On Rinuccini's career, see Martines, *op.cit.*, pp. 110-12.

[19] On Manetti, see Vittorio Rossi, *Il Quattrocento*, pp. 133, 152-54.

[20] Vespasiano was aware of the social and political distinction between Manetti and the humanists who served in the Florentine chancery. See *The Vespasiano Memoirs*, trans. William George and Emily Waters (London, 1926); reprinted as *Renaissance Princes, Popes and Prelates*, with an intro. by Myron P. Gilmore (New York, Evanston, and London, 1963), pp. 386-87.

[21] See A. Della Torre, *Storia dell' Accademia platonica di Firenze* (Florence, 1902), pp. 200ff.

tatis, the studies of humanity.[22] He thus did not reserve this term for the subjects taught by the professional humanists, as Salutati and Bruni did. Perhaps he regarded the scholastic disciplines as—in a broad sense—humanistic also. Gianozzo Manetti was certainly one of the most capable and accomplished Florentines of his day. Like Roberto de' Rossi and Cino Rinuccini, he belonged to the group of established families who guided the city's life.[23] Like them, too, he did not limit his view of true learning to those pursuits which were properly associated with the humanists.

One of the clearest appreciations of scholastic philosophy and theology to be found in mid-fifteenth-century Florence was penned by a man from whom we might not expect it: Benedetto Accolti, who succeeded Poggio as chancellor of Florence in 1458.[24] As chancellor, Accolti was closely associated with the professional humanists, and we might expect him to share their negative feelings about the scholastics. That he did not may have something to do with his distinguished family background, and with his interest in the history of the Middle Ages. Like Bruni, Accolti was born in Arezzo, but of a much more prominent family; his father was a doctor of law (Bruni's was a dealer in grain).

[22] *Dantis Petrarchae ac Boccaccii Vitae ab Iannotio Manetto Scriptae,* recensente Laurentio Mehus (Florence, 1747); reprinted in Philippi Villani, *Liber de civitatis Florentiae famosis civibus . . . et de Florentinorum litteratura principes fere synchroni scriptores,* ed. G. C. Galletti (Florence, 1847), p. 77: "Proinde non Etruria solum, sed universa quoque Italia derelicta, in Parisiensium urbem studiorum dumtaxat gratia se contulit, quippe in hoc loco humanarum et divinarum rerum studia ceteris Orbis Terrarum locis celebratiora, consensu omnium ferebantur, ibique ceteris omnibus posthabitis naturalium ac divinarum rerum studiis assiduam et pene incredibilem operam navavit, in quibus usque adeo profecit, ut in frequentissimis memoratarum rerum disceptationibus pro more civitatis et magnos quidem Philosophos, et quos etiam Theologos vocant, una voce omnium saepenumero superaret.
"Dum itaque in huiusmodi humanitatis studiis quietissime simul, atque securissime viveret, ecce nova quaedam cogitatio . . . quae quidem sua haec pertranquilla ac divina studia importune admodum perturbavit. . ." (the expedition of Henry VII).
[23] See Martines, *op.cit.,* pp. 135-38, 176-91.
[24] On Accolti's writings, see Rossi, *Il Quattrocento,* pp. 43, 172.

233

Before becoming chancellor of Florence, Accolti had a successful career as a lawyer—whereas most of the humanists were notaries. Even after he became chancellor he continued to practice law, and for a time his income from legal practice exceeded his salary as chancellor.[25]

Accolti had a higher opinion of medieval achievements in all realms than men like Salutati and Bruni did. One of his principal literary works was a history of the First Crusade in which he celebrated the virtues of the crusaders, judging their prowess equal to that of ancient warriors, and attributing well-wrought speeches to them in the manner of humanist historians. In a shorter work, *De praestantia virorum sui aevi*, Accolti spoke more generally about the attainments of men of the post-classical era.[26] In this dialogue, written around 1460, he expressed doubt that the accomplishments of men in antiquity had actually been of a higher order than those of medieval men. What caused his contemporaries to believe the ancients superior, Accolti explained, was the excellence of their literary art: Roman and Greek authors had written with an eloquence that made their subjects come alive to later readers, and that medieval writers had not been able to match. The period after the fall of Rome had not lacked for deeds worthy of memory, he assured his readers; this era only appeared undistinguished because its chroniclers lacked literary power. Accolti discussed the achievements of medieval and Renaissance Italians (particularly Florentines and Venetians) in all fields, from warfare to poetry (which had revived in the very recent past), and found them equal to the feats of the ancients.[27]

One implication of this view was that the reputation of

[25] On Accolti's family background and financial position, see Martines, *op.cit.*, pp. 343-44.

[26] *Dialogus de praestantia virorum sui aevi*, printed by Galletti, in his edition of Villani, *Liber de civitatis Florentiae famosis civibus*, pp. 105-28.

[27] *Dialogus, passim.* "Quamobrem non aetas nostra, aut superior culpanda est, quae multos habuerunt illustres viros, sed dolendum est potius, eis meritum scribendi praeconium defuisse; cuius defectu etiam praestantium veterum nomina non pauca obscurata sunt" (p. 112).

an age, a people, or a city depended on the eloquence which was employed in its service. Accolti himself proposed to further the reputation of the Middle Ages by writing eloquently about medieval achievements. But his understanding of the power of eloquence also led him to suspect it. Sometimes, he declared, ancient historians had aimed more at displaying their own talent and eloquence than at telling the truth. Therefore he refused to believe that the deeds of the Greeks and Romans had been as glorious as classical historians made them appear.[28] He extended the same analysis to his own century. Accolti praised Bruni's *History of Florence*, noting its similarity to the works of ancient writers. But one of the ways in which Bruni's narrative resembled classical histories was in its inclusion of many fictitious orations, speeches so carefully constructed and polished—in Latin—that the reader could not believe they had been given by the men to whom Bruni ascribed them.[29] Therefore, while Accolti believed that eloquence helped preserve the memory of noteworthy things, he also recognized that it was not committed to truth. At one point, referring to Bruni, Niccolò Niccoli, Carlo Marsuppini, and Poggio Bracciolini, Accolti described them as "men of great learning and luminaries of eloquence," but—in contrast to the humanists' descriptions of themselves—he did not attribute wisdom to them.[30]

[28] *Ibid.*, p. 111: ". . . id est, Auctores pro libito sua literis mendacia tradidisse, non veritati studentes, sed quemadmodum sua eloquentia sua ingenia celebrarentur. Itaque illa veterum gesta, quae solemus admirari, etsi magna fuisse crediderim, non tamen qualia scriptores ipsi demonstrarunt; nec etiam aliquando talia, quod non ab aliis postea maiora, vel paria saepenumero sint facta."

[29] *Ibid.*, p. 121: "An vero tu credis, quas *Leonardus* refert, conciones, easdem fuisse, quas illi quorum scriptae sunt nomine, protulerunt; quae (ut plurimum) materno sermone dictae sunt, et si ad eas, quas legimus, comparentur, proculdubio diversissimae videbuntur?" In this passage Accolti argued that, since the speeches found in Roman histories were actually the work of the historians rather than of the speakers, they could not be taken as evidence that ancient men had surpassed medieval men in practical eloquence.

[30] *Ibid.*, p. 118; "Nicolaum *Nicolum*, *Leonardum* et *Carolum* Arretinos, et *Poggium*, viros doctissimos, et eloquentiae lumina." Here Accolti praised Cosimo de' Medici for his patronage of these men.

He did, however, praise medieval philosophers for their devotion to wisdom. His evaluation of the scholastics supported his assertion that medieval men equaled the ancients in achievement. He praised them in spite of the defects the humanists found in them. Let us admit, he said, that the ancient philosophers, with a few exceptions, joined the knowledge contained in their books to a high level of eloquence, whereas contemporary philosophers, like those of the past three centuries, shun rhetorical embellishments. This meant simply that the moderns were zealous for truth alone. As Augustine said of Varro, they delighted as much in knowledge as the ancients had in language. Philosophy was the pursuit of wisdom, as its name indicated; so that a philosopher should be praised according to whether he furthered the search for wisdom, not for writing in a fine literary style. "If you are seeking the pure study of philosophy, therefore," Accolti wrote, "you will find that, in the last four hundred years, France, Germany, Italy and Spain have been full of teachers and pupils in this subject." The best of these, Albertus Magnus and Thomas Aquinas, he considered the equals of any of the ancients, with the exception of Plato and Aristotle. He praised even Averroës and Avicenna, together with a number of Christian philosophers. The latter included several important Italian scholastics. One of these, Ugo Benzi of Siena, we met earlier as a critic of Bruni's translation of Aristotle; a second, Luigi Marsili, was a friend of Petrarch and Salutati; something will be said about a third, Giovanni Dominici, below. In conclusion Accolti stated that while Greece had produced many schools of philosophers, the Romans, who had sometimes been suspicious of philosophy, had achieved less in this field than the medieval schools. Thus, despite his association with the humanists, Accolti differed sharply with them in his evaluation of medieval philosophic culture.[31]

[31] *Ibid.*, pp. 122-23: "Caeterum sicut in Rhetorica et Poesi parumper vincimur, ita in PHILOSOPHIA veteres (praeter admodum paucos) aut vincimus, aut adaequamus: dum tamen (sicut necesse est) verissime fateamur, veteres quidem Philosophos, paucis exceptis,

To find a patrician Florentine clearly stating that humanist learning should be supplemented by scholastic philosophy, it seems necessary to move further into the second half of the fifteenth century. Evidence from this period should be used with caution in connection with the earlier part of the century; but even taking account of the distance between the two historical moments, the testimony we shall cite retains its value. The writer in this case was Alamanno Rinuccini, a member of a group of Florentines who had campaigned in the 1450's to have the republic support the *studio*.[32] He had a number of teachers, but the one who influenced him most was Johannes Argyropulos, a Greek exile. The program of education described by Rinuccini

quae libris tradiderunt suis summa fere cum eloquentia iunxisse; eos vero, qui vel hoc tempore, vel a trecentis citra annis philosophati sunt, nequaquam orationis fuco deditos; solum inquirendae veritatis studium adhibuisse, qui, ut de Varrone Augustinus ait, tantum studiosos rerum, quantum diserti illi studiosos verborum delectarunt. Si enim, ut verbum indicat Philosophia sapientiae studium dicitur; non verborum ornatus, sed qui magis eam argumentis demonstret laudandus est, si res ipsa non autem orationis lenocinia inquiruntur. . . . Si ergo nudum Philosophiae studium spectas; reperies a quadringentis citra elapsis annis Gallias, Italiam, Germanos, Hispaniam, innumeris eius facultatis magistris, discipulisque scaturisse. . . . Nec sane intelligo, cui antiquorum, quorum libri extant, exceptis Platone et Aristotele, *Albertus Magnus*, et *Beatus Thomas* postponendi sint. . . . Et si apud Graecos quondam multae Philosophantium Scholae repertae sunt; nunc inter nationes plures eiuscemodi artes non minori frequentia, quam tunc in illa fere sola orbis parte increbuerunt. Aliis enim in locis rarum Philosophiae studium fuit, quod Romanis quoque diu incognitum fuisse, Auctores tradunt, a quibus etiam relatum invenimus, primum Catonem censuisse pellendos ex urbe Philosophos, quorum, opera iuventus ad nova quaedam et inutilia irritari videretur. . . . Si ergo vera fateri volumus, non minor hoc tempore, aut satis ante Philosophorum numerus fuit, quam in veteribus fuit seculis. . . ." Accolti also remarked on important achievements in the study of medicine during the Middle Ages.

[32] See Vito R. Giustiniani, *Alamanno Rinuccini, 1426-1499* (Cologne, 1965). See also *Lettere ed Orazioni di Alamanno Rinuccini*, ed. V. R. Giustiniani (Florence, 1953); Ferdinandus Fossius, *Monumenta ad Alamanni Rinuccini Vitam Contextendam* (Florence, 1791). Also, J. E. Seigel, "The Teaching of Argyropulos and the Rhetoric of the First Humanists," in the forthcoming Princeton book, *Action and Conviction in Early Modern Europe, Essays in Memory of E. H. Harbison*, ed. T. K. Rabb and J. E. Seigel.

in a letter to his son in 1474 gives a good idea of his cultural orientation.[33] The education he had in mind was one appropriate to the future citizen, and in many ways it followed humanist notions. Not only was Cicero given an honored place in the program; Bruni and Poggio Bracciolini were themselves placed next to the ancients as models of style. But their utility was limited. Rinuccini found their knowledge confined to rhetoric and history; for dialectic and even moral philosophy he urged his son to look elsewhere.[34] In another place, he stated more explicitly his view of the limitations of humanist learning:

> Of philosophy, in which the knowledge of natural and supernatural things is contained, only a short time ago few men had even a taste, thinking they had done enough and more in it, if they had studied Aristotle's *Moralia*. I am speaking of our fellow citizens; notwithstanding some who philosophized as members of a religious order, or because they wanted to teach medicine, you will find among those who taught the *studia humanitatis* before our own time, except for Gianozzo Manetti, the smallest number learned in philosophy, as their writings make clear.[35]

Rinuccini felt that the situation had been changed by the arrival of his own teacher, Argyropulos. But Argyropulos was not the only source of philosophical learning, in Rinuccini's eyes. The scholastics, he said, though they "wrote in a rather harsh manner," had "attained to knowledge about

[33] See the letter in *Lettere ed Orazioni*, ed. Giustiniani, pp. 86-104.
[34] *Ibid.*, pp. 94-95, 98-99.
[35] Letter of Rinuccini to Roberto Salviati, 24 November 1489, in *Lettere ed Orazioni*, ed. Giustiniani, pp. 188-89. "Philosophiam vero, qua naturae tum etiam supernaturalium rerum cognitio continetur, non multo ante pauci vix summis, ut ita dicam, labiis attingebant, satis superque in ea profecisse arbitrantes, si Aristotelis *Moralia* discerent. De civibus nostris loquor; atqui religioni cuidam addicti aut medicinam profiteri volentes philosophabantur, quod illorum scripta declarant, qui ante aetatem nostram humanitatis studia profitebantur, inter quos praeter unum Iannoctium Manettum paucissimos in philosophia peritos invenies."

many and great things."[36] While he was proud of the revival
of many arts, both literary and visual, in his own time, he
did not believe that it had been necessary to rescue all
learning from darkness. Speaking of "dialectic, philosophy
and knowledge of the sacred scriptures," he asserted: "The
more necessary zeal for such studies is to living well and
wisely, the more they have flourished without interruption
among all peoples in every age."[37] Therefore, while he certainly appreciated the humanists and their achievements,
Rinuccini set definite limits to the value of their cultural
program. He thought that the intellectual formation of an
educated man in his day should include a kind of learning
in which the schoolmen were superior to Bruni and Poggio.

This attitude, of which Alamanno Rinuccini's comments
are the clearest expression, must be kept in mind in considering the relationship between humanism and other forms
of culture within Renaissance society. Humanist culture
permeated fifteenth-century Italian life, but it was not the
only form of culture that men of the time pursued.[38] Before
seeking the ways in which it may have been characteristic
of Renaissance society as a whole, the historian should be
aware that it was primarily identified with a particular
group of men within that society: the professional humanists. There was always a distinction between the professional humanists, who taught grammar and rhetoric and
served in the chanceries of the towns, and the amateurs,
who were their students and audience. The first group was
the real source of humanist culture; its members were completely identified with it. The *studia humanitatis* was the

[36] *Ibid.*, pp. 107-08.
[37] *Ibid.*, p. 107: "In dialectica autem et philosophia, tum etiam
sacrarum litterarum peritia clarissimos viros enumerare longissimum
esset. Talium enim disciplinarum studia, quo magis ad bene beateque
vivendum sunt necessaria, eo magis apud quasque gentes quacunque
aetate nunquam intermissa viguerunt, unde etiam effectum est ut
superioribus quoque temporibus ad summam perducta subtilitatem,
plurimis iisdemque doctissimis hominibus abundarent."
[38] See, in general, Pearl Kibre, "The Intellectual Interests Reflected
in Libraries of the Fourteenth and Fifteenth Centuries," *Journal of
the History of Ideas*, VII (1946), 257-97.

basis not only of their intellectual orientation, but of their social position as well. The most prominent humanists of the Quattrocento did not come from patrician families like the Manetti of Florence or the Quirini of Venice. The great humanist chancellors of Florence—Salutati, Bruni, Poggio Bracciolini, Carlo Marsuppini—were not even native Florentines.[39] Each was born in the Tuscan hinterland and sought his fortune in the city. For such men, a place in the upper levels of Renaissance society was not guaranteed by birth and wealth, but attainable only by excelling in their profession. Many of them achieved striking economic and social success. But this success resulted from their professional eminence, not vice versa. To exalt humanist culture and declare its superiority to scholasticism was, for them, to justify both their own activity as intellectuals and the position which this activity had gained for them in society. From their point of view, the legacy of Petrarch bulked so large that it often obscured other elements of the intellectual scene. But it is not correct to read the history of Renaissance culture through their eyes alone. Men like Cino Rinuccini and Gianozzo Manetti in Florence, and

---

[39] The importance of this distinction is underestimated by Professor Martines. He notes that these men did not belong to the Florentine patriciate on their arrival in the city (*The Social World of the Florentine Humanists*, p. 265), but does not note that these four humanists were of special importance. In fact each of the four was the central figure of Florentine humanism in his day. Their social position was very different from that of a Rossi, a Rinuccini, or a Manetti. It is certainly true, as Martines suggests (*ibid.*, p. 279), that such "social climbers" may take over the dominant values of the class into which they rise. Salutati's growing respect for scholasticism after many years spent in Florence may reflect the influence of men like Rossi and Rinuccini. But neither the intellectual values of the humanists nor their social and political values can be simply equated with those of the "ruling class." Martines' suggestion (*ibid.*, p. 280) that the humanist expression of "the ideal of service to the community" was a reflex of the patrician desire for office may describe one reason for the popularity of the humanists, but it adds little to the understanding of humanist thought. Martines gives no evidence to justify his implied belief that the patrician desire for office was greater in the early fifteenth century than it was a hundred years earlier.

Lauro Quirini and others in Venice, all belonged to a different social group, and therefore had a different perspective. The same may be said also of Benedetto Accolti, despite his having served for a time as chancellor of Florence. To these members of already-established families, participation in intellectual life offered not sustenance and social advancement, but diversion, cultivation, and added prestige. They were not fully identified with the *studia humanitatis* in the way the professional humanists were. Humanism occupied an important place in their intellectual life, but it was not their only interest. They admired and respected the scholastic philosophers as well.

Why should this have been so? What did scholastic writers have to offer that was relevant to the concerns of active citizens in Renaissance towns? This question is too complicated to be dealt with in detail here. One answer to it, however, is quite simple: many Italian scholastic philosophers and theologians encouraged a positive attitude toward civic life. The schoolmen were not as far removed from the life of their time as some humanist polemics would lead one to believe. An early example of this is provided by Remigio de' Girolami, the most prominent Florentine teacher of theology in Dante's day.[40] Remigio belonged to a Florentine family of some prominence in the wool guild and in the factional struggles around 1300. He studied at Paris in the 1260's, when Thomas Aquinas was teaching there. His surviving writings give a picture of a man whose basic orientation was Thomistic, but whose primary interests reflected and interacted with the urban environment of Florence. He was deeply troubled by the problem of political factions, and he praised the Romans for placing the common good above private ambition.[41] Though he con-

[40] On Remigio, see Charles T. Davis, "An Early Florentine Political Theorist, Fra Remigio de' Girolami," *Proc. Am. Phil. Soc.*, CIV (1961), 662-76; Martin Grabmann, "Die Italienische Thomistenschule des XIII und beginnenden XIV Jh.," *Mittelalterliches Geistesleben*, I (Munich, 1926), 332-91, esp. 369; L. Minio-Paluello, "Remigio Girolami's *De Bono Communi*," *Italian Studies*, XI (1956), 56-71.

[41] Davis, pp. 665-66.

demned usury and feared the temptations of great wealth, he was still able to list among God's gifts to Florence such eminently practical advantages as an abundance of riches, a respected coinage, a large population, the wool industry, skill in arms manufacture, and the resources of the *contado* or countryside.[42] There was no contradiction between his respect for Aristotle and for scholastic logic on the one hand and his concern for the welfare of his city on the other.

A number of later schoolmen followed the lead of Remigio de' Girolami. The views of Marsiglio of Padua are too well known to require restatement here.[43] Other thinkers and writers of basically scholastic orientation also discussed practical questions of civic life in ways which were appreciated by laymen. Perhaps the best example in the later fourteenth century is Luigi Marsili, the Forentine Augustinian who studied at the University of Paris and who was a correspondent of Petrarch and a friend of Salutati. Together with other eminent schoolmen of the day, he played a major role in the discussions reported by Giovanni da Prato in his *Il Paradiso degli Alberti*.[44] Even if we accept the argument recently put forward that Marsili was not responsible for the theory of the founding of Florence by Sulla, which Salutati, Bruni, and other humanists later accepted, it can hardly be doubted that his interests em-

[42] *Ibid.*, p. 667.
[43] In addition to the standard works, see the recent comments of J. K. Hyde, *Padua in the Age of Dante* (Manchester and New York, 1966), pp. 210-12, 306ff.
[44] The picture of Marsili given in Bruni's *Dialogi* is famous; the one painted by Salutati in several of his letters has been noted above, in Chap. III. Poggio Bracciolini, in his funeral oration for Niccolò Niccoli, said of Marsili: "Frequentabatur ab optimis ac praestantissimis viris huius civitatis, qui ad eum velut ad divinum quoddam oraculum undique confluebant" (quoted by A. Della Torre, *Storia dell' Accademia platonica di Firenze*, p. 187). Among the other scholastic philosophers present in *Il Paradiso degli Alberti* was Francesco Landino, well known as a musician and a mathematician. Landino was the author of some verses in which William of Occam spoke in defense of scholastic culture, against his humanist detractors. Cesare Vasoli is correct to point out that these sentiments reflected "the opinions of a rather broad sector of Florentine culture" ("Polemiche Occamiste," p. 124).

braced such matters as the history of his native town, and that his learning was admired by her citizens.[45]

Marsili was a friend of the humanists; but one can also find a positive attitude toward civic life in a scholastic writer who opposed them, Giovanni Dominici. Dominici, a teacher in the Florentine *studio* and a popular preacher, wrote a long treatise against the dangers of classical literature entitled *Lucula Noctis* (in which, however, he displayed considerable knowledge of the classics himself). Salutati was engaged in drafting a reply to this work when he died in 1406. But Dominici also wrote a treatise on the ordering of personal and family life which contained much practical advice for everyday living.[46] The first two chapters contained traditional religious counsel on the care of soul and body, but the last two, on domestic economy and child-raising, showed much sympathy for the wealthy and politically active citizen. Dominici warned against taking the New Testament idealization of poverty too literally. It was wrong for a person with family obligations to give up his worldly goods to follow Christ, because "anyone who does not provide charitably for his own family is worse than faithless."[47] It was quite enough to refrain from valuing riches too highly. In the prologue, Dominici reminded his readers that men had found God in many ways; the rich, as well as the poor, could gain salvation. Throughout the treatise he revealed his belief that men should live and dress as their social rank, not ascetic counsels, dictated. In the last chapter he noted that "Since children, and especially boys, are to be members of the commonwealth, it is appropriate to raise them for its utility," and he enumerated many occupations necessary to the community.[48]

[45] Baron, *Crisis*, Chap. IV. On Marsili, see C. Vasoli, "La *Regola per ben confessarsi* di Luigi Marsili," *Rinascimento*, IV (1953), 39-44, as well as the literature cited above, p. 66, note 4.

[46] Giovanni Dominici, *Regola del governo di cura familiare* (Florence, 1927).

[47] *Ibid.*, p. 83: ". . . perchè è peggio che infedele qualunche non fa pietà a' suoi."

[48] *Ibid.*, p. 138: "E perchè i tuoi figliuoli, e massimamente maschi,

Another figure who combined a scholastic education with a practical awareness of the problems of everyday life was San Bernardino of Siena, the famous preacher. His success and popularity were in part the result of his characteristic "mixture of fervor and practical common sense."[49] He has been called "perhaps the ablest economist of the Middle Ages." Like other scholastic commentators on economic matters, he took a strikingly practical stand on the question of the just price, admitting the justice of the market valuation of a commodity.[50] An affirmative view of wealth was taken by other scholastics as well, even by so personally ascetic a one as San Antonino, the well-known archbishop of Florence. While Antonino regarded with suspicion the pursuit of money as an end in itself, he also described riches as "aids to blessedness, inasmuch as they support our corporeal life and serve as instruments for acts of virtue."[51] As we shall see, this attitude was essentially identical to that of Leonardo Bruni. In general, therefore, there is reason to doubt that scholastic thinking was fundamentally out of touch with practical-minded laymen in the fifteenth century.

This is not to say that laymen looked to figures like Luigi Marsili or San Bernardino primarily for affirmations of civic life. These churchmen represented the values of Christianity, not of business or government; judging contemporary life by religious standards, they found more to criticize than to praise. This seems to have been both expected and appreciated by their audiences. The laymen of Renaissance towns were men of trade and politics, but this was not their only identity: they, too, were committed Chris-

---

son membri della repubblica, convengonsi allevare ad utilità di quella. . . ."

[49] Iris Origo, *The World of San Bernardino* (New York, 1962), p. 19.

[50] Raymond De Roover, "The Concept of the Just Price: Theory and Economic Policy," *Journal of Economic History*, XVIII (1958), 423.

[51] Quoted by R. H. Tawney, *Religion and the Rise of Capitalism* (New York, 1926; reprinted 1947), p. 35.

tians. When San Bernardino, in a sermon of 1422, criticized the commercial practice of the Venetians, the Doge Mocenigo sought to reward, not punish, him.[52] The same preacher rebuked the Florentines, saying they were all usurers, but—like other Italians of the day—they turned out in droves to hear him.[53] For a fifteenth-century preacher or writer to judge worldly life by otherworldly standards did not make his message irrelevant as far as the ordinary men of the time were concerned.[54]

These remarks about the place of scholasticism in Renaissance life may help us to understand in turn the place of the humanists there. They remind us that humanism was not the only expression of Renaissance cultural life. They also suggest that in order to explain the popularity of humanism, or to show that the humanists expressed values implicit in the lives of less articulate men, we need not—and perhaps should not—limit our focus to those parts of their work in which the humanists specifically praised or served civic life. These aspects of humanist literature have been stressed by a number of recent scholars, who therefore speak of Quattrocento humanism as "civic humanism." The present writer has expressed elsewhere doubts about some of the interpretations of this school; these will not be repeated here.[55] Here we shall attempt only to outline what seems to us a more balanced view of the attitude—ex-

[52] See Origo, *The World of San Bernardino*, pp. 32-33.

[53] *Ibid.*, p. 90.

[54] The persistence of medieval attitudes toward economic life during the Renaissance has been emphasized repeatedly by Federico Chabod; see *Scritti sul Rinascimento* (Turin, 1967), pp. 68-69, 98ff.; p. 703: "Una mentalità 'capitalistica,' nel senso moderno, un pensiero in cui non rimanga forte l'influsso dei divieti ecclesiastici, de' criteri medievali . . . non gli verrà mai fatto di trovarli, neppure nel secolo XV, anche se storici ed economisti continuino con scarsa comprensione storica, a considerare l'uomo d'affari del Rinascimento come un uomo d'affari moderno."

[55] J. E. Seigel, " 'Civic Humanism' or Ciceronian Rhetoric? The Culture of Petrarch and Bruni," *Past and Present*, No. 34 (1966). Much of the material in this article has not been incorporated into the present study—in particular the criticisms of Professor Baron's work. For Baron's reply, see the same journal, No. 36 (1967), pp. 21-37.

pressed and implied—of the humanists toward civic life, and of the place they occupied in society. To do so within the general context of this book is appropriate because one important source of the humanists' civic attitudes was their belief that the best kind of learning required the combination of rhetoric and philosophy. It was as men who sought to be both orators and philosophers that the humanists discussed questions of civic participation and solitary withdrawal. In order to show how this was so, we must pause to recall some of the intellectual problems described in the earlier chapters of our study.[56]

The attempt to combine rhetoric and philosophy always involved a basic ambivalence, one which can be discovered in Cicero and in all his successors. Cicero devoted much effort to the projected union of wisdom and eloquence, but at the same time he recognized deep-seated tensions between the two. Not only did he present some of the greatest Greek philosophers as unfriendly to oratory, he even suggested that philosophy itself was fundamentally— and perhaps even irreconcilably—hostile to rhetoric. Cicero insisted that the orator respect not only the linguistic standards of his community, but its moral standards as well. Philosophy, however, was free of such restrictions. Philosophy was among those arts in which "that is most excellent which is farthest removed from the understanding and mental capacity of the untrained." The philosophic enterprise caused men to turn their backs on the mundane necessities of everyday life; the orator's search for persuasive speech could not succeed if he did the same. Given this primary opposition between the two arts, how could any union be achieved?

In large part, Cicero's answer lay in the differences between various ancient philosophical schools. The school for which he felt the greatest sympathy was Academic

[56] For what follows, see the relevant sections of Chaps. I-V, above. For more information about humanist moral philosophy, presented in a way that harmonizes in large degree with the present study, see Charles Trinkaus, *Adversity's Noblemen* (New York, 1940; reissued with a new preface, 1965).

246

skepticism, since its doctrines complemented and harmonized with the requirements of rhetoric. Both demanded of their followers a wide general culture, including a knowledge of diverse philosophical dogmas, but both also forbade a final commitment to the positive teachings of any philosophical school. The Academic skeptic, denying that any philosophical opinion could be accepted as true, at once trained his mind and supported his principles by arguing first for, and then against, various philosophical points of view. The orator, inspired by the traditional ideal of the combination of rhetoric and philosophy, also moved freely among the philosophic schools, demonstrating his ability to speak persuasively on every side of a question. Combining the roles of orator and skeptic, Cicero spoke at times on behalf of the moral philosophy of the Stoics, and at times for the Peripatetics.

While Cicero showed enthusiasm for both of these schools, he supported them on significantly different grounds. When he argued for the teaching of the Stoics he spoke of its superiority as a philosophical system per se: that is, of its perfect internal consistency, which resulted from its denial that any external circumstances could affect the happiness of the wise and virtuous man. In support of Peripatetic moral philosophy, however, Cicero adduced its greater relevance to actual human life—it admitted the moral importance of health and of external conditions— and therefore its suitability to the civic environment in which the orator lived. Stoicism was, Cicero admitted, the school of the "only true philosophers." Of all the dogmatic philosophical schools, however, it was Peripateticism that was most in harmony with oratory. Thus it was as orator that Cicero embraced Peripateticism, and as philosopher that he admired the Stoics. To support the two schools alternately was in a sense to try to combine rhetoric and philosophy. The perfect orator would be a Stoic in his most philosophical moments, a Peripatetic in his ordinary, common-sense moments, but fundamentally a skeptic at all times. In this way Cicero articulated a characteristically

247

rhetorical point of view toward moral philosophy and the various ancient schools.

Petrarch rediscovered this rhetorical perspective on philosophy. He often spoke of the need to combine wisdom with eloquence, both to make philosophy active and to enroll rhetoric in the service of truth. Even more explicitly than Cicero, however, Petrarch acknowledged the fundamental contradiction within this ideal. The orator's commitment to the everyday world of the city made it impossible for him to share in the solitary philosophic quest for true self-knowledge, free from the confusions and errors of ordinary men. Thus Petrarch's attempt to join wisdom and eloquence, like Cicero's, had to overcome his own recognition of the basic opposition between the two. Following Cicero, Petrarch sought to overcome this antagonism between philosophy and oratory. This objective underlay his approach to the ancient philosophical schools.

As a Christian, Petrarch could not of course entirely share Cicero's enthusiasm for Academic skepticism, though he sometimes showed considerable sympathy for that school in matters which did not touch on faith. Yet in a sense he did not need to enlist skepticism as a philosophical support for oratory. Christianity itself provided firm reasons for believing that no ancient philosopher had been able to distinguish truth from mere opinion. Thus Petrarch (followed closely by Salutati) made free use of both Peripatetic and Stoic maxims in his letters and treatises, and defended both Stoic and Peripatetic points of view. For this reason, although Petrarch sometimes praised consistency, his writings are filled with contradictions. These contradictions should be understood within the context of Petrarch's Ciceronian style of thought. There is as much of Cicero as of Petrarch in the affirmation that "Just as my reason is often Stoic, so are my feelings always Peripatetic." The ethical stance of the Ciceronian orator is well summarized in Petrarch's statement: "You will act differently as a philosopher than you do as a man. No one is so given to wisdom that he does not, when he returns to the common human state, condescend also to public ways of acting."

The attitudes of Petrarch and other humanists toward civic life—its problems and its values—were in large part conditioned by this Ciceronian style of thought. Petrarch spoke sometimes in favor of the life of solitude and silent contemplation; this was to speak as a philosopher. At other times he stood for an acceptance of the city with its noisy activity, and praised the humanity of the moral values which the give and take of community life required; here he spoke as an orator. Petrarch's statements moved continually back and forth between these two positions, between the claims of an abstract wisdom and the moral standards of the everyday world. This alternation did not arise because Petrarch experienced any fundamental change of heart about the two opposed lives of civic action and philosophic contemplation, but rather grew out of his attempt to combine the lives of philosopher and orator. In Petrarch's vision rhetoric and philosophy both attracted and repelled each other, and humanist thought embodied this dialectic. One result was the simultaneous affirmation and rejection of civic life.

As we have seen, Salutati's position on these questions closely followed Petrarch's: he too vacillated between a Stoic and a Peripatetic point of view. Bruni departed somewhat from his predecessors in this respect. He seldom specifically shared Petrarch's sympathy for the Stoics, though he included them in his "conciliation of philosophers." His basic source for the study of ethics was Aristotle. His attitude toward philosophy was no less Ciceronian because of this, however. It was Peripateticism, after all, that Cicero had singled out in *De oratore* and *De finibus* as the philosophical school which best met the needs of the orator. In his own *Life of Aristotle*, Bruni emphasized both the harmony of the Philosopher's doctrines with everyday life and his interest in rhetoric. The difference between Bruni's philosophical posture and Petrarch's was therefore not funda-

249

mental; both men were inspired by the Ciceronian combination of philosophy with eloquence. Whereas Petrarch interpreted this goal in a way which sometimes led to a distrust of rhetoric, however, Bruni's procedures did not allow this. His version of the ideal represented a more complete devotion to rhetoric, a more confident affirmation of the orator's own philosophical and ethical perspective. This was the meaning of his Aristotelianism, and of his slightly more consistent affirmation of civic life.

The close kinship between Bruni's position and that of Petrarch is clear in the attitude which Bruni adopted toward the active and contemplative lives. He wrote in his *Introduction to Moral Philosophy*: "Each life indeed has its own praise and commendation. The contemplative is surely more divine and more rare, the active however is more excellent by reason of its general usefulness."[57] Strictly speaking, this placed the contemplative above the active, since divinity was the highest attribute Bruni could have applied to either. Yet Bruni's emphasis in his treatise belied this conclusion; it was the life of action and the active virtue of *prudentia* which drew forth his enthusiasm. The noblest ideal, Bruni wrote here and elsewhere, was a combination of the two lives. But he was able to regard each as praiseworthy in itself. He joined his praise of Dante's involvement in civic affairs to a commendation of Petrarch's solitude.[58]

Thus Bruni's acceptance of civic life was not unqualified. His statements about wealth are an example of his varying attitudes toward the moral value of worldly success. Some recent writers have claimed great significance for Bruni's comments on wealth, and his apparent acceptance of riches as an aid to virtue.[59] In some places he did praise wealth

[57] *Schriften*, p. 39. Bruni defended Aristotle's allegiance to the life of contemplation in a letter he wrote near the end of his life to Lauro Quirini the Venetian. See Bruni, *Epistolarum Libri VIII*, ed. Mehus, II, 134-44.
[58] Bruni, *Le vite di Dante e di Petrarca*, in *Schriften*, pp. 68-69.
[59] Hans Baron, "Franciscan Poverty and Civic Wealth as Factors in the Rise of Humanistic Thought," *Speculum*, XIII (1938).

for the opportunity it afforded for the exercise of virtue, especially with regard to liberality and munificence, which by definition require large means. But this was not his only attitude. Writing to Cosimo de' Medici, Bruni cautioned that wealth was only an external good, not a good of the body or the soul. It therefore contributed to virtuous living even less than physical well-being did, and still less than wisdom. "To compare riches with wisdom is nothing else than to set the lowest grade of good against the highest."[60] Bruni admitted that wealth created some possibilities of virtuous action, but he cautioned against pursuing it for its own sake.

As long as humanism remained loyal to the ideal of the combination—on professedly equal terms—of rhetoric and philosophy, the humanists' affirmation of civic life could not be unconditional. From a Ciceronian point of view, to admit the value of a strictly philosophical perspective was to set limits to the moral value of everyday life. Only when the application of philosophical standards to ethics was completely rejected, as it was by Lorenzo Valla, could humanism arrive at a stage of complete and uncritical acceptance of the morality of ordinary men. Valla frankly subordinated philosophy to rhetoric. The corollary of this position was the rejection of any philosophical morality which contradicted the standards of common sense. Refusing altogether to accept the independent value of philosophical standards, Valla could regard wealth much more positively than Bruni did. Writing in the *Elegantiae* about the word "happy" (*beatus*), he observed: "He is happy who abounds in all things which pertain to the use and ornament of life. Therefore we rightly call all the rich

[60] *Schriften*, p. 135. Alison M. Brown, "The Humanist Portrait of Cosimo de' Medici, Pater Patriae," *Journal of the Warburg and Courtauld Institutes*, XXIV (1962), notes that Bruni had earlier praised Cosimo for his wealth, and asks whether the "change of emphasis from private family virtues to public political virtues does not reflect Cosimo's increasing authority in the city" (p. 188). Perhaps it may, but the fact remains that even in writing to so prominent a citizen as Cosimo, Bruni was capable of demeaning the "civic wealth" on which his position was mainly based.

251

happy, as in Juvenal: 'the purse of the happy old woman.' And in Cicero: 'Let them be wealthy, let them be happy!' And in another place: 'Formerly when the Crotons prospered with all kinds of riches and when they were celebrated as the happiest people in Italy. . . .'"[61] Here Valla implied that wealth had a much greater moral importance than Bruni ever attributed to it. Of all the humanists we have considered here, only Valla consistently affirmed the ethical values of the ordinary world. Only he openly and fully denied the value of philosophical contemplation separate from the active life.

This is certainly not to deny the importance of the contributions the other humanists made to the civic culture of their time. Even if they sometimes may have felt required by "philosophy" to temper their civic enthusiasm, at the moments when they gave free rein to their literary talents they celebrated civic life and its values in ways which were original, and which could not have been the product of any other form of contemporary culture. Bruni's *Panegyric on the City of Florence* and *History of Florence*, Salutati's chancery letters and *Invective against Antonio Loschi*, Petrarch's *De viris illustribus* and *Africa*—all these writings affirmed the life of action and civic participation with a depth of feeling and an enthusiasm unmistakably humanistic. To patricians seeking reassurance about the values implicit in their everyday activities—at least to those among them who could read Latin—these works must have spoken with genuine force. Giangaleazzo Visconti is said to have counted Salutati more valuable to the Florentines during their war against Milan than a troop of cavalry; no scholastic writer could match the service the humanists rendered to the city-state. In this regard, those who have emphasized the "civic" quality of humanist cul-

[61] *Elegantiae linguae latinae*, IV, cxiv (*Opera*, p. 159): "Beatus qui rebus omnibus ad vitae usum, ornatumque spectantibus abundat. Ideoque locupletes sane omnes Beatos vocamus, ut apud Iuvenalem: Vetulae vesica beatae. Et Cicero: sint florentes, sint beati. Et alibi: Crotoniatae quondam quum florerent omnibus copiis, et in Italia quum in primis beati nominarentur. . . ."

ture have cast light on important features of the humanist movement.

Important as it is to recognize the services which the humanists provided, however, it is also necessary to see that writings like Bruni's *Laudatio Florentinae Urbis* and the others mentioned above were examples of eloquence first of all, and that it was as rhetorical compositions that they contributed to civic sentiment. The humanists were willing and eager to place their pens at the service of the city-state, but they were conscious of the rhetorical nature of the declarations they made on such occasions. Bruni later excused some of his statements in the *Laudatio* on the grounds that the genre of panegyric "exalts many things above what is true." Bruni must have been aware of his exaggeration when he wrote that the fact that Florence was descended from Rome gave her the right to "the lordship of the world," and that in any war the city would be fighting only "for the defense or recovery of its own property." Given the rhetorical quality and purpose of such assertions, it is not surprising to find Bruni considerably detached from them in the following years, when he worked in the papal chancery at Rome, or to discover that Salutati could contradict his praises of civic life as easily as he could make them.[62] For the humanists, eloquent affirmations of the virtue of a city-state and its citizens were not primarily expressions of personal feelings; they were the performance of a professional task. To say this is to repeat a view stated by several of the humanists themselves: that to affirm the values of civic life was to speak as an orator.

This same line of reasoning may also clarify the relationship between the humanists' often vacillating comments on civic life, and the apparent feelings of broader segments of Renaissance society toward it. If the success of preachers

[62] On Bruni, see Seigel, " 'Civic Humanism' or Ciceronian Rhetoric . . . ," pp. 19-28. On Salutati, see Peter Herde, "Politik und Rhetorik in Florenz am Vorabend der Renaissance," *Archiv für Kulturgeschichte*, XLVII (1965), 141-220; also, Charles Trinkaus, "Humanist Treatises on the Status of the Religious: Petrarch, Salutati, Valla," *Studies in the Renaissance*, XI (1964), 7-45, esp. 20ff.

like San Bernardino (and, later, Savonarola) indicates that fifteenth-century men felt considerable uneasiness about the values embodied in their everyday activities, then it is doubtful that an ideology which merely affirmed civic values could have satisfied many of the humanists' contemporaries. One function of the noncivic or philosophical ideals retained by most of the humanists may have been to allow them—as in the case of Salutati or Bruni—to express those anxieties about civic life and doubts about the adequacy of a purely civic ideology which were more widely present among their contemporaries. If these speculations are not too wide of the mark, then it may be possible to understand something which otherwise remains puzzling: namely, the fact that it was Lorenzo Valla, a man much less at home in the civic society of his time than Bruni or Salutati, but more fully identified in his own eyes with the art of oratory, who produced the most insistent and extreme celebration of everyday life.

To understand the place of the humanists in the life of their time, therefore, one should regard them both under the general aspect of men of the fifteenth century, and under the specific aspect of intellectuals of a certain type. Their world view contained elements which were shared by other Renaissance men, as well as elements which were particularly and individually theirs. They participated in social and political life not simply as citizens, but rather as members of a distinguishable professional—and social— group. While their intellectual techniques contributed to both Renaissance education and politics, they were not the only intellectuals of the time, nor necessarily the most representative. These conclusions derive—as does the analysis of humanist thought earlier in this book—from the identification of the humanists as professional orators seeking to model themselves on the Ciceronian ideal. It was as men of eloquence that they found a place in the society of their day.

CONCLUSION

I N CONCLUDING our study, we shall give attention to some implications of the material presented here, and to some of its limitations, which have not yet been made explicit. Here we must take note of several aspects of the humanist movement not specifically dealt with in this book. This epilogue relates primarily to the first, more monographic part of the study, but refers to the later, more speculative part as well.

THE HUMANIST conception of the relationship between rhetoric and philosophy did not remain static in the late fourteenth and early fifteenth centuries. From Petrarch's union of the two arts, in which philosophical standards regarding man's intellectual and moral life retained considerable independence (as they had, with similar inconsistencies, in Cicero's writings), the humanist program evolved by way of Salutati's waverings into Bruni's more confident affirmation of the orator's philosophical perspective and, finally, into Valla's outright demand for the subordination of philosophy to rhetoric. The general direction in which Petrarchian humanism developed in the Quattrocento is hard to mistake: the humanists came to conceive of the combination of wisdom and eloquence in ways which granted increasingly less independence within it to philosophy. Petrarch had sought only to justify, in opposition to the scholastics, a rhetorical approach to moral philosophy, and had affirmed the genuine philosopher's right to criticize the style of living and thinking typical of the orator. Valla, however, tried to vindicate rhetoric against all philosophers, both ancient and medieval, and refused to admit that any "true" philosophy might be out of harmony with oratory. There may be an element of the arbitrary in presenting this development only through the thinkers treated here; had other humanists been included, the line of evolution might have been less clear. Yet this does not detract from the importance of the fundamental traits of humanist

255

thought which we have analyzed. Petrarch and his followers were conscious that their discussions of philosophical questions were those of men of eloquence. This consciousness influenced the philosophical positions taken by individual humanists, and finally contributed to the radical anti-philosophical polemic of Lorenzo Valla.

These observations may help to clarify a question which has been debated by recent students of the humanist movement: Were the humanists philosophers?[1] The answer depends in large part on how the term "philosopher" is defined. If, to earn the right to be called a philosopher, it is enough to discuss some of the traditional problems of philosophy, to enter into debate with philosophers, and to influence the subsequent course of the history of philosophy, then the humanists were certainly philosophers. But if, on the other hand, the name philosopher is reserved for men who seek to place themselves within one of the great philosophical traditions, or who actually try to find solutions to philosophical problems through reasoned and consistent discourse, then the claim of the humanists to the title is doubtful. The humanists were often careless or indifferent about the distinction between one philosophical position and another; what gave unity and a certain consistency to their thought, despite the fact that they often defended contrasting positions in moral philosophy, was their rhetorical approach to philosophical problems. They shared an identity as men of eloquence, not of reason. While they often claimed the title of philosopher, they sometimes admitted that it belonged more properly to their scholastic rivals. This was true—to a different degree and with different implications in each case—of Salutati in his defense of Petrarch against Poggio, of Bruni in the *Dialogues* inscribed to Pier Paolo Vergerio, and of Valla in numerous anti-philosophical passages. When we speak of

[1] Professor Kristeller has usually answered this question in the negative (but see his *Eight Philosophers of the Italian Renaissance*). Professor Garin stoutly maintains the affirmative.

256

the humanists as philosophers, therefore, we should remember that their first loyalties were to rhetoric.

Their ambivalence toward philosophy may help us to understand the boundaries within which the humanists carried on the revival of antiquity. Despite the great enthusiasm of Petrarch and his followers for ancient culture, certain segments of the ancient world were either misunderstood or ignored by them. Aristotle, as the author of those treatises bearing his name which survived the classical world, could not be easily reconciled with the humanist vision of antiquity. He remained a puzzle to Petrarch, was never clearly seen and accepted by Bruni despite the latter's knowledge of Greek, and could only be regarded as an enemy by Valla. The tensions which the figure of Aristotle created for the humanists were not merely the result of the place he occupied in contemporary scholastic culture; they were due equally to the humanists' conflicting feelings about philosophy. Bruni sought to claim Aristotle for the *studia humanitatis*, but his was an Aristotle constructed in part from Cicero's comments on the philosopher's lost youthful works, and in part from Bruni's own imagination. Valla's image of Aristotle was different still, recognizing the roughness of the philosopher's style and the primacy of logic and metaphysics among his interests; precisely for these reasons Valla regarded Aristotle with hostility, as he did the rest of ancient pagan philosophy. Plato did not fare much better among the early humanists. All repeated the praises of Plato which they found in Cicero and St. Augustine, and Bruni translated some portions of Plato's writings. But none of the humanists seem to have ever shown much understanding or sympathy for the genuine Plato of the dialogues and the *Republic*, with his many criticisms of sophistic rhetoric and his celebration of a philosophy based on critical dialectic. Bruni preferred Aristotle to Plato, as more suited to the everyday world of the orator. Valla once associated the Socrates of the *Gorgias* with the hated Stoics. The early humanists, in

CONCLUSION

their view of antiquity, either failed to comprehend or refused to sympathize with those aspects of ancient philosophical culture which were genuinely hostile to rhetoric.

To be sure, the enthusiasm of the early-fifteenth-century humanists for antiquity helped give impetus to the
Neoplatonic revival of the later fifteenth century. Ficino,
the leader of this movement, regarded his restoration of
ancient philosophy as part of a broader contemporary return to ancient culture. But the activities of Ficino and his
circle were far from being a simple continuation of the Ciceronian humanism of Petrarch and Bruni. Ficino and Pico,
in contrast to these earlier thinkers, both had extensive
training in scholastic philosophy, and neither of them entirely rejected medieval philosophical culture. Their scholastic background was an important preparation for their
study of ancient philosophy.[2] Moreover, both men placed
rather strict limits on the value of the rhetorical humanism
of the earlier Quattrocento. Ficino sometimes spoke of the
need to forsake a popular style in order to devote oneself
to the strict language of philosophy. He regarded a rhetorical approach as a possible, but not a properly philosophical, attitude toward philosophy.[3] Pico made his suspicion of the combination of wisdom and eloquence even
more explicit. In a well-known letter to Ermolao Barbaro,
he wrote in defense of the "barbarian" scholastics: "The
barbarians have had the god of eloquence not on the
tongue, but in the heart . . . if eloquence they lacked, they
did not lack wisdom; . . . eloquence should not have been
joined to wisdom; only their not being joined perhaps is
free from fault, so that it were wicked to join them."[4] The

[2] See P. O. Kristeller, "Florentine Platonism and its Relations with
Humanism and Scholasticism," *Church History*, VIII (1939), 201ff.;
idem, "The Scholastic Background of Marsilio Ficino," *Studies in
Renaissance Thought and Letters*, pp. 35-98.
[3] See the letter of Ficino (ed. A. Perosa and P. O. Kristeller) in
Kristeller, *Studies in Renaissance Thought and Letters*, p. 146; also
the *Laus Philosophiae oratoria, moralis, dialectica, theologica*, in Ficino, *Opera*, pp. 668-70.
[4] See the English translation of Pico's letter to Barbaro by Quirinus
Breen in *Journal of the History of Ideas*, XIII (1952), 395. Note

258

CONCLUSION

men whose interest lay in a revival of the more strictly philosophical aspects of antiquity felt their separation from their predecessors, whose return to the ancient world had been accomplished under the banner of eloquence.

But these recognitions should not lead one to belittle the early humanists, or to deny the important new elements which they contributed to European thought. Rhetoric is so unpopular in the twentieth century that to stress the humanists' commitment to it may seem an outright condemnation of them. Before condemning the humanists for their loyalty to rhetoric, however, we should consider the large degree to which Bruni and Valla were correct in seeing the orator as the central figure of classical culture, and were justified, furthermore, in their belief that a return to the cultural standards of the ancient world could be led by men who sought to revive ancient eloquence. Their identification with the Ciceronian orator made the humanists blind to some important features of classical thought, but at the same time it allowed them to see much that no one had glimpsed for centuries. By identifying themselves with the idealized figure of the classical orator and refashioning existing rhetorical culture in the Ciceronian image, the humanists radically changed—even revolutionized—the relationship of European culture to the classical past. Earlier medieval men had admired and respected classical literature, but they had shaped it to their own needs rather than letting themselves be molded by it. This was true of even so avid a medieval classicist as John of Salisbury. Petrarch and his successors, however, did not merely try to adapt Ciceronian rhetorical culture to existing needs; they sought to model themselves as men of eloquence after Cicero and Crassus. Where earlier enthusiasts for ancient culture had regarded the ancients from a

also the attitude of Giordano Bruno towards the humanists, analyzed by Frances Yates, "Giordano Bruno's Conflict with Oxford," *Journal of the Warburg Institute*, II (1938-39), 227-42, and by R. McNulty, "Bruno at Oxford," *Renaissance News*, XIII (1960), 300-05; and more recently, F. Yates, *Giordano Bruno and the Hermetic Tradition* (London, 1964), pp. 167-68.

perspective firmly fixed in their own time, the humanists sought to approach classical culture from a point of view within the ancient world itself. This point of view was particular rather than universal, but it was authentically ancient nonetheless.

Even when the humanists distorted or attacked ancient ideals—as in Bruni's image of Aristotle as a seeker of eloquence, and Valla's campaign against the classical ideal of philosophy as it appeared outside the rhetorical tradition— their views have a markedly different character from earlier misunderstandings and rejections of ancient achievements. Such features of medieval culture as the legend of Virgil the magician and the recurring suspicion of ancient philosophy or poetry show the distance between medieval men and the classical past, and indicate the contemporary frame of mind in which they approached it. The humanists' attempts either to reform or reject classical philosophy where it failed to harmonize with rhetoric had a contemporary resonance to be sure, but they also revived a problem of importance to ancient culture. Bruni distorted Aristotle, and Valla fought what he stood for, but in the name of the classical ideal of eloquence, not in the name of some medieval ideal. Their cultural polemics echoed those of the classical past itself; they carried on where Cicero and Quintilian had left off.

Furthermore, while the identification of the humanists with the classical art of rhetoric often limited their understanding or sympathy for other classical achievements, these limitations were neither permanent nor insuperable. In the first rush of enthusiasm for the rediscovered glories of eloquence, activities like poetry and history were often conceived of in rhetorical terms, and the distinction between the aims and procedures of these arts was often blurred. But in the very act of binding poetry or history to the ideal of eloquence, the humanists emancipated these arts from some of the restrictions which had previously hampered them. Early humanist historical writing did not achieve the realism later attained by, for instance, Guic-

CONCLUSION

ciardini, but it quickly distinguished itself from the medieval chronicle, and it created the forms within which a realistic historiography would be born. Similarly, early humanist notions of poetry failed to distinguish the poet's techniques and purposes from those of the orator, but the humanist enthusiasm for classical poetry led to the eventual recognition of the distinction between the two.[5]

The humanists' love of language served as a powerful spur to a clearer and more objective understanding of the classical world. Their belief that the eloquence of classical writers had been corrupted through medieval carelessness in preserving and translating texts inspired corrective activities. Petrarch and his followers sought to restore the classical corpus by rediscovering lost or mangled works of classical writers. In addition, they began the heroic task of textual emendation through which obviously corrupt passages were restored to something approaching their original sense. Whatever other differences of opinion exist about the humanists, most modern students agree in calling them the founders of philology and classical scholarship.[6]

These remarks should suffice to make clear why the identification of the humanists as professional rhetoricians does not belittle them. If the humanists' commitment to rhetoric was responsible for some of their limitations, it was also the source of many of their achievements. Their con-

[5] On poetry and its relations to rhetoric in the fifteenth and sixteenth centuries, see Francesco Tateo, "Retorica" e "Poetica" fra medioevo e rinascimento; Bernard Weinberg, A History of Literary Criticism in the Italian Renaissance (Chicago, 1961); Charles Trinkaus, "The Unknown Quattrocento Poetics of Bartolommeo della Fonte," Studies in the Renaissance, XIII (1966), 40-122. On the relations between history and rhetoric, see Felix Gilbert, Machiavelli and Guicciardini (Princeton, 1965), Part II.

[6] See J. E. Sandys, A History of Classical Scholarship (3 vols., Cambridge, Eng., 1903-38); R. Sabbadini, Le scoperte dei codici latini e greci nei secoli XIV e XV (2 vols., Florence, 1905 and 1914); B. L. Ullman, Studies in the Italian Renaissance (Rome, 1955); and most recently the extremely learned and informative studies of Giuseppe Billanovich, in particular "Petrarch and the Textual Tradition of Livy," Journal of the Warburg and Courtauld Institutes, XIV (1951), 137-208.

tribution was momentous: through their activity the European mind was gradually awakened to a new historical consciousness of the classical world and its values. The history of modern Western thought proclaims its debt to them with eloquence.

INDEX

Abelard, 185, 189-92; *Sic et Non*, 190-92
Academics, 16-17, 21-22, 25, 52, 74-75, 102, 135, 146, 246-48; in Petrarch, 57; in John of Salisbury, 188-89. *See also* skepticism
Accolti, Benedetto, 229, 233-36, 241
active life, 43, 73. *See also* everyday life, common sense
Aegidius Romanus, 81n
age, 82-83 and n
Alberti, L. B., 32n
Albertus Magnus, 81n, 236
Alcuin, 180-83
Alonzo of Cartagena, 123-33, 162
Antiochus of Ascalon, 21, 22
Antonino, San, 244
Antonio da Rho, 31n, 145, 155
Antonius, M., 5, 6, 41, 177
Arcesilas (Arcesilaus), 16
Arezzo, 99, 233
Argyropulos, Johannes, 237-38
aristocracy, 202-03
Aristotelianism, 59, 215-16. *See also* Aristotle, Peripateticism
Aristotle, 9, 21, 30, 62, 67, 90, 99-136 *passim*, 100-101, 103, 152, 159-60, 164, 193, 195-97, 211, 236, 238, 249-50, 257, 260; *Rhetoric*, 12-15, 133; his style, 13 and n, 109-10 and n, 112; his works, 13n, 41n, 110 and n; *Nicomachean Ethics*, 21, 100, 113 (*see also* Bruni); as seen by Petrarch, 35, 40f; *Economics* (pseudo-Aristotelian), 100; *Politics*, 100, 115; as seen by Valla, 143-44; *Posterior Analytics*, 230
ars arengandi, 208
ars dictaminis, 206-14, 220. *See also* notaries
ars notaria, 65, 69, 206ff, 220. *See also* notaries
Attumano, Simon, 117
Augustine, St., 37, 60, 62, 74-75, 90, 91, 236, 257; in Petrarch's *Secret*, 44, 46, 49, 51, 53-55, 58; *De doctrina christiana*, 45, 92n, 196; *Confessions*, 61, 66
Averroës, 66, 229, 236
Averroism, 228
Avicenna, 236

Barbaro, Ermolao, 258
Basel, Council of, 124
Beccadelli, Antonio, called Panormita, 145
Bene of Florence (?), 209n
Benzi, Ugo, 121, 129, 236
Bernard of Chartres, 185, 189, 190, 192
Bernardino of Siena, San, 244-45, 254
Blaise of Parma, 67n
Boccaccio, Giovanni, 31, 87, 88, 214, 215
Boethius, 152, 157-58
Bologna, 65n, 209; University of, 69, 207
Bonaventure, St., 194-95; *Art of Preaching*, 194; *Collationes in Hexameron*, 194; *De reductione artium*, 194-95
Boncompagno of Signa, 208
Bosco, Umberto, 60
Botticelli, Sandro, 174
Bracciolini, Poggio, 63, 86, 89-98, 140-41, 215, 229, 233, 235, 238, 240, 242n; view of Cicero, 3-4; view of Petrarch, 31, 89-98; method of translation, 118n
Bruni, Leonardo, xvi, 62, 63, 89-90 and n, 98, 99-136, 140-41, 143-44, 145, 159-60, 162, 168-69, 212, 215, 223, 227, 229, 232, 238, 240, 242, 244, 249-51, 254, 255-60; *Dialogues* (*ad Petrum Histrum*), 31, 61, 66, 88, 102-03, 109, 229, 231, 256; *History of Florence*, 99, 100, 235, 252; *Introduction to Moral Philosophy* (*Isagogicon moralis disciplinae*), 101, 104-

INDEX

Epicureanism, 23n; in Valla, 145-60
Epicureans, 18, 102, 105; in Cicero, 18-19
Epicurus, 105 and n
Erasmus of Rotterdam, 137-38, 146n
ethics, xii, 39-40, 184, 187, 188, 211, 227. See also philosophy, moral
Eugene IV, Pope, 124, 139
Evangelista of Pisa, 232
everyday life, 25, 29, 43, 53, 55-58, 75-76, 106, 144, 150-51, 198, 246, 248-49, 251-54. See also common sense

Faba, Guido, 212
Ficino, Marsilio, 258
Filelfo, Francesco, 133-34, 229
Florence, 63, 65, 99-100, 209, 217, 226, 229-41, 242, 252-53; University of (Studio Fiorentino), 66, 232; convent of Santo Spirito, 232
fortune, 19, 21, 23, 27, 52
France, 204, 216, 236
Frederick Barbarossa, Emperor, 200-201
Frederick II, Emperor, 65n, 209

Galland, Pierre, 168-69n
Garin, Eugenio, 132
George of Trebisond (Trapezuntius), 134-35
Gerbert of Aurillac (Pope Sylvester II), 176
Germany, 236
Gilbert de la Porrée, 185
Giotto, 221
Giovanni da Prato, 66; Il Paradiso degli Alberti, 242
Giovanni del Virgilio, 207n
Giovannino of Mantua, 218
Giraldus Odonis, 81n
Girolami, Remigio de', 241-42
Girolamo of Naples, 232
Giudici, Battista de', 122-23
glory, 47, 73, 82, 155, 209-10n
Gorgias, xii. See also Plato, Gorgias

grammar, xii, 42, 93, 139, 176, 178-79, 181, 185, 189, 192-93, 210, 213, 239
Greek language, and early humanism, 4, 99-100, 113ff
Grosseteste, Robert, 125, 131-32n
Guarino of Verona, 134, 158-59
Guicciardini, Francesco, 260-61

Heitmann, Klaus, 59
Henri d'Andeli, 193
history, xii, 50, 139, 238, 260-61
Homer, 113; Iliad, 116-18
honestas, 19-22, 27, 148, 149, 155
Horace, 34, 36, 91-92 and n; Ars poetica, 79

Iacopo da Uzzano, 67n
imitation, 50-51, 59, 95
induction, 164-65, 181
intellect, and will, 71, 73-74
Irnerius, 69
Isocrates, Antidosis, 7n, 8n, 12n; To Niccocles, xvn; his influence on Aristotle, 14-15n, 40-41, 112, 134

Jerome, St., 33, 85, 154, 156
John II, King of Castille, 124
John of Salisbury, 183-89, 191-92, 259; Policraticus, 117-18 and n; Metalogicon, 184-89
Julius Victor, 180

knowledge, 8, 9-11, 16-17, 38-39, 57, 74, 78-79, 88, 91, 92-94, 101, 167, 127, 197, 198, 236
Kristeller, Paul O., 132, 212, 213-14
Kuhn, Thomas S., 223

Lactantius, The Divine Institutes, 30n
Landino, Francesco, 67n, 242
language, 8, 11, 24, 114-15, 122-23, 126, 127, 129-31, 162, 166, 187, 191, 193, 236, 246, 258, 261
Latini, Brunetto, 209, 212, 217;